Corvette Buyer's Guide 1953–1967

Richard Prince

To my friend Frank Mitchell. While he knew very little about Corvettes, he knew so much about the things that really matter. I love him deeply and miss him more than words can describe, though I take some measure of comfort in the understanding that his infinite wisdom and boundless love will forever make a difference.

First published in 2002 by MBI Publishing Company, Galtier Plaza, Suite 200, 380 Jackson Street, St. Paul, MN 55101-3885 USA

MBI Publishing Company books are also available at discounts in bulk quantity for industrial or sales-promotional use. For details write to Special Sales Manager at Motorbooks International Wholesalers & Distributors, Galtier Plaza, Suite 200, 380 Jackson Street, St. Paul, MN 55101-3885 USA.

Library of Congress Cataloging-in-Publication Data Available

ISBN 0-7603-1009-2

On the front cover: The 1966 427 Corvette was among the fastest cars of its era.

Richard Prince has owned, restored, raced, and enjoyed dozens of different Corvettes over the past 30 years. A writer and photographer for editorial, advertising, and corporate clients worldwide, his work and personal interests involve a wide variety of cars, though Corvettes occupy a special place in his heart. Richard and his future wife went to their high school prom in a 1966 convertible. He lives in New York.

Edited by Chad Caruthers
Designed by Liz Tufte

Printed in China

Contents

Acknowledgments

A number of people very graciously assisted in the production of this book. Thank you to Alan Blay; Paul Blom; Angela Cox; Greg Cox; John Donato; Joe Lamberti; Mike Lombardi; Rich Luebkert; Larry Lukash; Rich Mason; Shar Mason; Dave Morgan; Bill Nichols; Greg Ornazian; Paul Pergamo; Tom Riccinto; Gary Roth; Dominick Salvemini; Bruce Silber; Ken Silber; Scott Sinclair; Chuck Spielman; Alvin Steinman; Ronnie Steinman; Greg Strassberg; Terry Strassberg; Renee Tringali; Bob Tringali; David Walters; Jo Walters; the dedicated crews at Professional's Choice Auto Body and at Vette Dreams Corvette Restorations, both in Babylon, New York; and the National Corvette Restorers Society, an organization that has done immeasurable amounts of good work in preserving the history of the Corvette. Thanks also to Paul Johnson, who was a great help. And finally, most important of all, thank you to my wife, Carolyn, whose love serves as my guiding light.

Introduction

Chevrolet's Corvette has occupied a special place in the hearts and minds of automobile enthusiasts since its introduction in 1953. For nearly half a century this marque's unique styling and outstanding performance have combined to attract buyers of all ages and from all walks of life. Those same endearing qualities continue to attract people to Corvettes old and new, making America's only true production sports car a cherished icon the world over.

In spite of the adoration people bestow upon them, Corvettes are not without their problems. Like all machines, they were engineered to have a finite life span. Though collectors and driving enthusiasts would like to think otherwise, Chevrolet did not intend for Corvettes to last forever, nor did the company expect people would want them to. Rubber components dry out and crack, ferrous items rust, interior colors fade, moving parts wear out, and so on.

In addition to the inevitable deterioration that results from old age and hard use, Corvettes sometimes suffer from another problem that is found among all collector cars: misrepresentation of one sort or another. Whether old or new, Corvettes typically have substantial value in the marketplace and as with other collectibles, worth is largely a function of originality, rarity, options, color combinations, and numerous other factors that are susceptible to alteration. Of course, money can bring out the worst in people, and some of the unscrupulous among us have made a habit out of altering the characteristics of Corvettes in order to increase value.

Originality

The originality of its engine is important to the value of any vintage Corvette. The practice of altering engine numbers and codes to make them appear original is somewhat common, and determining originality requires considerable knowledge and a trained eye. The information in this note and book will help you gain knowledge, but a trained eye can only be acquired by studying known-original examples and thoroughly familiarizing yourself with all of their nuances.

All Corvette engine blocks carry a casting number, a casting date, and a stamping. The casting number is a raised numeric sequence that was cast as part of the block when it was manufactured. Blocks with casting numbers correct for a Corvette were also used in other GM products, so a correct casting number does not ensure a correct engine. See Appendix 1 for casting numbers.

Casting dates begin with the letter "A" for January and end with the letter "L" for December. The letter is followed by one or two numbers representing the day and then by a number for the year, with 3 for 1953 and so on. With the exception of a small number of 1965 327s, all Corvette block casting dates utilize a single number to represent the year. If the date contains two numbers for the year (for example, 57 for 1957), then the block came from the Tonawanda engine plant rather than the Flint engine plant, and it is therefore not correct for a Corvette. The casting date must precede the build date of the car for the block to be considered correct. The generally accepted standard in the hobby is that engine blocks and all other components should not have been manufactured more than six months before the car was built.

Engine stampings contain some combination of letters and numbers that indicate the engine's original application. In later years, the stamping also contained the engine assembly date and the serial number of the car it was originally installed into. See Appendix 1 for engine codes.

The 1953–55 six-cylinder casting number is located in a recess just below and forward of the fuel pump mounting boss. The casting date is located at the right rear of the block adjacent to the starter motor solenoid.

Six-cylinder engine stampings are located in a boss immediately rearward of the distributor opening. Original Corvette engines were stamped with a two– or three–letter application code followed by a six-digit engine serial number. There is no discernible correlation between an engine serial number and the car's serial number, other than that higher serial number cars tend to have higher serial number engines.

All small block V–8 engine blocks have a casting number on the driver side rear on the flange, where the block attaches to the bellhousing. The casting date is located on the passenger side rear on the same flange. The 1955–56 V-8 engine stamping is on a boss just forward of the passenger side cylinder head. It contains a serial number that began with 0001001 at the beginning of each year and continued in sequence. The engine's serial number is not the same as the car's serial number, though higher serial number cars tend to have higher serial number engines. The engine serial number is followed by F55 (for 1955 and F56 for 1956) and a two-letter application code.

Beginning in 1957, continuous engine serial numbering was discontinued. Instead, the engine stamping contains a letter indicating where the engine was built (all Corvette engines begin with F to designate Chevrolet's Flint plant), three or four numbers designating the month and day the engine was assembled, and two application code letters.

Beginning early in the 1960 model year, the stamping contains a second sequence that is the latter part of the serial number of the car the engine was originally installed into. Prior to this there is nothing that links a specific engine to a specific car, so any given Corvette engine could be correct for many different Corvettes as long as the casting and assembly dates correlate to the car's build date. Also beginning in 1960, the assembly date contained in the stamping always has four numbers. Single digit months (January through September) are designated as 01, 02, and so on. Prior to 1960, they are simply designated as 1, 2, and so on.

Big block engines were offered as optional in Corvettes beginning in 1965. Big block stampings were similar to small block stampings except they contain the letter "T" to designate Chevrolet's Tonawanda engine plant. Also in 1965, and 1965 only, a very small number of small blocks may also contain a T in the stamping. It is believed that for a short time the Flint engine plant was unable to supply 327 blocks so the Corvette plant obtained them from the passenger car engine plant in Tonawanda.

All 1965–67 big blocks contain a casting number on the driver side rear on the flange where the block attaches to the bellhousing. Big block casting dates are located on the passenger side of the block in back of the area where the starter motor mounts.

Whether your interest lies with the original six-cylinder models, a raging big block from the late 1960s, or something in between, this color buyer's guide will show you what to look for and perhaps even more important, what to look out for. It is my sincere hope that you take to heart the advice contained herein and in so doing find the greatest possible measure of happiness from the Corvette you bring into your life.

1953 Corvettes engender intense passion among collectors.

Chapter 1 1953

The inaugural year for the Corvette was 1953. Following wildly enthusiastic public reaction to the prototype that toured the country in General Motor's 1953 Motorama, the stylish two-seater was rushed into production. In June, the first of only 300 1953 models rolled off a makeshift assembly line set up in an old GM truck plant in Flint, Michigan.

All of the 1953 models, like every production Corvette ever made, were assembled using a fiberglass body and a steel chassis. Without exception, exteriors were painted Polo White and interiors were fully trimmed in Sportsman Red vinyl.

Though of conventional design, the chassis was created from scratch specifically for the Corvette. Nearly all of the parts that bolted to it, including those constituting the steering, brake, and suspension systems, were nearly identical to those used on Chevrolet passenger cars and light-duty trucks.

The in-line six-cylinder engine that powered all 1953 Corvettes was also borrowed from Chevrolet's other vehicles, but with some important adaptations. Compression was increased by virtue of a new cylinder-head casting, a higher-performance camshaft was fitted, and three Carter side-draft carburetors were used. As a result of these changes, output was rated at a respectable 150 horsepower.

A two-speed cast-iron Powerglide automatic was the only transmission offered. It was essentially identical to the units used in other Chevrolets with the notable exception of its tail housing, which was unique to Corvette.

Earlier 1953 models were made almost entirely by hand and were extremely crude in many ways. The fit and finish of the bodies were particularly poor, with wide, erratically spaced gaps between adjacent panels, pronounced waves and lumps in the fiberglass surface, and the weave of the hand-laid fiberglass cloth used to make the panels showing through the paint.

This poor quality was present right from the car's beginning, as evidenced by a wealth of recently discovered documents pertaining to its initial development. In writing of his experiences driving an early car, Chevrolet development engineer (and three-time Indianapolis 500 winner) Mauri Rose reported, among other things, severe water leaks, rattles, body shake, and doors that unexpectedly popped open while the car was in motion. Some of the car's more blatant problems were corrected during the model year, but many other shortcomings persisted into 1954 and even beyond. These included a lack of such basic creature comforts as roll-up door windows or any sort of power assist.

In addition to keeping the model's endemic shortcomings in mind, the buyer of a 1953 should be aware that they are especially vulnerable to the ravages of time. The science of petroleum-derived plastics—such as the type of plastic used to make fiberglass body panels—was still relatively new in 1953. The same can be said for plastic manufacturing techniques. As a result, surviving 1953 Corvette bodies are often in very poor condition, with extensive crazing very common.

Another problem, even more severe, is frequently seen in the bodies of earlier cars, which were assembled using panels that were laid up by hand. With this technique, workers layered sheets of woven glass matting saturated with catalyzed resin into female molds, which were initially made from wood. When the resin hardened, the part was simply popped out of the mold.

The wooden molds could be made relatively quickly, and this was instrumental in getting Corvette from prototype to production in a record time of only six months. The time savings was very valuable to GM, and any problems that might result many years into the future were entirely irrelevant.

Of course, the future is now and the problem with hand-laid-up panels is no longer irrelevant. They are prone to delaminating in their old age, which is a genteel way of saying they tend to come apart as the layers of resin-soaked cloth that constitute them separate from one another. Not all 1953 bodies delaminate and those that do can be fixed, though to properly do so is extremely labor intensive.

Over the course of the 1953 model year and into 1954, Chevrolet shifted body-panel production over to an interim method called vacuum bag molding, and then finally to what's commonly called matched-metal die manufacturing. With the matched-metal die process, resin-saturated glass mat was sandwiched between a male steel die and a corresponding female steel die. Each pair of dies was forced together by an immense hydraulic press and heat was then applied to the resin and glass mixture. The end result, as you might expect, was a much stronger and longer-lasting panel.

The general superiority of 1954 body panels brings to mind another peril to beware of when shopping for a 1953 Corvette. Chevrolet made more than 10 times as many 1954 Corvettes as it did 1953s, and 1954s probably enjoy a better survival rate. At the same time, because they are the first year—and because of their scarcity—1953s are much more valuable than 1954s. The greater number of 1954s in combination with the greater value of 1953s has created an incentive for the unscrupulous among us to misrepresent 1954s as 1953s. The usual modus operandi for accomplishing this is to simply unscrew the 1954's serial number plate, which is located on the driver's side door-hinge pillar, and replace it with a 1953 serial number plate lifted from the remains of a severely damaged or destroyed 1953.

To avoid being victimized in this way, familiarize yourself with the many minute but important differences between a 1954 and a 1953, including those shown in the Garage Watch section. It is especially important to check the serial number stamping in the chassis, which is usually located on the top of the driver-side rail and on top of the central X-brace.

It is also advisable to investigate the ownership lineage of the car you are considering for purchase. Trace the 1953 serial number back as far as possible and contact previous owners to learn if the car you are looking at and the number that it wears have been united since the beginning. You should be suspicious if, for example, a previous owner tells you that the 1953 with that serial number was hit by a train or destroyed in a fire. These kinds of revelations often indicate that someone later "resuscitated" the number and applied it to a 1954.

In spite of their inherent crudeness and shortcomings, first-year Corvettes are not without their virtues. They represent the birth of a cultural icon that has endured longer than any other model in automotive history. The very fact that 1953 was the first year of production, and the fact that only 300 cars were sold, make them highly coveted by collectors. And for many, that classic 1953 styling is just as beautiful today as it was when the car was brand-new.

All 1953 (and 1954) Corvettes were powered by Chevrolet's reliable old six-cylinder engine. When installed in Corvettes it got a high compression head, special camshaft, and triple Carter side-draft carburetors for increased performance.

Valve cover differs from all other six-cylinder Chevys: Front area is lower to provide hood clearance, oil filler cap is located more toward the rear, studs are fastened to the lower left side to aid in attaching ignition shielding, and areas beneath where the retention nuts go are inverted rather than raised. Original 1953 Corvette covers would likely sell for at least $5,000. Reworked non-Corvette Covers for about $1,500.

1953 Corvette Specifications and Major Options

Specs

Base Price When New	$3,498.00
Production	300
Engine Type	Overhead valve 6-cylinder
Bore x Stroke (inches)	3.562x3.937
Displacement	235.5 cubic inches
Compression Ratio	8:1
Horsepower	150 @ 4200 rpm
Transmission	Chevrolet two-speed Powerglide
Wheelbase	102 inches
Overall width	70 inches
Overall height	47 inches
Overall length	167 inches
Track, front	57 inches
Track, rear	59 inches
Weight	2,900 pounds
Tires	6.70x15 bias ply
Suspension, front	Unequal-length control arms, king pins, coil springs, telescoping shock absorbers
Suspension, rear	Semi-elliptic leaf springs, telescoping shock absorbers
Brakes	Bendix duo-servo hydraulic with 11.0-inch drums front and rear
Steering	Worm and ball-bearing roller, 16:1 ratio
0–60 miles per hour	11.10 seconds
Top speed	108 miles per hour

1953 Options

	Price	Quantity
FOA 101A Heater	$91.40	300
FOA 102A Signal-Seeking Radio	$145.15	300

1953 Garage Watch

All 1953 Corvette engine blocks originally came with an identification stamping located in a boss immediately rearward of the distributor opening. Original Corvette engines were stamped "LAY" followed by a six-digit engine serial number.

Engine block casting number is located in a recess just below and forward of the fuel pump mounting boss. Casting date is located at the right rear of the block, "A" for January through "L" for December, followed by one or two numbers representing the day then a "3" for 1953. Block's casting date must precede the build date of the car to be considered correct for that car.

All 1953s came with three Carter side-draft model YH carburetors. Correct carburetors have 1088 stamped into the flange and can be further identified by a brass tag. Early cars used 2066S carburetors. Between serial number 122 and 136, a change was made to 2066SA. Tags also contain a date code, here E 3 7 for May 7, 1953.

The 1953 Corvette's 3836066 cylinder head was not used elsewhere. As such, original heads are extremely rare and valuable. Reproduction heads, made from passenger car heads whose casting number has been altered, are available. To check the authenticity of a head remove all paint and examine the casting number for evidence of alteration.

Rather than roll-up windows, all 1953 Corvettes came with Plexiglas "side curtains". Each piece of Plexiglas contained a stamped-in manufacturing date, the example here reading 7 53, for July 1953. A properly restored pair of side curtains costs about $4,000.

Verify that the chassis has the correct 1953 serial number, found on top of the central X support below and rearward of the driver's seat. It is also usually on top of the driver's side rail.

1953

Careful examination reveals a distinguishing characteristic of 1953 wheel covers: The hole for the air valve lines up with a retention tang on 1953 wheel covers, while on later wheel covers the hole falls between retention tangs. Note also that 1953 wheels were painted Sportsman Red.

Serial number plates for the 1953 Corvette were held to the driver's-side door hinge pillar with two screws. Generally, the screws and plate were covered at the factory with fiberglass resin, which made it more difficult to remove or tamper with the plate.

1953

1953 Corvette Replacement Costs for Common Parts

Convertible top	$220.00 (functional replacement)
	$1,000.00 (correct replacement)
Windshield	$450.00 (correct reproduction with date code)
Door glass	$105.00 (correct replacement with date code)
Seat upholstery (per pair)	$350.00
Carpet	$225.00 (reproduction)
Hood	$900.00 (reproduction)
Front fender	$450.00 (reproduction)
Wheel	$125.00 (used original)
Wheel cover	$1,000.00 (used original)
Front outer horizontal bumper	$120.00
Front grille assembly (minus oval)	$425.00 (reproduction)
Front grille oval	$1,000.00 (reproduction)
Headlamp switch	$60.00 (functional replacement)
Engine compartment wiring harness	$80.00
Dash wiring harness	$475.00
Exhaust system	$325.00
Shock absorbers	$115.00 (replacement set of four)
Front wheel bearing	$60.00 (outer)
	$40.00 (inner)
Front-wheel brake cylinder	$35.00 (functional replacement)
Master cylinder	$115.00 (functional replacement)
	$800.00 (original)
Front springs (pair)	$80.00
Lower control arm	$350.00 (used original)
Radiator	$350.00 (functional replacement)
Radiator support	$250.00 (reproduction)
Bullet air cleaners	$375.00 (for set of three reproductions)
Water pump	$2,000.00 (reproduction)
	$3,000.00 (used original)
Ignition shielding	$1,200.00 (reproduction)
	$2,500.00 (used original)
Cylinder head	$7,500.00 and up (used original)
Chassis	$4,000.00 (reproduction)
Rear leaf springs (pair)	$200.00 (functional replacements)
Complete tune-up kit (ignition points, condenser, plugs, distributor cap, rotor)	$50.00
Fuel tank	$200.00 (reproduction)

1953 Corvette Ratings Chart

Collectibility ★★★★★
Smoothness of Ride ★★★
Reliability ★★★
Comfort Cruising Speed: 55 miles per hour
Passenger Accommodations ★
Part/Service Availability ★★★

All genuine 1953 models are highly collectible. The three side-draft carburetor system is problematic and sometimes leaks fuel. If the carburetors are working properly, 1953 Corvettes run well and are a pleasure to drive. Correctly numbered and dated parts unique to 1953s, such as the cylinder head, water pump, master cylinder, distributor, transmission, and carburetors, can be very difficult to locate and extremely expensive to buy.

All six-cylinder Corvette engines, including 1953s, use a special water pump that was not used on any other vehicles. It positions the fan lower to clear the Corvette's low hood line.

In 1953 and very early 1954 models, brake and fuel lines run along the outside of the chassis, while in later 1954 models, along the inside. This is another way to authenticate a 1953. Note the large brass block toward the rear of the fuel line and the coupling in the brake line, both of which are correct.

Because the Corvette's plastic body provided inadequate shielding against radio interference emanating from the ignition system, radio-equipped cars had shielding around the distributor and coil. Original shielding was made from steel and is very rare. Many years ago fiberglass reproductions were sold, and more recently a limited number of steel reproductions were manufactured.

All 1953 through 1955 Corvettes came with a radio antenna in the form of a metal mesh bonded to the underside of the trunk lid. Check the connection, seen here in the lower right, to make sure it is not broken or missing.

While the fiberglass bodies are immune to corrosion, the same is not true for the car's steel frame and various other steel parts. Areas particularly prone to rust include the rear-most cross member of the chassis and the radiator support. A rotted radiator support is seen here through the grill opening, with the grill and radiator removed.

1953

What They Said in 1953

The Corvette, the sport car Chevrolet began as a long term experiment, has become a production item due to terrific public response. First shown at General Motors Motorama in New York around the first of the year, the initial models are expected off the lines in June.

Company officials estimate 300 Corvettes will be available this year. Price, although not announced, is expected to be in the $3,000.00 range.

Low slung—it is only 33 inches high at the door—the Corvette body is made of fiberglass, and mounted on a 102-inch wheelbase. Fitted with a Chevrolet engine souped up to put out 150 horsepower, this 2,900-pound model has been clocked at more than 100 mph at the GM proving ground.

The power plant is basically the reliable 6-cylinder, overhead valve Chevrolet displacing 235 cubic inches and running a compression ratio of 8 to 1, a dual exhaust system and triple side-draft carburetors. This is coupled with Chevrolet's improved Powerglide transmission.

Suspension is by coil springs at the front and conventional leaf springs in the rear.

A 2-seater, the doors are hinged ahead of the trailing edges of the wrap-around windscreen. The gas filler cap has been located just behind the door on the left side and the wheels are fully exposed.

The speedometer is located directly in front of the driver and is housed in a quadrant. Other instruments and control knobs are spaced across the dashboard.

Having caught the public's fancy design-wise, the Corvette faces another challenge . . . competition. —*Cars of Today,* 1953

The Chevrolet will become the first volume-produced sports car made in America in over a decade.

The power plant is a modified 1953 assembly, which has full pressure lubrication and aluminum pistons. The power output has been stepped up to 160 bhp at 5200 rpm by virtue of higher compression ratio, a special camshaft, side-draft Carter carburetors, and a dual-exhaust system.

The specification of a Powerglide transmission has been met with considerable

derision, but a torque converter has potential advantages for road racing that have not been fully explored.

The chassis is specially designed for this car, and one notes that Hotchkiss drive is used, a drastic step for Chevrolet. There is independent front suspension, and a special gear ratio of 3.27 is specified.

A close examination of the fiberglass body reveals excellent workmanship and careful attention to detail. The fabric top is much better in appearance than most imported cars and folds neatly into a flush compartment behind the bucket-type seats. The instrument panel is very neat and includes a tachometer placed in the center of the dash. —*Road & Track,* August 1953

I Bought a 1953 Corvette

I have owned over two dozen Corvettes since buying my first, a 1962 I acquired in 1969. I always admired the 1953–55 body style and finally bought a 1954 in 1973. Number 75 was my first 1953 Corvette. This car, which I had known about since 1975, was sold new in Danbury, Connecticut, and was driven in that area until 1966, when it was removed from service. Its first owner was an executive with U.S. Rubber, a company that manufactured tires used on GM cars. The car had been poorly stored and needed extensive restoration.

I began passionately seeking and collecting early Corvette parts in 1970, knowing that one day I would perform the "dream restoration" on one of the original 300 1953s. Number 75 gave me that opportunity. After four years and thousands of man-hours Number 75 has been returned to "as new" condition.

I drive it regularly and have gone as far as [from] New York to Carlisle, Pennsylvania, where, by the way, it won an NCRS Top Flight award. In addition to this and many other awards, Number 75 has enjoyed the honor of touring Canada as part of General Motors' introduction of the fifth-generation Corvette in 1997. And most recently, it has been chosen to be displayed in the Brooklyn Museum of Art as part of the exhibit of American Art Forms of the Atomic age from 1940 to 1960. *—Alan Blay*

1953 Corvettes will always be special because that was the first year for America's celebrated sports car. I have owned my car for almost six years and have enjoyed it every step of the way. It was restored in the early 1980s and though there are some signs of age here and there, overall it still looks very good.

I have made some cosmetic improvements including installing a new convertible top and seat upholstery. Mechanically the car is quite sound, and I stay on top of normal maintenance like oil changes and tune-ups. When the car sits for long periods of time, as it usually does through the winter months, it drips a small amount of oil from the engine and the rear end. Otherwise, I have no problems with it.

I can't honestly recommend taking a 1953 on very long trips but it is a lot of fun to drive around town. I've been caught in the rain with it twice and everything you've ever heard about them leaking like crazy is true. The steering and handling have a very 1950s feel and acceleration is surprisingly peppy for a six-cylinder engine. A stick shift would be more fun than the Powerglide, but that's all they came with, so in the interests of leaving my car original I live with the automatic. *—John Barley*

Many people believe first-generation Corvettes look even more beautiful with their distinctive soft tops raised. All 1954 tops were originally beige (1953 tops were black) and hardtops were not available from the factory until 1956.

Chapter 2 1954

The initial use of fiberglass for the Corvette's body in 1953 occurred simply so the car could be put into production sooner. From the very beginning, however, 1954 plans called for a changeover to steel bodies. But despite rumors of steel-bodied Corvettes that have circulated for decades, the changeover never came to pass. High tooling costs, lack of time, the public's apparent acceptance of fiberglass, the many advantages it offered, and uncertainty about the Corvette's future led Chevrolet to continue using glass-reinforced plastic in 1954 and right up through the present day.

For 1954, the temporary Flint assembly line utilized in 1953 was replaced with a dedicated Corvette factory in St. Louis, Missouri. Engineers and line workers all learned a great deal during 1953 production, and many important improvements can be found in 1954 models. Perhaps the most notable is the improved quality of body panels, which, while still not particularly good, were quite a bit better than they had been in 1953.

It is important to keep in mind that making improvements to the Corvette was a very fluid process that did not always conform to the model-year calendar. Hence, improvements did not necessarily begin the day 1954s began rolling off their assembly line. Many appeared toward the end of 1953 production, while others filtered in after 1954 production began. It is common, therefore, to find many similarities between late 1953s and early 1954s, and many differences between early 1954s and late 1954s.

As a result of Chevrolet moving the Corvette factory to St. Louis, and of continuously improving manufacturing and assembly methods, production increased dramatically during the 1954 model year. By year's end 3,640 cars had been built, compared with only 300 for 1953. This increased production obviously makes 1954 models far more plentiful today, and hence far more affordable, when compared with 1953s.

As in the previous year, all 1954 Corvettes were powered by Chevrolet's in line six-cylinder engine, which was fed fuel by a trio of Carter side-draft carburetors. And again, the only available transmission was the reliable but heavy cast-iron two-speed Powerglide, which was never a favorite with sports car enthusiasts.

As with many of the remainder of the car's mechanical components, the Corvette's Powerglide was almost identical to what General Motors used elsewhere. To accommodate the Corvette's shorter wheelbase, however, a shorter tail section was used on the transmission.

Many early Powerglide Corvettes were converted to three- and four-speed manuals, and changing them back is relatively straightforward as long as you have the correct transmission. A Powerglide out of a Chevy passenger car of the era will function well in a Corvette, but it must have a correct Corvette tail section in order to fit. As you would expect, the Corvette-only tail section is quite difficult to find and expensive.

As with the 1953 Corvette, much of the 1954 model was assembled from Chevrolet passenger car parts. This is why it is relatively easy and inexpensive to buy items like kingpins, brake drums, steering linkage components, and internal engine parts. In addition to finding their way into a few thousand Corvettes, these parts were used in hundreds of thousands of regular passenger cars.

On the other hand, a number of highly specialized parts were used exclusively on these early Corvettes. As a result, they are very difficult to find today and are typically quite expensive. Understandably, aftermarket parts suppliers are resistant to reproducing many parts for these early cars, since so few were made and even fewer survive to this day, making demand for parts relatively low.

Very limited supply and correspondingly high prices for parts make it quite important for a buyer to seek out as complete a car as possible when shopping for a 1954. Difficult and expensive-to-replace items that are often missing include the convertible top frame, radiator expansion tank, ignition shielding, correct casting number cylinder head, shifter, wheel covers, headlamp bucket assemblies, exhaust tips, and side curtains. Other often-missing parts, such as exterior chrome, spare tire tools and jack, and correct gauges, are only slightly easier to find and can be quite expensive as well.

The unique look of first-generation Corvettes, including, of course, the 1954 model, has endeared them to enthusiasts for nearly half a century. The sight of one motoring down the street is often enough to stop anyone in his tracks. In many ways, the design is clearly a product of its era, but it was also so futuristic that it looks exotic even today.

While the appearance of a 1954 and its brethren was way ahead of its time, the same cannot be said for their performance. The chassis design was already somewhat antiquated by the mid-1950s, and though handling compared favorably with passenger cars of the day, it does not inspire great confidence today. Another area that does not inspire great confidence is its six-volt electrical system. A common problem encountered with six-volt systems is a slow-ranking starter motor and corresponding difficulty in starting. Inadequately sized, loose, and corroded battery cables, as well as excessive internal resistance in the starter motor, are often to blame for this.

Higher compression, more carburetion, and a racier camshaft profile boosted the 1954 Corvette engine's power output noticeably compared with Chevrolet's passenger car engines, but it was certainly not overwhelming. And though the side-draft Carter carburetors increase horsepower and look rather exotic, they are prone to fuel leaks. Besides presenting a fire hazard, the leaking fuel can accelerate engine wear by washing oil off the cylinder walls and thinning the oil in the pan when it runs down the throat of the carburetor and into the engine.

While it can't offer blinding acceleration or go-cart-like handling, 1954 Corvettes are still a lot of fun to drive, at least around town, to local car shows, and in parades. Long-distance touring is certainly possible, but profuse wind noise, water leaks, and a nearly complete lack of even basic creature comforts such as roll-up windows, exterior door handles and door locks, and any sort of power assist relegate long drives to only the most devoted enthusiasts.

This interior was created in an era when styling counted at least as much as function.

In keeping with their era, there was no shortage of chrome on 1954 Corvettes. All of the exterior brightwork is readily available, but none of it is inexpensive. Buy as complete a car as you can to begin with.

1954 Corvette Specifications and Major Options

Specs

Base Price When New	$2,774.00
Production	3,640
Engine Type	Overhead valve 6-cylinder
Bore x Stroke (inches)	3.562x3.937
Displacement	235.5 cubic inches
Compression Ratio	8:1
Horsepower	150 @ 4200 rpm (later 1954s are rated at 155 horsepower owing to a camshaft change)
Transmission	Chevrolet two-speed Powerglide
Wheelbase	102 inches
Overall width	70 inches
Overall height	47 inches
Overall length	167 inches
Track, front	57 inches
Track, rear	59 inches
Weight	2,900 pounds
Tires	6.70x15 bias ply
Suspension, front	Unequal-length control arms, kingpins, coil springs, telescoping shock absorbers
Suspension, rear	Semi-elliptic leaf springs, telescoping shock absorbers
Brakes	Bendix duo-servo hydraulic with 11.0 inch drums front and rear
Steering	Worm and ball-bearing roller, 16:1 ratio
0–60 miles per hour	11.10 seconds
Top speed	108 miles per hour

1954 Options

	Price	Quantity
FOA 100 Directional Signals	$16.75	3,640
FOA 101A Heater	$91.40	3,640
FOA 102A Signal-Seeking Radio	$145.15	3,640
RPO 290B 6.70-15 Whitewall tires	$26.90	3,640
RPO 313M Powerglide Transmission	$178.35	3,640
RPO 420A Park Brake Alarm	$5.65	3,640
RPO 421A Courtesy Lamps	$4.05	3,640
RPO 422A Windshield Washer	$11.85	3,640

As originally equipped, the 1954 trunk contained a spare tire and jack in a circular well covered by a circular plywood board. On top of that went the rubber mat seen here. The red vinyl bag hanging at the back of the trunk is for stowing the side curtains when they are removed from the doors. The black rod behind the bag is the tool used to turn the car's jack.

The rear chassis cross member is prone to rusting, so check it carefully. Also check the side rails that connect to this cross member.

The underside of the trunk lid is painted to match interior color. The box assembly toward the top of this photo is the rear license-plate housing. The wire connected to the trunk in the lower right of this photo is the radio-antenna cable. The antenna is a wire mesh that is bonded into the fiberglass trunk lid.

Most cast components can be identified as correct for a 1954 Corvette by virtue of their casting number and/or casting date. The number 5451233 with the larger 233 characters seen here identify this as an original 1954 master cylinder. A greater number of correct components makes any vintage Corvette more valuable.

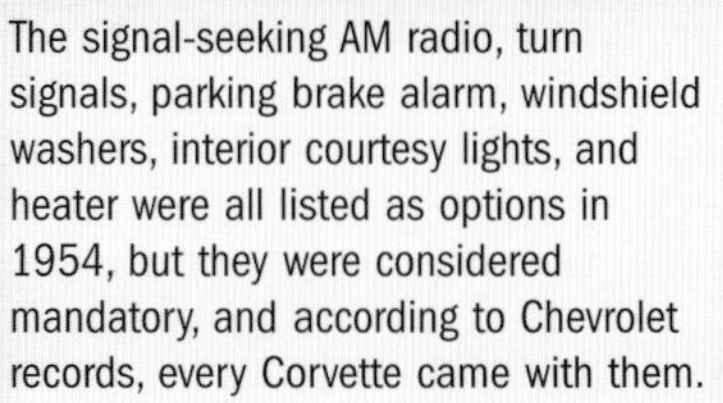

The signal-seeking AM radio, turn signals, parking brake alarm, windshield washers, interior courtesy lights, and heater were all listed as options in 1954, but they were considered mandatory, and according to Chevrolet records, every Corvette came with them.

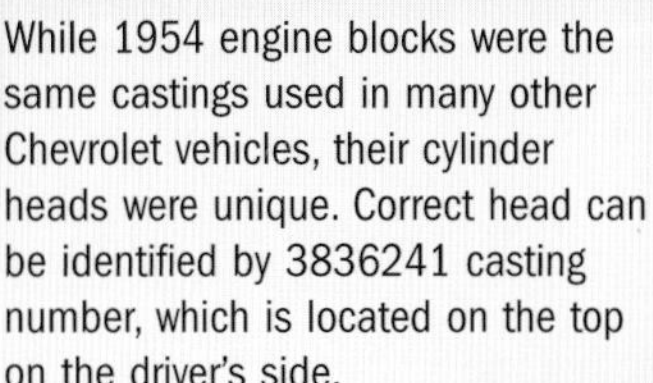

1954

While 1954 engine blocks were the same castings used in many other Chevrolet vehicles, their cylinder heads were unique. Correct head can be identified by 3836241 casting number, which is located on the top on the driver's side.

Numerous mechanical components found in vintage Corvettes, including the starter motor, generator, and radiator, had identification tags attached. As shown on this 1954 generator, the tag contains a part number and assembly date. This 1102793 generator was assembled on 4E27, which translates to May 27, 1954.

Engines in 1954s used unique twin-pot air cleaners atop their three side-draft Carter YH carburetors. A small triangular brass tag on each carburetor has the model number (2066SA) and assembly date code stamped in. The carburetors look beautiful but can leak profusely, so beware of fuel leaking into the engine as well as out of it. Original 1954 aluminum intake manifold bears no casting number or date. Later service replacements contain casting number 3706064 and the symbol of Winters Aluminum Casting Company, a "W" inside a snowflake.

1
9
5
4

1954 Corvette
Replacement Costs for Common Parts

Convertible top	$220.00 (functional replacement)
	$750.00 (correct replacement)
Windshield	$950.00 (correct replacement with date code)
Door glass	$105.00 (correct replacement with date code)
Seat upholstery (per pair)	$350.00
Carpet	$225.00 (reproduction)
Hood	$900.00 (reproduction)
Front fender	$450.00 (reproduction)
Wheel	$125.00 (used original)
Wheel cover	$1,000.00 (used original early design)
	$500.00 (used original late design)
Front outer horizontal bumper	$120.00
Front grille assembly (minus oval)	$425.00 (reproduction)
Front grille oval	$1,000.00 (reproduction)
Headlamp switch	$60.00 (functional replacement)
Engine compartment wiring harness	$80.00
Dash wiring harness	$475.00
Exhaust system	$325.00
Shock absorbers	$115.00 (replacement set of four)
Front wheel bearing	$60.00 (outer)
	$40.00 (inner)
Front-wheel brake cylinder	$35.00 (functional replacement)
Master cylinder	$115.00 (functional replacement)
	$400.00 (original)
Front springs (pair)	$80.00
Lower control arm	$350.00 (used original)
Radiator	$350.00 (functional replacement)
Radiator support	$250.00 (reproduction)
Water pump	$1,200.00 (used original)
Ignition shielding	$2,500.00 (used original)
	$1,200.00 (reproduction)
Cylinder head	$2,000.00 (used original)
Chassis	$4,000.00 (reproduction)
Rear leaf springs (pair)	$200.00 (functional replacements)
Complete tune-up kit (ignition points, condenser, plugs, distributor cap, rotor)	$50.00
Fuel tank	$200.00 (reproduction)

1954 Corvette Ratings Chart

Collectibility ★★★★
Smoothness of Ride ★★★
Reliability ★★★
Comfort Cruising Speed: 55 miles per hour
Passenger Accommodations ★
Part/Service Availability ★★★

All 1954 models are quite collectible. In addition to Polo White, which was the only exterior color available in 1953, 1954 models could be had in Black, Sportsman Red, or Pennant Blue. The vast majority of 1954s were originally painted White, though it is often impossible to tell what color a given car was originally, since Corvettes did not come with trim tags affixed until 1963. As with 1953s, the three-side-draft carburetor system used in 1954 is problematic and frequently leaks fuel, and correct numbered and dated parts unique to 1954s, such as the cylinder head, water pump, and master cylinder, can be very difficult to locate and expensive to buy.

All 1954 Corvette engine blocks originally came with an identification stamping located in a boss immediately rearward of the distributor opening. Original Corvette engines are stamped with a seven-digit engine serial number that runs in sequence starting with 0001001. The engine serial number is followed by "F 54" for model year 1954, and the two letter suffix code "YG."

1954 Corvette engines were similar to inline six-cylinders found in other Chevrolet products but gave more performance as a result of higher compression, increased carburetion, and a racier camshaft profile.

As with any vintage Corvette, originality of major components such as the engine block, transmission, chassis, and body are very important. Check the serial number plate, which is held to the driver-side door hinge pillar with Phillips-head screws.

Wheel covers are highly polished stainless steel, while two spinner ears toward the middle are chrome plated. These are not being reproduced and original examples are difficult to find and quite expensive. All 1954 Corvettes came with 15"x 5"steel wheels painted Sportsman Red on the outside. Some wheels were also red on the reverse side while others were black.

The 1954 engine-block casting number is located in a recess just below and forward of the fuel pump mounting boss; the block casting date is at the right rear of the block adjacent to the starter motor solenoid. Casting dates begin with the letter "A" for January and end with the letter "L" for December, followed by one or two numbers representing the day and then by one number representing the year, with "3" for 1953 and "4" for 1954. Note correct chrome-plated radiator overflow tank and two-section ignition shielding held below it with wing nuts.

The space age was in its infancy when first-generation Corvettes were created but there's no mistaking its influence on their design.

Rather than roll-up windows all 1954 Corvettes came with Plexiglas "side curtains" that were held in place by a tang fore and aft and a chrome-plated thumbscrew attached to an inboard side brace. Original Plexiglas contains a logo and a manufacturing date, which should precede the car's final assembly date. The date in this example, 1-54, translates to January 1954.

1954

What They Said in 1954

Chevrolet stands alone in the American sports car field, with a true production automobile priced at a figure John Doe can comprehend.

Relatively few Americans can afford the staggering prices asked for many imported models; if they could, there is still more money to shell out—for another car, one that can contain the family.

With this dare flung in their faces by the European invaders, Chevrolet took up the challenge. The result is proof that a "compromise" car can be built; while the Corvette won't hold but two, this GM product combines the best features of a foreign sports car without its stark simplicity of purpose.

The Corvette goes! . . . the Corvette was driven side by side through acceleration and high-speed runs against a well-known and popular European make of sports car. . . . From a standing start—and bear in mind that the Corvette has automatic transmission—the new member of the Chevrolet family took off like a scalded dog, and left its competitor five car lengths behind at the end of a quarter mile!

A driving impression not entirely favorable concerns cornering. However, it must be explained first that for average driving the Corvette behaves itself around corners very nicely, turning flat, with a proper seat-of-the-pants feeling in the cockpit.

The Corvette does not offer the riding comfort its more conservative Chevy family members do. However, this is not to be expected and next to impossible to achieve hand-in-hand with superior handling qualities.

The arrangement of the instruments on the dash is good except for the location of the tachometer; rather than in its present location in the center of the panel, the tach would serve its important purpose better if relocated directly in front of the driver, next to the speedometer.

The cockpit of this two-seater is plush in the American fashion, with handy door compartments and plenty of space—maybe too much space.

The use of fiberglass as body substance is a revolutionary move—production-wise—on Chevrolet's part. The resin-glass combination is definitely out of the experimental stage and has proved a worthy successor to sheet steel, offering lightness and strength.

To sum it up, the Chevrolet Corvette is a true sports car, offering the prospective buyer tops in performance. It has a few "bugs," as does any model first or last, but none are so extreme as to discredit the car to any degree. The Corvette is a beauty—and it goes! —*Motor Life,* June 1954

Named after the naval patrol vessels of World War II. The new car has an engine which is basically a 1954 Chevrolet aluminum piston valve-in-head "Blue Flame" of 235-cubic-inch displacement, but with added power obtained through modifications such as increased compression ratio, triple side draft carburetors and a dual exhaust system.

The transmission is a 1954 Powerglide automatic with a floor-mounted quadrant in sports car tradition.

The car carries an experimentally molded body, hood and fenders, and has a manually adjusted lightweight fabric top that folds into a flush compartment behind the bucket seats of driver and passenger.

The driving compartment has two low doors, which are wide in cross section and are equipped with saddle-type compartments for driver's accessories. . . . Windows are stored in the luggage compartment when not in use.

The car's instruments include a center-mounted tachometer in addition to the usual speedometer, oil, water, fuel, and generator gauges. —*Automobile,* 1954

I Bought a 1954 Corvette

I have owned several different models over the years including a 1969, 1978, and a 1986 that I bought new. None were quite as enjoyable from an all-around perspective as the 1954.

When I acquired the 1954, in 1992, it was in good general condition, needing only some cosmetic freshening to be brought up to current show standards. Two owners before me had done a fairly extensive restoration in the early 1980s, and then the gentleman I bought it from made various improvements.

I found that letting the car sit for too long a time, like through the whole winter, caused various problems. The most troublesome of these were leaks from the carburetors, transmission, and rear end. The carburetors were particularly bad, requiring a rebuild every spring. I cured this problem for the most part by using the car on a regular schedule throughout the year.

The car's ride is surprisingly smooth and comfortable and handling is good, considering the technology of the time period. The brakes work fine and don't require an undue effort even though there is no power assist. Power and acceleration are nowhere near the other Corvettes I have owned, but the car can still get out of its own way when the gas pedal is pushed. The old inline six can rev up pretty good and is what I would call peppy rather than fast. I would say the biggest area where improvement can be made is with the transmission, which always feels like it could use a third speed.

I don't drive in the rain but know from washing the car that it leaks quite a bit. There is nothing that I can see that is obviously wrong, but water seems to come in from just about everywhere if I'm not careful with the hose. —*Charles Burraca*

My car was acquired from the second owner, who had had it since early in 1975.

The car has been repainted three times and had the seat covers and carpet changed in the late 1970s. Aside from the seats and carpet the interior is all original. Everything works, including the radio—although it does sound rather anemic compared with a more modern stereo.

The original mileage is 77,000, which isn't even an average of 1,500 miles per year. Aside from installing new brakes, having the transmission resealed and having the carburetors rebuilt (twice), I have not done any mechanical work to the car.

I am very attracted to the styling of these first Corvettes. I was a young boy when they were new, and to me they are reminiscent of some of the rocket ships and other space-theme toys I enjoyed as a child. One of the truly amazing things about the design is its longevity. As I mentioned before, the car caused quite a stir when the high school principal brought it to work or drove it around town, and I can speak from personal experience when I say that nearly 50 years later the car still causes quite a stir whenever and wherever it goes.

I try to get out in the car a minimum of once a month because it's detrimental to cars, especially collector cars, if they are not exercised regularly. Of course, living in an area with very mild winters makes that much easier.

While driving this car can only be described as a blast, the fun actually begins with starting the engine. We're so used to jumping into our newer cars, turning the key and going—but that's not the way it was in the good old days. You have to manually set the chokes, pump the gas pedal, and then turn the key. Then once it fires up, you have to incrementally open the chokes while the engine warms up.

The car is comfortable puttering around town or cruising at reasonable highway speeds, and it gives quite a solid ride. There is a lot of wind noise with the soft top up and it is something of a chore to put it up and down, so I always leave it in the down position. I would prefer a stick shift to the two-speed Powerglide but wouldn't ever change it over because that would really alter the character of the car.

Overall, early Corvettes like my 1954 are great fun, reliable, and as history has shown, solid investments to boot. —*Dennis McGill*

First-generation Corvette styling looks as futuristic and beautiful today as it did 50 years ago! As seen here, correct 1955 exhaust tips are longer than those used previously, a change made to eliminate soot buildup on the body.

Chapter 3 1955

By all accounts, 1955 was a pivotal year in the evolution of the Corvette. Unbeknownst to most enthusiasts, the car that in subsequent years grew into a legend recognized and admired the world over came within inches of extinction before it really had a chance to demonstrate its viability.

To the surprise of Corvette's supporters within Chevrolet, many of the 3,640 cars assembled in 1954 had difficulty finding a willing buyer. It was reported that as of January 1, 1955, nearly one-third of the entire previous year's production—1,076 Corvettes—sat on dealers' lots unsold.

Chevrolet's inexperience in marketing a low-volume sports car, as well as the Corvette's numerous shortcomings, had become readily apparent to consumers, and many within the ranks of upper management at GM saw no reason to continue pouring money, time, and other resources into an obvious loser. But at the same time, a handful of dedicated men at Chevrolet, including brilliant engineers Ed Cole and Zora Duntov, as well as legendary designer Harley Earl, recognized the Corvette's potential and refused to let it die an unceremonious death. Just before it was too late they realized Corvette's salvation lay with dramatically improved performance and initiating a more focused marketing strategy.

Though the more focused marketing strategy would not really blossom until the following year, 1955 saw a very important leap forward in performance. The improved performance came by way of Chevrolet's revolutionary V-8, which was not only relatively light in weight compared with other production engines, but it was also inexpensive to produce, reliable, high revving, and impressively powerful. Whether coupled to the old cast-iron two-speed Powerglide or the new three-speed manual transmission, which became available very late in the model year, it turned the otherwise rather anemic Corvette into a credible if not outstanding performer. And perhaps most important, at least in the short term, it put Corvette on an equal footing with its newest competitor in the marketplace, Ford's aggressively styled and V-8 powered Thunderbird.

In spite of its considerable performance gains, many of the problems that had hampered Corvette sales the previous year continued to hurt it in 1955. These included prodigious water leaks when it rained, considerable wind noise at highway speeds, the inconvenience of plastic "side curtains" rather than roll-up windows, the awkward convertible-top system, and the absence of exterior door handles, door locks, and any power assists or other luxury options.

But in spite of its many shortcomings, the Corvette's new V-8 did address the problem of lackluster performance, even if it did not solve it altogether. And perhaps even more important than the raw performance gains, the installation of the V-8 signified a major move forward by replacing an engine whose design dated back to the Great Depression era with the newest, most innovative technology.

While Corvette's V-8 was almost identical to the engine that revolutionized Chevrolet's passenger car line in 1955, there were a number of differences worth noting. When installed in a Corvette the 265-ci power plant was fitted with a chrome-plated ignition shield over the distributor to reduce radio interference, chrome valve covers, and a chrome air cleaner cover. It also utilized an unusual, chrome-covered ignition coil and a unique shut-off valve spliced into the heater hose.

As you would expect, all of those items that were unique to Corvettes, such as the above-described engine parts, are quite difficult to find and expensive to buy. It is important, then, to seek out as complete a car as possible when shopping for a 1955.

As with all Corvettes, originality and technical correctness of components are also important when shopping for a 1955. Most major components, including engine block, cylinder heads, transmission, carburetor, generator, distributor, and radiator, contain one or more casting numbers, casting dates, stamped-in part numbers, assembly dates, and other identifying features. It pays to familiarize yourself with the location, appearance, translation, and significance of these many numbers and codes.

1955

While the new power under the hood was by far the most dramatic improvement, 1955 Corvettes are also distinguished by a number of other important changes. Fit and finish of the body, which had been an issue since the very beginning in 1953, continued to improve as it had in 1954, and a number of new exterior colors were added. In April 1955, Pennant Blue, which first became available in 1954, was discontinued while Harvest Gold, Gypsy Red, and Corvette Copper were introduced.

To signify the new engine powering the car, all V-8-equipped 1955 Corvettes were fitted with a new side emblem featuring an enlarged "V" in the word "Chevrolet." The very small handful of 1955s that were built with six-cylinder engines did not have this new side emblem.

Inside, 1955 Corvettes looked virtually identical to their predecessors, with the same centrally located speedometer and array of smaller instruments spread across the dash. There was, however, an important but unseen difference with the gauges, the radio, and all of the car's other electrical components when compared with previous years. The 1955 model heralded the substitution of a 12-volt electrical system in place of the previously used 6-volt configuration. The increased voltage made engine starting easier and laid the foundation for meeting the increased electrical demands future accessories would impose.

For those who are attracted to the futuristic and well-proportioned styling of first-generation Corvettes, 1955s hold a special allure. They combine that unique, dynamic styling with a wider range of lively colors. And perhaps even more important, they offer the practicality and reliability of V-8 power and a 12-volt electrical system, making them especially friendly to use on today's fast-moving highways. In spite of the fact that only 700 1955s were manufactured owing to the large quantity of unsold 1954s, their prices in today's marketplace are still relatively reasonable.

1955s came with blackwall tires as standard equipment and whitewalls as an extra-cost option. Wheel color was keyed to exterior color, with Polo White and Pennant Blue cars getting Sportsman Red wheels, Harvest Gold cars getting Harvest Gold wheels, Gypsy Red cars getting Gypsy Red wheels, and Corvette Copper cars getting Corvette Copper wheels. Correct 1955 wheel covers are identical to those used in 1953–1954 with the exception of the attaching tangs and valve stem hole location, which were slightly different in 1953.

Though it does not guarantee anything, the fact that a Corvette has earned the coveted NCRS Duntov Mark of Excellence Award is a very good indication that it is probably a correct, high-quality car.

1955 Corvette Specifications and Major Options

1955

Specs

Base Price When New	$2,774.00 (6-cylinder)
	$2,909.00 (V-8)
Production	700
Engine Type	V-8
Bore x Stroke (inches)	3.75x3.00
Displacement	265 cubic inches
Compression Ratio	8.0:1
Horsepower	195 @ 4600 rpm
Transmission	Chevrolet two-speed Powerglide
Wheelbase	102 inches
Overall width	70 inches
Overall height	47 inches
Overall length	167 inches
Track, front	57 inches
Track, rear	59 inches
Weight	2,900 pounds
Tires	6.70x15 bias ply
Suspension, front	Unequal-length control arms, kingpins, coil springs, telescoping shock absorbers
Suspension, rear	Semi-elliptic leaf springs, telescoping shock absorbers
Steering	Worm and ball-bearing roller, 16:1 ratio
Brakes	Bendix duo-servo hydraulic with 11.0 inch drums front and rear
0–60 mph	8.7 seconds
Quarter-mile	16.3 seconds @ 85 mph
Top speed	119 mph

1955 Options

	Price	Quantity
FOA 100 Directional Signals	$16.75	700
FOA 101 Heater	$91.40	700
FOA 102 Signal-Seeking Radio	$145.15	700
RPO 290B 6.70-15 Whitewall tires	$26.90	700
RPO 313 Powerglide Transmission	$178.35	n/a
RPO 420A Park Brake Alarm	$5.65	700
RPO 421A Courtesy Lamps	$4.05	700
RPO 422A Windshield Washer	$11.85	700

1955 Garage Watch

This unusual shielded ignition coil was used on 1955 Corvettes only. The coil was originally silver cadmium plated and has "086" and "12-V" embossed in its case. The radio interference shield is chrome plated. Both the correct coil and its shield are frequently missing and very difficult to find.

Most underhood components, including the distributor shown here, contain a part number and manufacturing date. Correct parts for a given car contain the right part number and a date that precedes the assembly date of the car by no more than about six months.

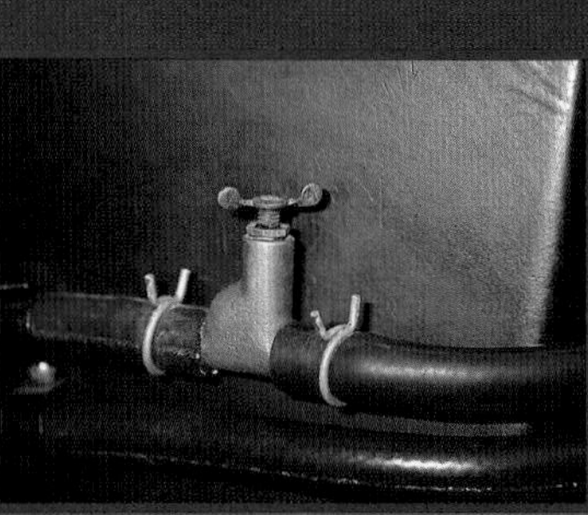

This unusual engine-coolant shutoff valve was used on 1955 Corvettes only. The correct valve is frequently missing and very difficult to find.

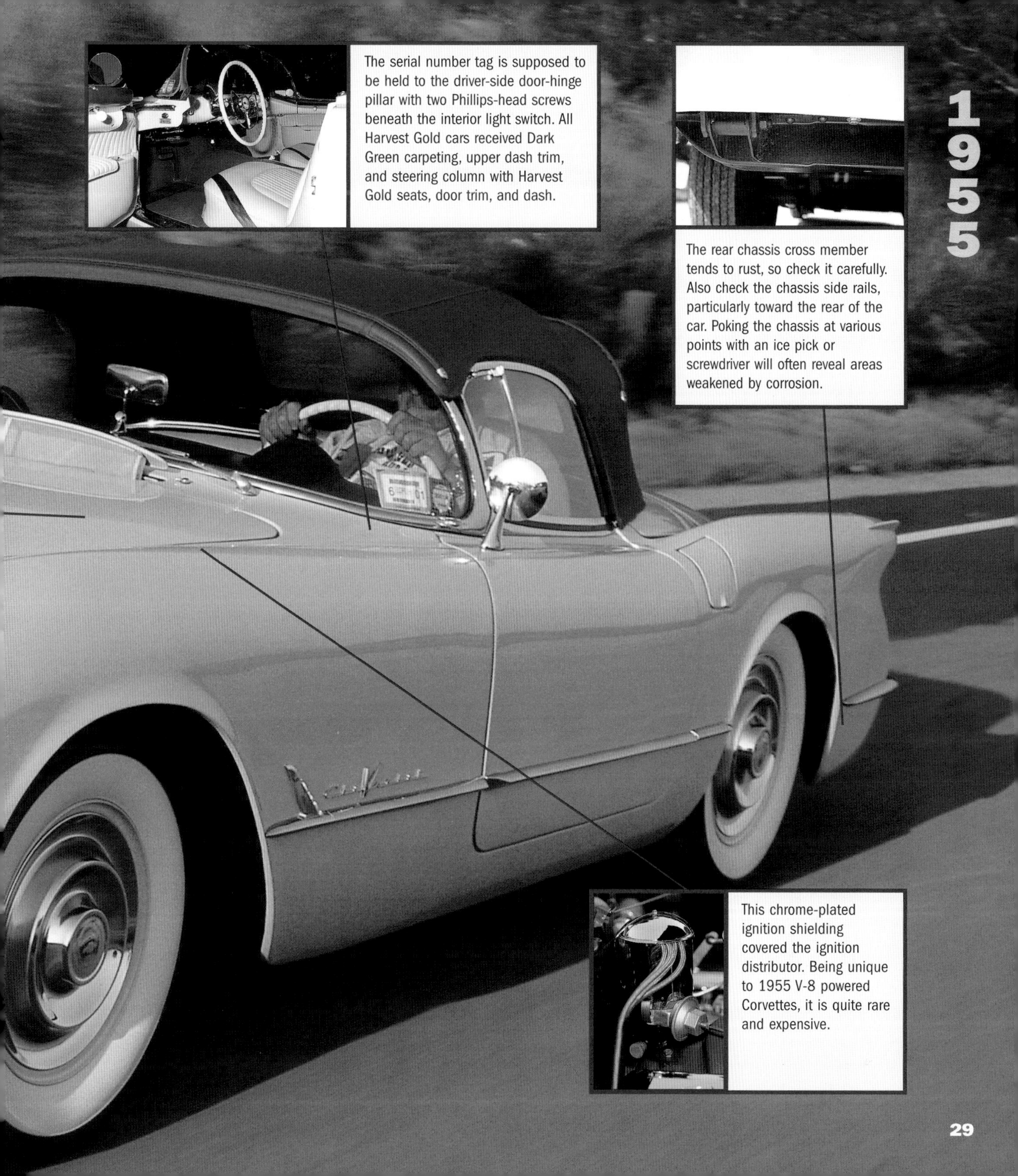

The serial number tag is supposed to be held to the driver-side door-hinge pillar with two Phillips-head screws beneath the interior light switch. All Harvest Gold cars received Dark Green carpeting, upper dash trim, and steering column with Harvest Gold seats, door trim, and dash.

1955

The rear chassis cross member tends to rust, so check it carefully. Also check the chassis side rails, particularly toward the rear of the car. Poking the chassis at various points with an ice pick or screwdriver will often reveal areas weakened by corrosion.

This chrome-plated ignition shielding covered the ignition distributor. Being unique to 1955 V-8 powered Corvettes, it is quite rare and expensive.

1955

1955 Corvette Replacement Costs for Common Parts

Convertible top	$220.00 (functional replacement)
Windshield	$950.00 (correct replacement with date code)
Door glass	$105.00 (correct replacement with date code)
Seat upholstery (per pair)	$350.00
Carpet	$225.00 (reproduction)
Hood	$900.00 (reproduction)
Front fender	$450.00 (reproduction)
Wheel	$125.00 (used original)
Wheel cover	$500.00 (used original)
Front outer horizontal bumper	$120.00
Front grille assembly (minus oval)	$425.00 (reproduction)
Front grille oval	$1,000.00 (reproduction)
Headlamp switch	$60.00 (functional replacement)
Engine-compartment wiring harness	$80.00
Dash wiring harness	$475.00
Exhaust system	$325.00
Shock absorbers	$115.00 (replacement set of four)
Front wheel bearing	$60.00 (outer) $40.00 (inner)
Front-wheel brake cylinder	$35.00 functional replacement)
Master cylinder	$115.00 (functional replacement) $400.00 (original)
Front springs (pair)	$80.00
Lower control arm	$350.00 (used original)
Radiator	$350.00 (functional replacement)
Radiator support	$250.00 (reproduction)
Water pump	$90.00 (rebuilt original)
Ignition shielding	$1,500.00 (used original)
Cylinder head	$400.00 (used original pair)
Chassis	$4,000.00 (reproduction)
Rear leaf springs (pair)	$200.00 (functional replacements)
Complete tune-up kit (ignition points, condenser, plugs, distributor cap, rotor)	$60.00
Fuel tank	$200.00 (reproduction)

1955 Corvette Ratings Chart

Collectibility ★★★★
Smoothness of Ride ★★★
Reliability ★★★★
Comfort Cruising Speed: 65 miles per hour
Passenger Accommodations ★
Part/Service Availability ★★★

The 1955 Corvettes are quite collectible, but selling prices have never reflected their extreme rarity, with cars usually fetching only a little bit more than comparable 1954s. As with the previous year's models, the vast majority of 1955s were originally painted Polo White, with only a handful being blue, gold, red, or copper. It is sometimes impossible to tell what color a given car was originally, however, since Chevrolet did not install trim tags. Owing to the V-8 engine and 12-volt electrical system, 1955 Corvettes are the most drivable of the first-generation cars. They still exhibit much of the crudeness inherent in the 1953 to 1955 series, including the absence of roll-up windows or external door handles, the absence of any power assists, and marginal fit and finish quality. As in 1954, a number of items were listed as options for 1955, but since almost every car built came with them, they can be better described as "mandatory" options. It wasn't until 1956 that buyers had a genuine choice of options.

All 1955 Corvettes came with Plexiglas side curtains rather than roll-up glass windows. The side-curtain assembly is held to the door with a latch and a thumbscrew. The vent window pivots freely and provides access to the interior door-opening lever when the curtains are in place and the soft top is up. Side-curtain assemblies are rather delicate and are often damaged, if not missing altogether. They are not reproduced and an original, well-restored pair typically sells for about $4,000.

The engine-block casting date is located on the passenger-side rear of the block. All 1955 V-8 dates begin with a letter representing the month, followed by one or two numbers representing the day, and then by a single number representing the year. The 1955 V-8 engine stamping is on a boss just forward of the passenger-side cylinder head. The engine serial number is followed by "F55FG" for V-8 Powerglide combinations and "F55GR" for V-8s coupled to manual three-speeds.

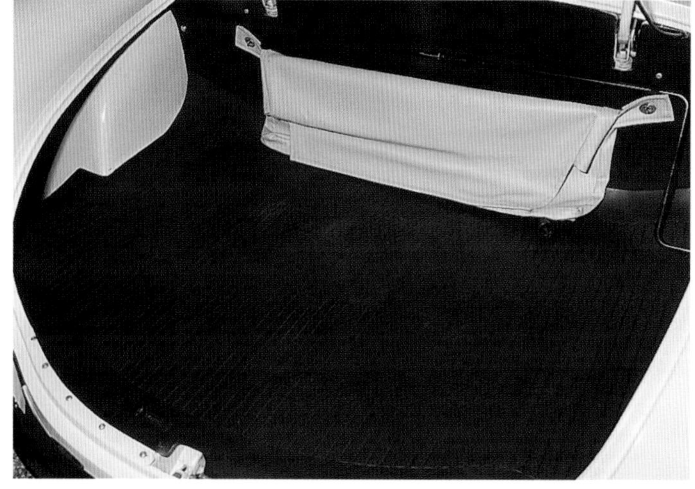

The 1955 trunk was spacious enough for two large pieces of luggage or a full set of golf clubs. The rubber mat covers the spare tire and jack.

The door treatment for 1955 was somewhat crude but was typical of 1950s-era sports cars.

Harvest Gold was available one year only and it is estimated that 120 1955 Corvettes were originally this color. Trim tags were not installed on Corvettes until 1963, but sometimes the original color was written in grease crayon on the rear bulkhead of the trunk toward the passenger side. Carefully scrape the paint off this area with the edge of a coin and you may find this information.

What They Said in 1955

For 1955 there are no changes in the car's specifications except that the new Chevrolet V-8 engine, tuned to 195 bhp, is optional, and the output of the 6 has been upped to 155 bhp (5 more). The V-8 powered version gives truly startling performance, as might be expected, but the transmission and brake deficiencies still will not satisfy the demands of either competition or of the true sports car enthusiast, no matter how loyal he may be to American engineering know-how.

The amazing thing about the Corvette is that it comes so close to being a really interesting, worthwhile and genuine sports car—yet misses the mark almost entirely.

Watching a Corvette in an airport race coming into a corner with fast company, we have observed that the brakes show up poorly, but the actual cornering is done just as fast, flat and comfortably as several imported sports cars we could name.

Chevrolet says the Corvette has "quick" 16:1 steering, but 3-3/4 turns, lock to lock, is not quick-steering "for experts," nor fast enough for a sports car that merits our wholehearted and unreserved recommendation.

Riding qualities are excellent and directional stability at high speeds is near-perfect. One does wonder why the much advertised ball-joint front suspension of the 1955 passenger cars was not applied to the sports car to give the reduced brake dive, easier maintenance and longer life of the ball joints.

Externally the Corvette scores heavily because it has well-executed sports car styling. . . . The instrument panel layout of the Corvette commits a cardinal sin by using a very small tachometer and placing it in the center of the panel rather than alongside the speedometer. Real oil-pressure and ammeter gauges are a saving grace in this day of warning indicators. . . . The seats are beautifully done and very comfortable but no provision has been made for seat belts." —*Road & Track*, July 1955

The Corvette V-8 is an outstanding performer and is a lot of fun to drive. In this sense it's a real sports car, although the purists will argue this point. It is still not quite a serious competition car, although it probably could be modified to give some of the more expensive foreign iron a rough time in road races.

It has some flaws—it's not the ideal car for driving in a heavy rain, I found. However, for those interested in a car of this type, the virtues should make up for any minor shortcomings.

Now for the interesting part: the way it performs! To give you an idea, it turned 0–60 in an average of 8.5 seconds, with a couple of runs being even a couple of tenths of a second less than that.

One of the things that contributes to the Corvette's excellent performance is its relatively light weight. With two passengers (total 325 pounds), a half-tank of gas and a few other odds and ends aboard, the car weighed 3,075 pounds.

In handling and roadability the Corvette V-8 rates very high. Steering ratio is 16:1 and it's very light . . . the steering and feel of the car was one of its highlights and was a special joy in these days when power steering is coming to be regarded as almost a necessary accessory.

In corners the Corvette felt great. It can be whipped around with ease and remains remarkably flat in the tightest turns.

The ride is good by sports-car standards, rather hard by normal passenger-car standards. Roll and sway are practically nonexistent. Even when going flat out, there is no wander. —*Motor Life*, September 1955

I Bought a 1955 Corvette

The 1955 Corvette was the very first car that truly made a lasting impression on me. I'll never forget the first time I saw one.

1955 was the second year that Corvettes could be ordered with other colors besides white, but very few of these other colors were made. In fact, with production of only 700 total cars, very few 1955s of any color were made.

I looked for more than four years before finding my 1955, because I was determined to find a real red one. Corvettes from that era didn't have trim tags, so you need to be quite a detective to figure out the car's original color. What really convinced me about mine was the original red paint that was found underneath the windshield and in other "hidden" areas of the car that never got touched when it was repainted.

The car was restored before I bought it, and everything that could be done to it was done. A professional took the body off the frame and stripped down every nut and bolt. Even the underside of the body was cleaned off so that it looks brand-new again.

The year 1955 was the first year for the Chevy V8, and it was a considerable improvement over the in-line six used in 1954 and 1953. For the first time Corvette had the muscle to match its gorgeous looks. *—Lou Valente*

I always paid particular attention to the beauty of the original styling of the 1953–1955 Corvettes. As a Corvette hobbyist and collector, I always believed that any collection was enhanced by the presence of the first-generation Corvette. My preference was a 1955, given the combination of its low production numbers and its V-8 and 12-volt enhancements. When I had the opportunity to purchase a 1955, I seized it, later purchasing a second.

Given the fact that I had driven many later models, which included the big blocks, I was certainly not interested in a 1955 for its power. The attraction of the 1955 is what I describe as the "Cute Corvette" appeal. It's not big and bold, nor even simple and elegant—it's just cute.

Even though the new "American Sports Car" was somewhat revolutionary, compared to the 1956 and later successors, it is somewhat tantamount to comparing a Victorian "granny porch" house to a contemporary one. As with no other Corvette, this perception of its being cute may be a part of its attraction and appeal, as the 1953s through 1955s will always be the only models with that aura.

The 1955 was GM's and its new Corvette chief engineer, Zora Duntov's, springboard toward Corvette's attaining recognition as a true sports car. It was the model year in which the "Corvette Concept" truly began, affording it the opportunity to attain the legacy it has today. *—Terry Strassberg*

Though much rarer than 1957 models, 1956s are not quite as valuable or sought after. This is undoubtedly due to the fact that more-powerful engines, including those featuring fuel injection, as well as a four-speed transmission, became available in 1957. 1956s are still excellent collectibles and are typically more affordable than 1957s.

Chapter 4 1956

If 1955 marks the birth of Corvette as a high-performance machine, 1956 signifies the beginnings of its maturation into a world-class sports car. Consistent with its increased performance and Chevrolet's marketing strategy, 1956 also marks the beginning of Corvette's racing legacy. Zora Duntov, John Fitch, and Betty Skelton drove a trio of 1956s to a number of new speed records on the sands of Daytona Beach in February 1956. The following month one of four factory-entered cars won its class at the grueling 12 Hours of Sebring. And by year's end the famous "Flying Dentist," Doctor Richard K. Thompson, won the first of his five SCCA National Championships behind the wheel of a Corvette.

Externally, Corvette was entirely restyled in 1956, with a more rounded rear end, striking curved coves breaking up the slab sides found on earlier models, simulated scoops perched atop each fender, and a more aggressive front end. Onyx Black, Aztec Copper, Cascade Green, Arctic Blue, Venetian Red, and Polo White were available colors. And for the first time, buyers could have the side coves painted in either Silver or Beige for an extra cost of $19.40.

Corvette took a significant leap forward in 1956 in terms of comfort and convenience. Gone were the removable Plexiglas side curtains, which most people found to be poor protection against the weather, burdensome to remove and install, and a nuisance when taking up storage space in the trunk. They were replaced by proper roll-up glass windows, which offered a number of advantages, including ease of operation, better sealing properties, and increased sound insulation. Also, rather than having a single, interior door release that could be accessed only by reaching through a pivoting vent window in the side curtains, Corvettes now had ordinary external door handles and locks.

Interestingly, though neither power steering, power brakes, nor air conditioning were offered, beginning in 1956 buyers could have power windows and a power-operated soft top—both at extra cost. Any sort of power assist was really rather remarkable when you consider that only the year prior the car didn't even have roll-up windows! The entire soft-top frame was redesigned for 1956, making it easier to put up and down even without the optional power assist.

As in previous years, a convertible was the only available body style, with fixed roof coupes not offered until 1963. What was new beginning in 1956 was a removable hardtop, which could be had in place of the standard soft top for no additional cost, or in addition to it for an extra $215.20. The 1956 hardtop is distinguished from later examples by its anodized header trim.

The adoption of roll-up glass side windows in concert with the redesigned soft-top assembly made 1956 Corvette interiors much quieter and more resistant to wind and water infiltration. Installation of an optional hardtop, which latched to the windshield header and bolted to the body, went even further in insulating the car's occupants from the vagaries of wind and weather.

Performance took a big step forward in 1956 with the introduction of two optional engines in addition to the standard 265-cubic-inch 210-horsepower unit. The first featured two four-barrel carburetors on an aluminum intake manifold and delivered 225 horsepower, while the second relied on a special high-lift camshaft in addition to dual quads on an aluminum intake to produce 240 horsepower. Both of the optional engines used a dual-point distributor instead of the base engine's single-point arrangement, and were dressed up with cast alloy valve covers in place of the base engine's painted steel covers.

Though officially an option, the 225-horsepower engine was automatically installed into all cars until approximately April 1956, which explains why it was in 3,080 of the 3,467 Corvettes sold in 1956. The 240 horsepower high-lift cam engine is much rarer, having found its way into only 111 cars.

Available transmissions included a cast-iron two-speed Powerglide automatic and a three-speed manual. All automatic-equipped cars came with a 3.55:1 standard (non-limited slip) differential while three-speeds could be had with a standard differential fitted with a 3.27:1, 3.70:1, or 4.11:1 gear ratio.

Though Corvette's body and interior were redesigned and its engine lineup was expanded, the car's underpinnings were largely unchanged for 1956. With the exception of modifications necessary to fit the V-8 engine, the chassis was virtually identical to what was used on the first Corvettes in 1953. Minor revisions introduced in the intervening few years, including stiffer springs and shocks and a suspension geometry altering front cross-member shim, did, however, improve handling somewhat.

As before, for 1956 most mechanical items including wheel bearings, brake drums, U-joints, engine and drive-train parts, shocks, springs, and the like are shared with other GM products of the era and thus remain readily available today. Unlike 1953–1955, however, there are few parts on a 1956 Corvette that are unique and therefore difficult and expensive to obtain. In that sense 1956 really marks the starting point for widespread availability of reproduction components. Compared with an earlier Corvette, then, this typically makes it less challenging and somewhat less expensive to own and restore.

Just like with all other Corvettes, the collector appeal and monetary value of a 1956 is almost always linked to its originality and technical correctness. Most collectors want the casting numbers, casting dates, part numbers, assembly dates, and other codes found on most major parts and assemblies to be correct for the car. This means the part numbers should correlate to what originally was installed on the car and the manufacturing dates should precede the final assembly of the car itself by no more than about six months. When evaluating a car for prospective purchase, you should be familiar with the location, appearance, and significance of the many part numbers and date codes found on older Corvettes, or alternatively should enlist the assistance of an expert who is familiar with them.

Especially important areas to evaluate include the VIN tag, which in 1956 was attached to the driver-door hinge pillar with two screws, and the chassis number, which is typically stamped in two places on the top of the driver-side rail.

1956 interiors were fully trimmed in either red or beige vinyl. When evaluating a car for purchase, don't forget to check the operation of all components, including gauges, radio, windshield wipers, horns, turn signals, and lights. In most instances early Corvettes are relatively simple to repair but parts can be quite expensive.

1956 Corvette Specifications and Major Options

Specs

Base Price When New	$3,120.00
Production	3,467
Base Engine Type	V-8
Bore x Stroke (inches)	3.75x3.00
Displacement	265 cubic inches
Compression Ratio	9.25:1
Horsepower	210
Base Transmission	Three-speed manual
Wheelbase	102 inches
Overall width	70.5 inches
Overall height	51.9 inches
Overall length	168 inches
Track, front	57.0 inches
Track, rear	59.0 inches
Weight	2,900 pounds
Tires	6.70x15 bias ply
Suspension, front	Unequal-length control arms, kingpins, coil springs, telescoping shock absorbers
Suspension, rear	Semi-elliptic leaf springs, telescoping shock absorbers
Brakes	Bendix duo-servo hydraulic with 11.0 inch drums front and rear
Steering	Worm and ball-bearing roller, 16:1 ratio
0–60 mph	7.5 seconds (with optional 265/225 horsepower engine and standard 3.55:1 rear axle)
Standing 1/4-mile	15.9 seconds @ 91 mph (with optional 265/225 horsepower engine and standard 3.55:1 rear axle)
Top speed	120 mph (with optional 265/225 horsepower engine and standard 3.55:1 rear axle)

1956 Options

		Price	Quantity
FOA 101	Heater	$123.65	n/a
FOA 102	Signal-Seeking Radio	$198.90	2,717
FOA 107	Park Brake Alarm	$5.40	2,685
FOA 108	Courtesy Lamps	$8.65	2,775
FOA 109	Windshield Washer	$11.85	2,815
RPO 290	6.70-15 Whitewall tires	$32.30	n/a
RPO 313	Powerglide Transmission	$188.50	n/a
RPO 419	Auxiliary Hardtop	$2,076.00	
	In place of soft top	no chg.	629
	In addition to soft top	$215.20	1,447
RPO 426	Power Windows	$64.60	547
RPO 440	Two-tone Body Paint	$19.40	1,477
RPO 449	225 hp engine w/special cam	$188.30	111
RPO 469	225 hp engine w/2x4	$172.20	3,080
RPO 471	3.27:1 rear axle	no chg.	n/a
RPO 473	Hydraulic Folding Top	$107.60	2,682

1956 Garage Watch

Only 276 Corvettes came with the base engine in 1956. These cars, as well as base engine 1957s, used this chrome-plated air cleaner. The internal element was meant to be cleaned by running kerosene or a solvent through it and then blowing it out with compressed air. Reproduction air cleaners are not exactly the same as an original. Originals are difficult to find and quite valuable, with decent ones typically selling for about $800 and restored ones bringing about $1,400.

Check for signs of obvious body damage. Fiberglass repairs are often evident when seen from the reverse side. Also, check for continuity along the seams where the original factory body panels were bonded together. This photo of a body stripped of paint clearly shows the original panel seams.

1956

Many engine compartment components, including the radiator, generator, carburetor or fuel-injection unit, and distributor shown here, have an identification tag affixed. The tag typically contains a part-number and assembly-date code. This distributor is part number 1110869, and it was assembled on "5L23," which translates to December 23, 1955.

All 1956 Corvettes use this master cylinder, casting number 5450233, with the last three numbers the same size as the first four. Other vehicles use a master with the "233" in larger characters. Though dual reservoir master cylinders weren't mandatory until 1967, it is usually a good idea to install one on a vintage Corvette that will be driven frequently, because dual units are safer. If you do replace the original master cylinder with a more modern unit, be sure to save the original one.

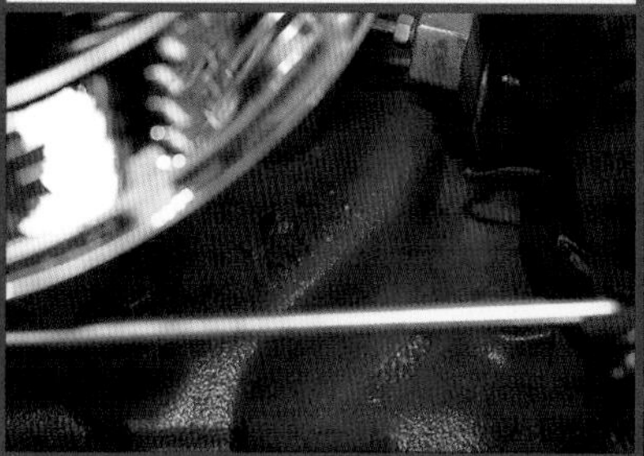

Most cast components contain a part number and manufacturing date code. This intake manifold, for example, is part number 3837109. It was cast on "C286," which translates to March 28, 1956.

The standard 210-horsepower engine came with a single Carter four-barrel carburetor. Optional 225- and 240-horsepower engines both came with two four-barrel Carters. Note the correct choke assembly, glass bowl fuel filter, and steel distributor advance vacuum line. Vintage Corvettes with original components are more desirable to collectors and generally perform better as well.

1
9
5
6

1956 Corvette
Replacement Costs for Common Parts

Convertible top	$230.00 (correct dated reproduction)
Windshield	$450.00 (correct dated reproduction)
Seat upholstery (per pair)	$245.00
Carpet	$400.00 (correct reproduction)
	$225.00 (functional replacement)
Door Panels (pair)	$400.00 (correct reproduction basic door panels minus all trim)
	$1,250.00 (correct reproduction basic door panels including all trim, sheet metal, and upper rail covers)
Hood	$700.00 (correct press molded reproduction)
Hood surround panel	$900.00 (correct press molded reproduction)
Wheel	$125.00 (used original)
Wheel cover	$200.00 (used original)
Front grille assembly (minus oval)	$500.00 (reproduction)
Front grille oval	$1,100.00 (reproduction)
Headlamp assembly (including bucket, cup, ring, adjusters, bezel mount kit, and bulb)	$50.00
Tail-lamp assembly (including housing, lens, gasket, and hardware)	$300.00
Exhaust system	$300.00
Front brake cylinders (pair)	$80.00
Rear brake cylinders (pair)	$60.00
Shock absorbers	$115.00 (replacement set of four)
Front wheel bearing	$60.00 (outer)
	$40.00 (inner)
Front springs (pair)	$90.00
Radiator	$325.00 (functional replacement)
Radiator support	$250.00 (reproduction)
Water pump	$50.00 (functional replacement)
	$85.00 (rebuilt original)
Ignition shielding	$300.00 (complete reproduction set)
Rear leaf springs (pair)	$200.00 (functional replacements)
Complete tune-up kit (ignition points, condenser, plugs, distributor cap, rotor, ignition wires)	$60.00
Fuel tank	$200.00 (reproduction)
Speedometer rebuild kit	$75.00

1956 Corvette Ratings Chart

Collectibility ★★★★
Smoothness of Ride ★★★
Reliability ★★★★
Comfort Cruising Speed: 65 miles per hour
Passenger Accommodations ★★
Part/Service Availability ★★★★

The 1956 Corvettes were the first to feature conveniences such as roll-up glass windows, exterior door handles and locks, and, at extra cost, a removable hardtop, power windows, and power soft top. They were also the first to feature widespread availability of a manual three-speed transmission. These facts, in concert with clean, classic styling and relatively low production, make 1956s highly collectible. They are, however, not quite as collectible nor as costly as 1957s, even though the two model years look extremely similar. This is primarily due to the expanded engine lineup for 1957 as well as the availability of numerous high-performance options that year such as Positraction and fuel injection.

The 1956 base engines came with red steel valve covers as shown here. Optional engines came with cast aluminum covers that say "Corvette" on top. Note the Phillips-head screws and reinforcing tabs retaining the valve cover, tachometer drive cable coming off the back of the generator, and spring-type hose clamp on the upper radiator hose, all of which are correct for 1956.

1956 marked the first year that buyers had a choice of optional engines. The condition of an unrestored, deteriorated engine compartment like this one will normally detract from the car's value. Incorrect components such as the valve covers and air cleaner shown here will also reduce value.

Engines in 1956 did not originally have the car's serial number stamped in, making it very difficult to determine if a particular engine came in a specific car. Engine serial numbers start at 0001001 and continue upward from there. The number is followed by the letter "F" for Flint (the city where the engines were manufactured), "56" for the model year, and two suffix code letters indicating which of the available engines that particular one is.

Almost all of the components needed to restore a 1956 interior are available new, but they are typically not inexpensive. A complete, correct set of door panels costs over $1,200, a fact that emphasizes the importance of carefully evaluating the completeness and condition of every area in a car you are considering for purchase.

Excessive wear and broken parts are common problems with 1953–1962 Corvette steering boxes. The internal steering box parts are available but expensive, and the labor required is considerable. Excessive play, tight spots when turning, and a "notchy" sensation when turning are all signs of trouble.

Replacing the windshield in a 1953–1962 Corvette is a time consuming and somewhat difficult undertaking. Plan to spend about $1,000 to buy new glass and pay a competent shop to perform the labor. Take this into consideration if the car you are considering for purchase has a damaged windshield.

1956

What They Said in 1956

The Corvette's seat is firmly padded and fits your back contour snugger than the T-Bird because of its semi-bucket shape.

The Corvette's speedometer, in its above-the-column position, is legible, but the position of the smaller tachometer in the center of the panel makes it almost useless. To see the fuel and water temperature gauges, you have to take your eyes well off the road.

Glove compartments are about a toss-up: the smallish T-Bird's compartment is a far right reach for the driver; the Corvette's upright box, in the center between the seats, is not useful except for the few things you can stack in it.

The stiffer steering of the Corvette is one of the features I like about it, though I dislike winding the wheel 3-3/4 turns to make a U-turn.

From scratch the T-Bird surges ahead, but two shifts (from low range to intermediate to high) against one (from low to drive) for the Corvette allows the latter to catch and barely nose out the T-Bird at the quarter-mile mark. In the passing speed ranges, the Corvette was the Thunderbird's master. . . .

Acceleration runs and mountain driving always bring out the shortcomings, if any, of the brakes. Both systems were quite responsive and could be easily applied with the left or right foot.

The general feel of the Thunderbird is unlike what you might expect from the car's size and appearance. Through turns it leans considerably, but after it reaches its maximum point of lean it settles down and takes the corner quite well.

The Corvette, on the other hand, feels more like a sports car, with more steadiness and not as much apparent lean.

The Corvette is less of a personal car and closer to being, or easily becoming, a sports car. *–Motor Trend,* June 1956, comparison between 1956 Corvette and 1956 Thunderbird

The Powerglide car gets away from a standstill better than the stick-shift, on the initial "jump". . . . The stick shift model takes off unimpressively too, primarily because of the very "high" first gear. However, at 25 mph in first gear, the power really comes on like a blast and 60 mph can be touched in very close to 7 seconds dead by over-revving somewhat.

The general handling qualities and cornering ability of the Corvette remain "good to excellent" as compared to other dual-purpose sports cars. We did notice, for the first time, a certain amount of body and cowl shake at over 100 mph, which may be due to the very high speeds the new car attains so readily. The more powerful engine is smooth all the way to nearly 6,000 rpm, but it did seem a trifle noisier, under full throttle, than last year's car.

The interior treatment is impressive but the new winding windows and power-operated top have forced some curtailment in elbow and leg room. *–Road & Track,* July 1956

I Bought a 1956 Corvette

I acquired my 1956 in September 1977. At the time of that purchase, the car was in what I would call a strong number-three condition. It was a little bit rough around the edges but was very much in drivable condition.

There are not many 1956s here in Canada and we enjoyed the rarity and the fun we had driving it for a number of years after we acquired it. After quite a few years of use it began to show its age more and more but was still solid and original enough to merit a full restoration. We performed a full body off-the-frame restoration, rebuilding all of the mechanical components to their original level of function and returning all cosmetics to factory-new condition.

The longest trip was when we took it on the 1999 National Corvette Restorers Society road tour to Idaho, an adventure that totaled 6,200 miles round trip! Over twenty-five years of ownership and tens of thousands of miles, the car has been a pure pleasure. It is very reliable and comfortable to drive and feels as familiar as a good pair of old shoes! *—Scott Sinclair*

I had been looking for a 1956 or 1957 for about a year before finding the right one. I wanted a car to restore but was set on finding one that was complete and solid. Also, I wanted one with a dual quad engine and two tops, if possible.

We began the process of restoring a 1956 in December 1995. With help from some very knowledgeable friends, I took everything apart and lifted the body off the frame in my two-car garage at home.

Once we got it down on a custom dolly we [had] made from 2x4 lumber, the real work began. It took five weeks of working nights and weekends to strip off what must have been 10 different paint jobs! Once the body was stripped I turned to the chassis. Again, with lots of help from friends, I disassembled it until there was nothing left attached.

The chassis and all suspension pieces were degreased and then sandblasted. Everything got painted with semi-flat black per NCRS specifications and then reassembled with new bushings, bearings, seals, etc. The dual quad 225 horsepower engine was rebuilt and balanced with all new internal parts. One cylinder head was cracked between two valves and I chose to locate another one with a good date rather than have the old one welded.

I did all of the body preparation but had a professional shop actually do the painting. The body went back onto the chassis in January 1997, two years almost to the day after we removed it. Seeing the body go back on gave me quite a feeling of pride and satisfaction and made me feel like I'd be driving down the road in my restored 1956 in no time. How wrong I was!

Restoring the interior took five times longer than I thought it would. It took almost another two years before everything was really done and the car looks so beautiful that it was worth all of the time and expense.

I get a great thrill from driving the car and getting honks and "thumbs ups" from people who appreciate it. I also love just going into the garage and tinkering with it or just looking at it sitting there. There were plenty of minor setbacks during the restoration, but overall the experience was wonderful and driving the car is truly thrilling. *—Robert Lee*

With a high-performance dual quad or fuel-injected engine, a 1957 has absolutely no trouble keeping up with modern freeway traffic! Generally speaking, unaltered cars are more desirable and hence more valuable. Simple bolt-on items like custom wheels don't usually diminish value beyond the cost to replace them with stock wheels and wheel covers.

Chapter 5 1957

The year 1957 is considered by many collectors to be a high-water mark in Corvette's history. The beautiful body redesign introduced the preceding year was continued essentially unchanged, as was the interior layout. To the previous year's color palette of Onyx Black, Aztec Copper, Cascade Green, Arctic Blue, Venetian Red, and Polo White was added Inca Silver.

Corvette's transformation into a true high-performance sports car, begun in 1955 with the introduction of V-8 power and continued in 1956 with the addition of optional, more-powerful engines, was advanced dramatically in 1957. The many important lessons that Chevrolet had learned in 1956 from the John Fitch-led Sebring race program and Dick Thompson's SCCA championship season were incorporated into the 1957 Corvette.

Engine design remained unchanged but for added power displacement increased from 265 to 283 cubic inches. The base engine utilized hydraulic lifters, a cast-iron intake manifold, a single four-barrel Carter carburetor, and painted steel valve covers with Chevrolet script. As always, cars equipped with an optional radio had metal shielding over the ignition distributor to reduce interference. The base engine delivered a respectable 220 horsepower.

At extra cost buyers could have a wide variety of optional engines. The first on the list was essentially the base engine fitted with an aluminum intake manifold and twin four-barrel carburetors, resulting in 245 horsepower. Next up the ladder was the same basic engine with new-for-1957 Rochester mechanical fuel injection instead of carburetors. It was rated at 250 horsepower. For those wanting still more, two truly high-performance optional engines fitted with solid lifters and high-compression pistons were available. The first of these, rated at 270 horsepower, used an aluminum intake and dual four barrels. The same engine with optional fuel injection instead of carburetion delivered an impressive 283 horsepower, making it one of the first mass-produced engines to produce at least one horsepower for each cubic inch of displacement.

Besides a Powerglide automatic (which was $188.30 extra) and three-speed manual box (which was standard with all engines), buyers could also, beginning in approximately May 1957, opt to have a four-speed manual at a cost of $188.30. Only 664 Corvettes were originally built with four-speeds, but many were converted to this more desirable transmission over the years.

To assist in getting Corvette's added power to the ground, a number of important chassis changes were made in 1957. One of the more popular was Chevrolet's version of a limited-slip differential, which was called Positraction. It was offered with either a 3.70:1, 4.11:1, or 4.56:1 gear ratio.

For even greater performance the factory offered a heavy-duty Brakes and Suspension option. Called RPO (for "regular production option") 684, this package included wider wheels (15x5.5 inches instead of 15x5 inches), stiffer springs, bigger shocks, quick-ratio steering, Cerrametallic brake linings, vented brake backing plates, and numerous other revised components. No doubt due in large measure to the $780.10 price tag, only 51 cars were built with RPO 684 in 1957. The few authenticated examples that survive today are highly coveted by collectors.

For the ultimate road-race-ready Corvette, Chevrolet offered an additional option package called RPO 579E. Enthusiasts often call this the "air box" package and refer to the 43 cars so equipped as "air box cars." RPO 579E cars had a number of very unusual components in addition to all of the items found in the RPO 684 heavy-duty Brakes and Suspension package, which was required when RPO 579E was ordered. Interestingly, RPO 579E cars had to have RPO 684 but RPO 684 cars were not required to have RPO 579E.

In addition to the parts included with RPO 684, RPO 579E cars also had a high-compression, solid-lifter, 283-horsepower fuel-injected engine, a steering column-mounted tachometer, and a rather complicated arrangement of ducts that fed outside air to the engine's intake and to the brakes at all four wheels.

While the expanded list of high-performance equipment captured the attention of racers in 1957, there were also a number of significant comfort and convenience options available to Corvette buyers. As in 1956, windshield washers, a removable hardtop, power windows, and a power-assisted soft top could be had. Still missing were real luxury items like air-conditioning, power steering and brakes, and leather interior trim, but this did little to deter buyers, as evidenced by the record sales of 6,339 cars.

In a continuing trend, overall quality once again improved in 1957. Fit and finish of body panels was better than it had been in prior years, and reliability of mechanical systems also progressed.

Certain shortcomings, which were endemic to the car's design, did not become apparent until many years later and should be considered when shopping for a 1957. Included among these is the propensity of the chassis to rot in certain locations, most notably the rear cross member and the areas of the side rails that connect to it. The bottom of the radiator support and fuel tank are two more areas that should be carefully evaluated for corrosion.

Another problematic item is often the steering box, which is bolted to the chassis adjacent to the engine on the driver side. The box's internal components are prone to failure due to lack of lubrication, high mileage, and hard use. Problems in the box typically manifest themselves with excessive play, tight spots, roughness, or a notched feeling when turning the wheel. The components needed to rebuild the box are now available but they are expensive, and it is very laborious to remove and reinstall the unit in the car.

Though not endemic to the car's design nor unique to 1957s, another area to evaluate when purchasing a Corvette is the presence or absence of important components. Items that have often been changed or are missing for one reason or another, such as factory wheel covers, the radio, and correctly numbered cylinder heads, can be remarkably expensive to replace. Familiarize yourself with all of the characteristics of the car's original components, including casting numbers, casting dates, part numbers, assembly codes, and the like before making a purchase.

Something to keep in mind when shopping for a vintage Corvette is that rarity does not always equate to value. For example, only 379 1957s came with power windows, and while this is a desirable option, it is not nearly as important as fuel injection, which found its way into 1,040 cars.

All 1957 dual carburetor engines used Carter four-barrel units with individual air cleaners as shown here. Dual quad engines, as they are called, add considerable value. Note the small brass triangular tag attached to the top of each carburetor. Visible on the tag to the left is part number 2613S, which denotes it as correct for the front carburetor for a 1957–1961 Corvette 283/270 horsepower engine.

1957

1957 Corvette Specifications and Major Options

Specs

Base Price When New	$3,176.32
Production	6,339
Engine Type	V-8
Bore x Stroke (inches)	3.875x3.00
Displacement	283 cubic inches
Compression Ratio	9.5:1 (base engine)
Horsepower	220 (base engine)
Base Transmission	Three-speed manual
Wheelbase	102 inches
Overall width	70.5 inches
Overall height	51.9 inches
Overall length	168 inches
Track, front	57.0 inches
Track, rear	59.0 inches
Weight	2,900 pounds
Tires	6.70x15 bias ply
Suspension, front	Unequal-length control arms, kingpins, coil springs, telescoping shock absorbers
Suspension, rear	Semi-elliptic leaf springs, telescoping shock absorbers
Brakes	Bendix duo-servo hydraulic with 11.0-inch drums front and rear
Steering	Worm and ball-bearing roller, 16:1 ratio
0–60 mph	5.7 seconds (optional 283/283 horsepower engine, four-speed transmission, and 3.70:1 rear axle)
Standing 1/4-mile	14.3 seconds @ 96 mph (optional 283/283 horsepower engine, four-speed transmission, and 3.70:1 rear axle)
Top speed	132 mph (optional 283/283 horsepower engine, four-speed transmission, and 3.70:1 rear axle)

1957 Options

	Price	Quantity
FOA 101 Heater	$118.40	5,373
FOA 102 Wonderbar Radio	$199.10	3,635
FOA 107 Park Brake Alarm	$5.40	1,873
FOA 108 Courtesy Lamps	$8.65	2,489
FOA 109 Windshield Washer	$11.85	2,555
RPO 276 15x5-1/2K Wide Wheels	$15.10	51
RPO 290 6.70-15 Whitewall tires	$31.60	5,019
RPO 313 Powerglide Transmission	$188.30	1,393
RPO 419 Auxiliary Hardtop		4,055
In place of soft top	no chg.	931
In addition to soft top	$215.20	3,124
RPO 426 Power Windows	$59.20	379
RPO 440 Two-tone Exterior Paint	$19.40	3,026
RPO 473 Hydraulic Folding Top	$139.90	1,336
RPO 469A 245 hp engine w/2x4	$150.65	2,045
RPO 469C 270 hp engine w/2x4	$182.95	1,621
RPO 579A 250 hp engine w/FI & Manual	$484.20	182
RPO 579C 250 hp engine w/FI & Powerglide	$484.20	102
RPO 579B 283 hp engine w/FI	$484.20	713
RPO 579E 283 hp engine w/FI - Special	$726.30	43
RPO 677 3.70:1 Positraction	$48.45	327
RPO 678 4.11:1 Positraction	$48.45	1,772
RPO 679 4.56:1 Positraction	$48.45	n/a
RPO 684 Heavy Duty Brakes & Suspension	$780.10	51
RPO 685 Close-Ratio 4-Speed	$188.30	664

1957 Garage Watch

Contrary to what many assume, cylinder heads used on 220-, 245-, 250-, and 270-horsepower 1957 Corvettes are much rarer than those used on 283-horsepower fuel-injected 1957s. The former contain casting number 3740997, and a good original pair can sell for $4,000 and up. The casting number, along with the casting date, can be found beneath the valve cover.

Another important engine number to check is the block casting date, located on the passenger side of the flange at the back of the block where it mates to the bellhousing. If the date contains two numbers for the year, as it does in this example ("57" for 1957), then the block came from the Tonawanda passenger-car engine plant rather than the Flint Corvette engine plant, and it is therefore not correct for a Corvette.

All 1957 Corvettes came with a serial number plate held to the driver-side door-hinge pillar with two Phillips-head screws. Don't buy a car that is missing this plate. The serial number can also usually be found stamped into the chassis in two places along the side rail on the driver's side of the car: in the areas below the door and above the rear wheel. You can normally see these stampings by placing a small mirror between the top of the chassis and the underside of the floor.

1957

Continuous engine serial numbering was discontinued in 1957. Instead, the engine stamping contained a letter indicating where the engine was built ("F" for Flint, Michigan, for example), three or four numbers designating the month and day the engine was assembled, and two letters commonly called the engine-suffix code, which in general indicates the type of vehicle the engine originally came in, its horsepower, and the type of transmission. This example, stamped "F415EG," is a 283/270 horsepower with manual transmission, assembled on April 15th.

In the course of determining whether a particular engine is correct for a given car you should check the engine-block casting number. The casting number is located on the driver side of the flange at the back of the block where it mates to the transmission or bellhousing. All 1957 Corvette engines used block #3731548.

1957

1957 Corvette Replacement Costs for Common Parts

Convertible top	$230.00 (correct dated reproduction)
Windshield	$450.00 (correct dated reproduction)
Seat upholstery (per pair)	$245.00
Carpet	$400.00 (correct reproduction)
	$225.00 (functional replacement)
Door Panels (pair)	$400.00 (correct reproduction basic door panels minus all trim)
	$1,250.00 (correct reproduction basic door panels including all trim, sheet metal, and upper rail covers)
Hood	$700.00 (correct press molded reproduction)
Hood surround panel	$900.00 (correct press molded reproduction)
Wheel	$125.00 (used original)
Wheel cover	$200.00 (used original)
Front grille assembly (minus oval)	$500 (reproduction)
Front grille oval	$1,100.00 (reproduction)
Headlamp assembly (including bucket, cup, ring, adjusters, bezel mount kit, and bulb)	$50.00
Tail-lamp assembly (including housing, lens, gasket, and hardware)	$300.00
Exhaust system	$300.00
Front brake cylinders (pair)	$80.00
Rear brake cylinders (pair)	$60.00
Shock absorbers	$115.00 (replacement set of four)
Front wheel bearing	$60.00 (outer)
	$40.00 (inner)
Front springs (pair)	$90.00
Radiator	$325.00 (functional replacement)
Radiator support	$250.00 (reproduction)
Water pump	$50.00 (functional replacement)
	$85.00 (rebuilt original)
Ignition shielding	$300.00 (complete reproduction set)
Rear leaf springs (pair)	$200.00 (functional replacements)
Complete tune-up kit (ignition points, condenser, plugs, distributor cap, rotor, ignition wires)	$60.00
Fuel tank	$200.00 (reproduction)
Speedometer rebuild kit	$75.00

1957 Corvette Ratings Chart

Collectibility ★★★★★
Smoothness of Ride ★★★
Reliability ★★★★
Comfort Cruising Speed: 65 miles per hour
Passenger Accommodations ★★
Part/Service Availability ★★★★

The 1957 Corvettes are perennial favorites with collectors owing to the expanded engine lineup as well as the availability of numerous high-performance options such as Positraction and fuel injection. Their outstanding performance combined with beautiful styling characterized by the utmost in proportioning, balance, and refinement combine to create a timeless classic.

Don't underestimate the cost of replacing missing parts. A beautiful set of original wheel covers typically sells for about $800, and a complete reproduction grille oval and grille assembly will cost you in the neighborhood of $1,600. Another expensive item, and one that is often missing, is a correct, complete, working radio, which will set you back at least $1,500.

1957

When evaluating a car for purchase, don't forget to check the operation of all components, including the engine, transmission, brakes, gauges, radio, windshield wipers, horns, turn signals, and lights. In general, early Corvettes are relatively simple to repair, but parts can be quite expensive. This rare factory fuel-injected Corvette does not have ignition shielding over the distributor, ignition wires, and spark plugs. Cars not equipped with the optional Wonderbar radio did not come with shielding.

The front upper body panel of all 1956 to 1962 Corvettes extends from the front all the way to the instrument cluster and comprises the top surface of the dash. Beware of poor collision repairs wherein only a portion of this panel was replaced, with a seam between old and new. Even when a car is painted and fully assembled you can spot repairs and seams by scrutinizing the underside of the panel.

1957 interiors were available in either red or beige vinyl. Aztec Copper and Cascade Green could be ordered only with beige while all other exterior colors were available with either interior color. All 1957 (and 1956) Corvettes came with seat-belt anchors installed in the interior but not with the seat belts. Note the radio block-off plate, in place of where the optional radio would go, and the chrome shifter ball.

Correct reproduction interior trim, including seat covers, door panels, and carpet, is readily available. Other items, such as gauges, knobs, windshield frame, and seat frames are not being reproduced, and good original examples can be quite expensive. Take this into consideration when evaluating a car that is missing components. Note the location of the serial number tag on the driver-door hinge pillar.

This clever "before and after" display was created by the artisans at Vette Dreams Restorations. There is something very satisfying about the final result when you undertake a restoration project, but the cost in dollars and time will often exceed the car's present fair market value. Take this into consideration when negotiating to buy a restoration candidate.

What They Said in 1957

After driving the fuel-injection Corvette many miles and under all sorts of conditions, it was very evident that this new fuel system has great possibilities with further refinement. Its present appeal would not be to the majority of the motoring public. The sporty individual, who enjoys instantaneous throttle response and a surge of power that never seems to run out no matter how tight you wind the engine, will be enthusiastic in his praise of the fuel-injection unit.

However, grandma wouldn't be the least bit impressed with the necessity to shift into second gear at cruising speeds under 30 mph.

The greatest praise for the Chevy fuel-injection unit (from the driver's standpoint) comes from its insensitivity to motion.

The acceleration and top speed of this car is fantastic for a stock car that is available to the public.

The Corvette has all the markings of a wonderful sports car, and it is very gratifying to see Chevrolet developing this model to the extent that it has. But the stock brakes are woefully inadequate to cope with the power and speed built into the engine, and the stock suspension leaves a lot to be desired. *—Motor Life,* June 1957

Even the Anglophiles now readily admit that the Corvette will go. The only question left is how well it goes. Our figures in the data panel are, as usual, the mean of several runs in opposite directions, and corrected for speedometer error. . . . The data are unequalled by any other production sports car.

The fuel-injection engine is an absolute jewel, quiet and remarkably docile when driven gently around town, yet instantly transformable into a roaring brute when pushed hard. . . . Its best feature is its instantaneous throttle, completely free of any stutter or stumble under any situation. . . . With suitable gears the Corvette can approach 150 mph, as has been proven at Bonneville and at Daytona.

Chevrolet said, back in 1954, that they were in the sports car business to stay, and their competition successes of the past two years certainly show that they meant it. – *Road & Track,* August 1957

The 1957s with fuel injection are among the most valuable vintage Corvettes, and fakes are rather common. Unfortunately, there is nothing in the car's serial number that identifies it as a fuelie, making it fairly easy for anyone with the requisite knowledge and appropriate parts to transform a carbureted car into a fuel-injected one. The best insurance is to enlist the services of an expert thoroughly familiar with 1957 fuelies and, if possible, trace the history of the car back to earlier owners to verify its authenticity.

I Bought a 1957 Corvette

My love for 1957 Corvettes began at about age nine when my neighbor had one that he was restoring. When I was eighteen I sold a one-year-old Trans Am to purchase the first of 31 1957s I have owned.

Because I enjoyed restoration so much, and with encouragement from Bob Gold, a good friend and well-known personality in the Corvette hobby, I went into the Corvette Restoration business in the early 1980s.

In 1986 I bought one of my more memorable '57s from Bob Gold. It was an original, unrestored car that he nicknamed "St. Bird." Its original black paint was flaking off and it had an old, musty smell that I loved. For several years I drove that car every day regardless of what the weather was. I'd pull up to a stoplight in a snowstorm and people would look at me in disbelief!

After many more 1957s came and went I bought another memorable one when my first daughter was born in September 1992. Like St. Bird, it was unrestored and had that musty, old car smell. I installed a car seat for the baby and drove it just about every day. I have a lot of fond memories of my daughter and me going to the beach, going to the playground, and just cruising around.

My restoration shop does everything for vintage Corvettes ranging from simple repairs to Bloomington Gold/NCRS quality restorations. But as perfect as these cars are when we are finished with them, I still prefer my 1957 with that musty old smell! *—Dominick Salvemini*

When I first became interested in cars as a teenager, a 1957 Corvette was the coolest car under the sun. When it was new it was the best-looking and the best-performing car, bar none. How many other cars throughout history can we say that about?

Like a lot of other people I was lucky to afford any kind of car when I got out of the service, let alone a new Corvette. It would take many years and many mortgage payments and college-tuition payments before I could treat myself to the dream car.

I had heard from several different people that there were a lot of problems with older Corvettes and that it was important to get one with "matching numbers," whatever that meant. The more warnings I heard the more I thought I'd better learn a lot more about the Corvette hobby before diving in and spending a lot of money. I joined a local Corvette club and began reading everything I could get my hands on that had anything to do with old Corvettes.

After learning a lot about the cars I began my search, looking through Hemmings every month and spreading the word around the car circles that I was a serious buyer for a good car. After looking for about four months I wound up finding the right car at the show in Hershey and buying it there. Even though I am far from an expert, the car was so clean that it largely spoke for itself.

I am the fifth owner of the car and it was obviously well cared for by all of the previous owners. I had it painted in the original color of Venetian Red about six years after I bought it and other than that have done only normal maintenance and minor repairs as needed.

I get the most enjoyment driving the car and have only had the soft top up two or three times over the years. The original 283/220 single-carb engine has a lot of miles on it but still runs smooth and quiet, and even the radio works. It's been a lot of years since I was that teenager in love with the 1957 Corvette but to me it's still the coolest car under the sun! *—Dave Aliberti*

This side view emphasizes the clean lines and perfect proportions of 1958 Corvettes. The chrome emblem on the front fender denotes this car's optional fuel-injected engine. The contrasting color in the side cove was also an extra-cost option.

Chapter 6 1958

Corvette underwent a fairly extensive and readily apparent styling change in 1958. Almost all of the car's body panels were altered in some way and quad headlights were substituted for the previous model's dual arrangement. In addition to the headlight change, 1958 Corvettes are easily distinguished from both earlier and later models by virtue of two chrome strips on the trunk and a series of raised ridges on the hood, both of which were 1958-only embellishments.

As with the outside, Corvette's interior underwent a rather dramatic redesign in 1958. Rather than having the speedometer in front of the driver and all of the other instruments spread out across the dash, 1958s utilize a curvaceous instrument pod mounted above the steering column. And instead of a flat dash face stretching across the entire width of the interior, 1958 Corvettes foreshadowed the future with their central console.

Besides being stylish, the new center console design was also functional. It housed the optional AM radio, the standard clock, and the heater and defroster controls.

In 1956 and 1957 seat belt anchors were installed at the factory, but installation of the actual belts was an extra-cost dealer accessory. For the first time in Corvette's then short history, seat belts were installed as standard equipment by the factory in 1958. Webbing for the belts was dyed to match interior color, but all buckles were painted a color called Hammertone.

Displacement for the 1958 Corvette's base engine and all optional engines remained at 283 cubic inches. Horsepower for the base engine was increased to 230 from the previous year's 220, that mostly by virtue of a new cylinder head casting and a different Carter four-barrel carburetor.

Output of most of the optional engines offered in 1958 remained the same as the previous year. A low compression, hydraulic lifter, dual four-barrel 283 was rated at 245 horsepower while a high-compression, solid-lifter, dual-quad version gave 270 horsepower.

Rochester mechanical fuel injection, first introduced in 1957, was again offered on engines featuring two different levels of tune. A mild version, rated at 250 horsepower, was fitted to an engine having low compression, a tame camshaft profile, and hydraulic lifters. Corvette's power leader, quoted at 290 horsepower (seven more than the previous year), featured a stout 11.0:1 compression, a racy cam, and high revving solid lifters.

As before, a three-speed manual transmission was standard fare with all engines. For additional cost either a four-speed manual or two-speed Powerglide automatic was also available. The four-speed could be put behind any of the engines offered, but the automatic could only be had with the base, 245-, or 250-horsepower engines. This was because the automatic would not hold up as well with the high-revving 270- or 290-horsepower engines.

All of the high-performance options that became available during the 1957 model year, including the heavy-duty suspension and brake package, Positraction, and wide wheels, were again offered in 1958. The underhood fiberglass air box, which was part of the very rare 1957 579E option package, was no longer used in 1958. All of the complex and rather exotic ductwork that fed cooling air to the brakes at all four wheels was still offered as part of RPO 684. Only 144 Corvettes were equipped with this option in 1958 and very few examples survive today. As you would expect, they are highly desirable to collectors and command top prices when they sell.

In addition to a long list of performance equipment, the option list for 1958 also included some comfort and convenience items. The power-operated soft top assembly found its way onto 1,090 cars while power windows made it into only 649. Both are desirable to collectors today and will generally add to the selling price of a car. The power windows are quite sturdy and reliable but the power-top systems are complex and rarely work unless they have been restored. Virtually all of the parts that the system comprises are available (though most differ cosmetically from their original counterparts), but their cost can add up quickly. Take this into consideration when contemplating a purchase that includes a non-functioning power top.

The same general advice applies to some of the other options that were available in 1958. The Wonderbar radio, for example, was a popular option that is frequently not working decades after it was first installed. There are a number of specialists around the country who have the expertise, equipment, and necessary parts to repair a 1950s era Wonderbar, but their services are not inexpensive.

Fuel injection is another example of an option that can be surprisingly costly to repair. The injection system was rather exotic in its day and few people understood how to adjust and service it. It was not uncommon for car owners to get fed up with problems resulting from the service technician's ignorance and replace the fuel injection unit with a good old reliable carburetor. The injection setup was relegated to a spot under the work bench or on a dusty out-of-the-way shelf, only to re-emerge decades later at a swap meet or in the trunk of the car when it was sold. It might look like a good cleaning is all it needs to function properly, but in reality it will likely take a whole lot more. That whole lot more typically includes the trained eye and careful hand of an experienced specialist and a laundry list of rather expensive parts.

Another thing to keep in mind when considering a 1958 for purchase has nothing to do with nonfunctioning components, but rather with the subject of corrosion. Corvette body panels are made from fiberglass, which is virtually immune to rust. Unfortunately, the same cannot be said for the chassis and various underbody supports, all of which are made from steel. Pay particular attention to the chassis's rear cross member and side rails in the areas where they connect to the rear cross member. Also take a good look at the radiator support, which is prone to rust along the bottom.

As is always the case with Corvettes, originality and technical correctness of components is important to the car's value and desirability to collectors. Familiarize yourself with the correct location, appearance, and significance of the many casting numbers, casting dates, part numbers, and assembly codes that are found in most major components and assemblies. Especially important areas to evaluate include the VIN tag, the chassis number, and the engine numbers.

All interior soft-trim items, including seat covers, carpet, dash pads, and door panels, are being reproduced. Other interior parts, such as door sills, grab-bar insert, and steering wheels are also being made. None of these items are inexpensive, however, a fact that should be taken into consideration when considering a purchase in need of interior restoration.

1958 Corvette Specifications and Major Options

Specs

Base Price When New	$3,591.00
Production	9,168
Engine Type	V-8
Bore x Stroke (inches)	3.875x3.00
Displacement	283 cubic inches
Compression Ratio	9.5:1 (base engine)
Horsepower	230 (base engine)
Base Transmission	Three-speed manual
Wheelbase	102 inches
Overall width	70.5 inches
Overall height	51.9 inches
Overall length	168 inches
Track, front	57.0 inches
Track, rear	59.0 inches
Weight	2,900 pounds
Tires	6.70x15 bias ply
Suspension, front	Unequal-length control arms, kingpins, coil springs, telescoping shock absorbers
Suspension, rear	Semi-elliptic leaf springs, telescoping shock absorbers
Brakes	Bendix duo-servo hydraulic with 11.0 inch drums front and rear
Steering	Worm and ball-bearing roller, 16:1 ratio
0-60 mph	6.9 seconds (optional 283/290 horsepower engine, four-speed transmission, and 4.11:1 rear axle)
Standing 1/4-mile	15.6 seconds @ 95 mph (optional 283/290 horsepower engine, four-speed transmission, and 4.11:1 rear axle)
Top speed	118.7 mph (optional 283/290 horsepower engine, four-speed transmission, and 4.11:1 rear axle)

1958 Options

	Price	Quantity
FOA 101 Heater	$96.85	8,014
FOA 102 Wonderbar Radio	$144.45	6,142
FOA 107 Park Brake Alarm	$5.40	2,883
FOA 108 Courtesy Lamps	$6.50	4,600
FOA 109 Windshield Washer	$16.15	3,834
RPO 276 15x5-1/2K Wide Wheels	no chg.	404
RPO 290 6.70-15 Whitewall tires	$31.55	7,428
RPO 313 Powerglide Transmission	$188.30	2,057
RPO 419 Auxiliary Hardtop		5,607
In place of soft top	no chg.	2,215
In addition to soft top	$215.20	3,392
RPO 426 Power Windows	$59.20	649
RPO 440 Two-tone Exterior Paint	$16.15	3,422
RPO 469 245 hp engine w/2x4	$150.65	2,436
RPO 469C 270 hp engine w/2x4	$182.95	978
RPO 473 Hydraulic Folding Top	$139.90	1,090
RPO 579A 250 hp engine w/FI & Manual	$484.20	400
RPO 579B 250 hp engine w/FI & Powerglide	$484.20	104
RPO 579D 290 hp engine w/FI	$484.20	1,007
RPO 677 3.70:1 Positraction	$48.45	1,123
RPO 678 4.11:1 Positraction	$48.45	2,518
RPO 679 4.56:1 Positraction	$48.45	370
RPO 684 Heavy Duty Brakes & Suspension	$780.10	144
RPO 685 4-Speed Transmission	$215.20	3,764

1958 Garage Watch

The ridged hood (often called a "washboard" hood) is another item unique to 1958. The color of this particular car, called Charcoal, was replaced late in the model year by Black. Note the silver-painted wheel and small "dog dish" style hubcap, which is unique to the 15x5-1/2K Wide Wheels option.

Two-thirds of all 1958s were equipped with the optional Wonderbar signal-seeking AM radio. When the "Wonderbar" is pushed, the radio tuner is supposed to automatically move until it locates a sufficiently strong signal. Original Wonderbar radios are difficult to find and quite expensive. They also tend to be expensive to repair.

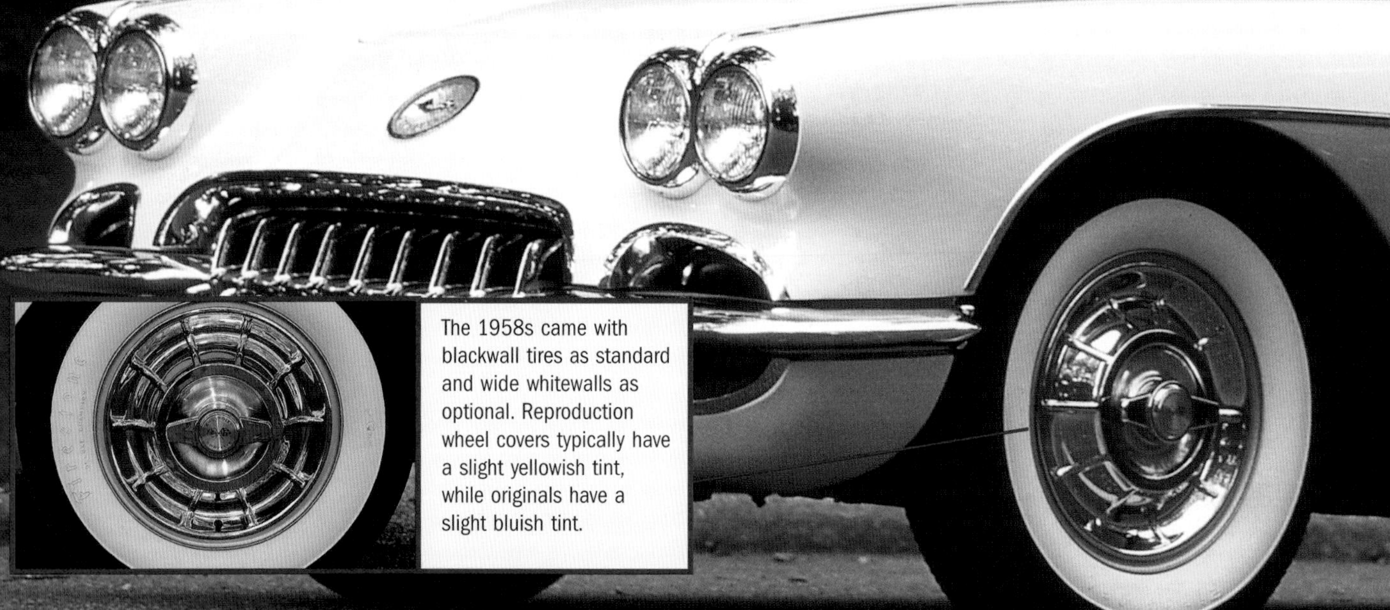

The 1958s came with blackwall tires as standard and wide whitewalls as optional. Reproduction wheel covers typically have a slight yellowish tint, while originals have a slight bluish tint.

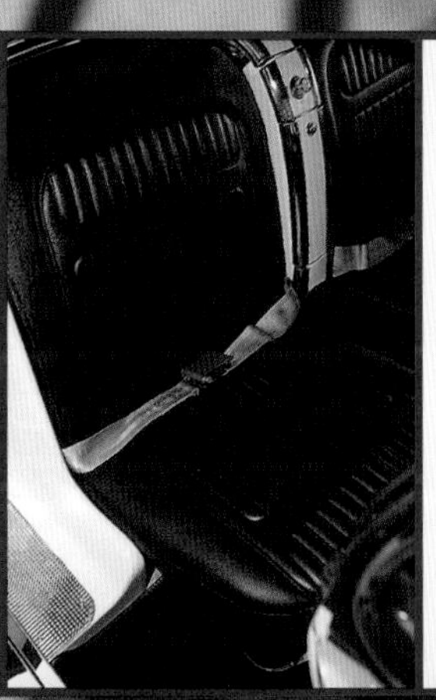

The 1958 seat upholstery has a pebble-grain pattern. Available interior colors included Charcoal, Blue-Gray, and Red. Seat-belt webbing was color keyed to the interior, but all buckles came with a finish called Hammertone, which gives them a mottled gray appearance. The year 1958 marks the first year Corvettes came from the factory with seat belts.

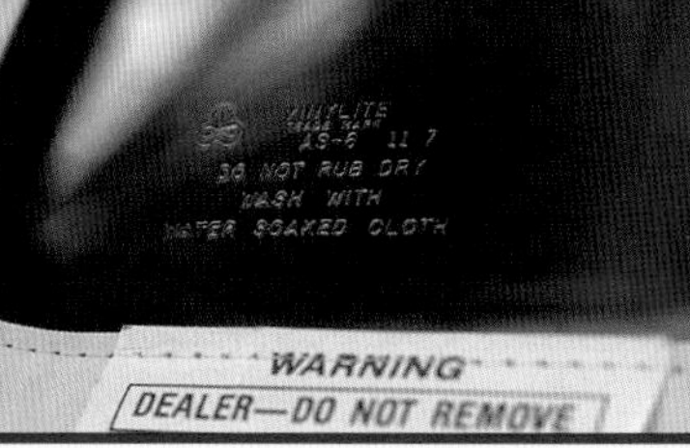

The 1958 soft tops originally contained a manufacturer's logo and various other information heat-stamped into the plastic rear window. The white tag sewn into the top beneath the window is also correct. Note the date code in the upper right portion of the heat stamping, "11 7" for November 1957. Correct soft tops like this one are being reproduced.

Items unique to 1958 include chrome-plated trunk irons. They dress up the rear of the car and are emblematic of the time period, when chrome was king in Detroit. As is usually the case, these one-year-only parts are costly to replace, so make sure they are present or that the price you are paying reflects their absence.

All 1958s should have a serial-number tag attached to the driver-side door-hinge pillar with two Phillips-head screws. Make sure the serial number on the tag matches the serial number on the title and on the chassis. It is normally stamped into the chassis in two places along the top of the side rail on the driver's side. These stampings can normally be seen by placing a small mirror between the top of the chassis and the underside of the floor.

1958

1958 Corvette Replacement Costs for Common Parts

Convertible top	$230.00 (correct dated reproduction)
Windshield	$450.00 (correct dated reproduction)
Seat upholstery (per pair)	$245.00
Carpet	$400.00 (correct reproduction)
	$225.00 (functional replacement)
Door Panels (pair)	$400.00 (correct reproduction basic door panels minus all trim)
	$1,250.00 (correct reproduction basic door panels including all trim, sheet metal, and upper rail covers)
Hood	$700.00 (correct press molded reproduction)
Hood surround panel	$900.00 (correct press molded reproduction)
Wheel	$125.00 (used original)
Wheel cover	$200.00 (used original)
Front grille assembly (minus upper and lower moldings)	$500.00 (reproduction)
Front grille molding, upper and lower	$350.00 (reproduction)
Headlamp assembly (including bucket, cup, ring, adjusters, bezel mount kit, and bulb)	$50.00
Tail-lamp assembly (including housing, lens, gasket, and hardware)	$300.00
Exhaust system	$300.00
Front brake cylinders (pair)	$80.00
Rear brake cylinders (pair)	$60.00
Shock absorbers	$115.00 (replacement set of four)
Front wheel bearing	$60.00 (outer)
	$40.00 (inner)
Front springs (pair)	$90.00
Radiator	$325.00 (functional replacement)
Radiator support	$250.00 (reproduction)
Water pump	$50.00 (functional replacement)
	$85 (rebuilt original)
Ignition shielding	$300.00 (complete reproduction set)
Rear leaf springs (pair)	$200.00 (functional replacements)
Complete tune-up kit (ignition points, condenser, plugs, distributor cap, rotor, ignition wires)	$60.00
Fuel tank	$200.00 (reproduction)
Speedometer rebuild kit	$75.00

1958 Corvette Ratings Chart

Collectibility ★★★★★
Smoothness of Ride ★★★
Reliability ★★★★
Comfort Cruising Speed: 65 miles per hour
Passenger Accommodations ★★
Part/Service Availability ★★★★

The 1958 Corvettes fell somewhat out of favor with collectors in the 1970s and 1980s owing to their gratuitous use of adornment. They have become increasingly popular in more recent years, however, precisely because their extra chrome and embellishment so aptly represent the era in which they were created.

Almost all underhood components contain a part number and manufacturing date. Sometimes, as with this generator, the date and numbers are on an attached tag while at other times they are stamped or cast into the part itself.

All early Corvettes used safety glass for the windshield. This type of windshield consists of two pieces of glass laminated together with a layer of adhesive material between them. Sometimes the lamination separates in areas, resulting in this appearance. The only way to fix this is to replace the windshield.

This original paint, unrestored 1958 has had only two owners. Shown here with its optional removable hardtop, the car's sculpted body contours render it a work of art!

Modifications usually detract from the value and desirability of vintage Corvettes, but there are exceptions to this rule. This beautiful 1958 fuelie is wearing Halibrand magnesium knock-off wheels, period racing parts that are worth about $2,000 each.

To authenticate factory fuel injection, look for components unique to fuelies, including an electric choke, passenger-side exhaust manifold not drilled for a mechanical choke's heat riser tube, an oblong opening in the firewall behind the distributor for the tachometer cable (which for fuelies is driven by the distributor rather than the generator), and riveted steel plates on the inner fender wells that receive the fuelie air cleaner attaching bolts.

The originality of its engine is important to the value of any vintage Corvette. When determining the originality of an engine, evaluate the block casting number, the assembly stamping, and the block casting date.

There is no shortage of chrome on early Corvettes. Most exterior chrome-plated trim, including the grille assembly, is being reproduced but is understandably expensive. As always, you are better off buying as complete a car as possible to begin with rather than spending a fortune on parts afterward to make what initially seemed like a bargain into a complete car.

What They Said in 1958

This month's cover car has been the subject of sundry improvements, as well as the corrosive influence of the "stylists." Chevrolet has gone farther than ever before in attempting to please, via the option route, all potential Corvette buyers. Those who want a real sports car will lean toward the dual 4-barrel carburetors or the fuel-injected engine, with or without the special camshaft; compression ratios go up to 10.5:1, and an 8,000-rpm tachometer comes with the top performance combination.

The cockpit . . . is a highly satisfactory job of pleasing buyers with different tastes. The most glaring fault of the previous models, the too-small tachometer placed low in the center, has been rectified. It is now in front of the driver, where it belongs, though it is still too small.

The first mass-production use of a central "control tower" is here haltingly pioneered. No true car controls are mounted in this spot, which has the advantage of not being reachable, on purpose or accidentally, by a passenger. There are true gauges for oil pressure and generator charge. –*Road & Track,* December 1957

Chevrolet's 1958 Corvette incorporates several improvements to the body and a few minor ones to the engine.

Options that do not change the basic car's essentially "boulevard" character include: Powerglide transmission and with it, a 3.55:1 rear end; electric operating window equipment; a hydraulic mechanism for the folding top; and for the belt-and-braces types, both the hard and soft tops may be ordered on one car.

To improve performance, one can order either two Carter four-choke carburetors or fuel injection. . . . For the man who is really serious about racing, a heavy-duty brake and suspension specification is offered in an all-or-nothing deal. To get this you must also order the "D" engine and the limited-slip differential. But what a package!

We were able, in a very short time, to discover how the 1958 Corvette behaves in nearly every conceivable road situation. It may be summed up as "very well indeed."

Once under way, the limited-slip differential really earns its keep and the acceleration is quite breathtaking. The gear ratios in the four-speed gearbox are well spaced. . . . It is at least the equal of any box we've ever tried, not only with respect to the suitability of the ratios to the engine performance, but the smoothness of the synchromesh brings to mind the old metaphor about a hot knife and butter.

The brakes were so good that we extended our punishing test for twelve stops instead of the usual ten, and it was only in the last two that a slight but definite weakening showed up. –*Sports Cars Illustrated,* January 1958

The rarest 1958s of all are those equipped with RPO 684, the Heavy Duty Brakes and Suspension option. This extra-cost package included stiffer springs and shocks, a fast steering adapter, 15x5-1/2 Wide Wheels, and a completely revised braking system. Shown here are two features of that braking system, a finned brake drum and ductwork that directs cooling air to the assembly.

I Bought a 1958 Corvette

The most important fact about the car my sons and I located was that it was an original 290 HP fuel-injection model. All of the important parts, including the correct engine block, fuel-injection unit, high horsepower tachometer, and undrilled (no heat choke hole) exhaust manifold were there. The car needed much work, but we decided that this was the car we would restore.

We began in November 1990 with the goal to be ready for Gold Certification at the June 1991 Bloomington event. The aim was to restore the car to its original factory condition. All original parts were refinished. My son's & my job would be to research what was correct to the car & hunt down any missing parts. The restoration and assembly was done at a professional shop where the body, engine, interior, chassis, etc., were returned to new condition.

The engine was completed nine days before Bloomington and the body mounted to the chassis 7 days before the event. My restorers worked tirelessly to finish the car. We were all exhausted at Bloomington where some last-minute details were attended to, but it all seemed worth it when the car achieved the "Gold" standard.

Over the next two years we entered a number of events and earned an NCRS National Top Flight. At each event we met many new faces and always enjoyed sharing the Corvette experience. The best part of that experience has been the friendships I've made and the time that I've spent with my sons. *—Terry Strassberg*

In the late 1970s I made a conscious decision to follow my real interest in Corvettes, and that was to procure and race the older Corvette factory-prepared race cars. My good friend Mike Pillsbury, who was very well known in Corvette circles, had much to do with the purchase of many of these cars.

The first Corvette I purchased with vintage racing in mind was a 1958 with RPO 684, of which Chevrolet had made only 144. This car was bought through Mike in 1979, and it came from the Los Angeles area. In addition to the very rare RPO 684 heavy-duty brakes and suspension package, the car was fully optioned with Wonderbar radio, heater, power windows, power soft top, auxiliary hardtop, four-speed transmission, and fuel injection.

Before restoration of this very rare 1958 was completed, I purchased a 1962 Corvette with RPO 687 and a 37-gallon fuel tank. It had been raced out of Johnson Chevrolet in Dallas, Texas; at Sebring, Daytona, and elsewhere. I raced that car for two years and then purchased a 1957 Corvette with RPO 579E, an "air box" car that I am still racing to this day.

The restoration of the 1958 was ultimately completed with vintage racing in mind, but on those occasions when I race a solid-axle Corvette, I always wind up choosing the 1957 air box car.

The 1958 is beautifully finished and a pleasure to drive, but it has yet to see the racetrack again since restoration was completed. I street drive it somewhat regularly and simply enjoy owning it. The headlight fairings and Halibrand magnesium wheels are period correct and in my opinion really add to the car's purposeful look.

One of the benefits of having purchased a car like this some 20-plus years ago is that all of the unique ducting, heavy-duty brake system, and heavy-duty suspension parts were intact and still on the car. The condition and originality made it relatively easy to verify the authenticity of its very rare RPO 687 option package. *—Rich Mason*

Though it would be four more years before Chevrolet would offer creature comforts like air conditioning, power steering, and power brakes in Corvettes, 1959s still make for very enjoyable drives.

Chapter 7 1959

The 1959 model year saw continued refinement of the first-generation Corvette design. Exterior body appearance is the same as 1958, with the exception of the hood and trunk areas. The hoods are smooth between the two spears rather than ridged like in 1958, and the trunks lack the two chrome strips found on the trunk in 1958.

Besides the smooth hood and unadorned trunk, another exterior feature new to 1959 was the wheel cover design. It is similar to the 1958's but incorporates 10 small rectangular cutouts around the periphery to aid brake cooling.

The redesigned interior introduced in 1958 continued in 1959 with a number of welcome improvements. Seats were slightly reshaped for increased support, and the vinyl upholstery had a smoother texture. Door-release handles were moved forward for easier access, and door-panel armrests were relocated to increase elbow room.

All of the instruments were made a bit easier to see in 1959 by virtue of glare-reducing concave lenses. Tach faces were revised for greater legibility. To prevent the likelihood of accidentally going into reverse gear, the shifter was given a "T-handle" that served as a positive lockout. The transmission could not be put into reverse unless the spring-loaded T-handle was held in its upward position.

The paucity of interior storage space that was a common complaint among owners prior to 1959 was addressed with the addition of an open tray beneath the passenger-side grab bar. The tray is not huge but it does provide someplace to toss a pair of gloves, a map book, and the like.

The same design chassis that the Corvette was born with in 1953 continued through 1959. A number of effective changes were made to the underpinnings, however, with the end result being a better handling car. At the rear, two trailing radius rods were added, each anchored at one end to a bracket on the axle and at the other end to a bracket on the chassis. By anchoring the axle housing to the chassis, the trailing radius rods did a great deal to suppress axle hop under hard acceleration. In addition, shock absorbers were redesigned to reduce fluid foaming, another problem sometimes encountered during hard use.

Engine selection remained virtually unchanged from the previous year. The base unit used a cast-iron intake four-barrel carburetor and hydraulic lifters to deliver 230 horsepower. The same basic engine fitted with an aluminum intake and two four-barrel carburetors was rated at 245 horsepower. When equipped with Rochester mechanical fuel injection instead of carburetors, this same package delivered 250 horsepower.

For increased performance on the street and on the track, buyers had their choice of two high-output engines. A twin four-barrel version relied on high compression, solid lifters, and an aggressive camshaft profile to make 270 horsepower. For maximum power production Chevrolet offered the same high-compression, solid-lifter engine with fuel injection. As in 1958 this option was rated at 290 horsepower.

Once again a three-speed manual transmission was standard fare, regardless of which engine the car came equipped with. The base engine and any of the optional engines could be ordered with a four-speed manual transmission and the base, 245-, and 250-horsepower engines could be coupled to the available two-speed automatic Powerglide. The Powerglide was not available with either the 270 or the 290 horsepower engine.

All of the high-performance options that first became available during the 1957 model year, including Positraction differential, wide wheels, and the heavy-duty suspension and brake package, were again offered in 1959.

The heavy-duty brake and suspension package was called RPO 684 in 1959. When installed in very early 1959s, this rare option package included all of the complex and somewhat exotic brake-cooling ductwork seen in 1957 and 1958. This was dropped during the 1959 model year in favor of much simpler scoops bolted to the reverse side of each wheel assembly.

In addition to the brake and suspension/steering package, Positraction differential, wide wheels, and fuel injection, another racing-oriented option appeared on the order form beginning in 1959. Called LPO 1625 (for "limited production option"), it was a 24-gallon fuel tank that presumably was helpful in endurance racing. When equipped with this oversize tank, the car had to be ordered with a hardtop only, since the tank prevented a soft top from fitting in its folded away position. Production figures are uncertain but it is likely that no more than two or three dozen Corvettes were originally built with the big tank.

As in the previous year, a limited number of comfort and convenience options were offered to Corvette buyers in 1959. These included a rather complex hydraulic-assist power-top system, electric power windows, a windshield washer system, and signal-seeking AM radio. It would be a few more years before luxury options like AM/FM stereo, air conditioning, power steering, and power brakes would be offered.

As is always the case with Corvettes, originality and technical correctness of components is important to the car's value and desirability to collectors. Familiarize yourself with the correct location, appearance, and significance of the many casting numbers, casting dates, part numbers, and assembly codes that are found in most major components and assemblies. Especially important areas to evaluate include the VIN tag and the chassis number, which is typically stamped in two places on the top of the driver-side chassis rail. Other important things to consider are the engine numbers, which include the block casting number, casting date, and stamped-in assembly code. The stamped-in assembly code should be located on the front of the passenger-side block deck surface, just forward of the cylinder head. Keep in mind that "restamping" or otherwise altering the engine stampings has been a common practice in the hobby for a number of years, and the originality of a stamping should be determined by a qualified expert if it is important to you.

To today's collectors 1959 Corvettes occupy a niche all their own. Their performance and various appointments are nearly identical to the years immediately before and after, so people's preferences are almost always based on aesthetics. Many enthusiasts prefer either the 1958s for their additional adornment or 1961–1962s because of the revised rear-body design, but still others simply prefer the clean look and curvaceous lines seen in 1959.

Old Corvettes are generally quite simple, especially compared with today's vehicles, but that does not mean they are inexpensive to repair. When considering a car for purchase don't forget to check the function of everything, including the radio, heater defroster, lights, gauges, etc.

1959 Corvette Specifications and Major Options

Specs

Base Price When New	$3,875.00
Production	9,670
Engine Type	V-8
Bore x Stroke (inches)	3.875x3.00
Displacement	283 cubic inches
Compression Ratio	9.5:1 (base engine)
Horsepower	230 (base engine)
Base Transmission	Three-speed manual
Wheelbase	102 inches
Overall width	70.5 inches
Overall height	51.9 inches
Overall length	168 inches
Track, front	57.0 inches
Track, rear	59.0 inches
Weight	2,900 pounds
Tires	6.70x15 bias ply
Suspension, front	Unequal-length control arms, kingpins, coil springs, telescoping shock absorbers
Suspension, rear	Semi-elliptic leaf springs, telescoping shock absorbers
Brakes	Bendix duo-servo hydraulic with 11.0-inch drums front and rear
Steering	Worm and ball-bearing roller, 16:1 ratio
0–60 mph	6.6 seconds (optional 283/290 horsepower engine, four-speed transmission, and 4.11:1 rear axle)
Standing 1/4-mile	14.5 seconds @ 96 mph (optional 283/290 horsepower engine, four-speed transmission, and 4.11:1 rear axle)
Top speed	128 mph (optional 283/290 horsepower engine, four-speed transmission, and 4.11:1 rear axle)

1959 Options

	Price	Quantity
FOA 101 Heater	$96.85	8,014
FOA 102 Wonderbar Radio	$144.45	6,142
FOA 107 Park Brake Alarm	$5.40	2,883
FOA 108 Courtesy Lamps	$6.50	4,600
FOA 109 Windshield Washer	$16.15	3,834
RPO 121 Clutch-type Radiator Fan	$21.55	67
RPO 261 Sunshades	$10.80	3,722
RPO 276 15x5-1/2K Wide Wheels	no chg.	214
RPO 290 6.70-15 Whitewall tires	$31.55	8,173
RPO 313 Powerglide Transmission	$199.10	1,878
RPO 419 Auxiliary Hardtop		5,481
In place of soft top	no chg.	1,695
In addition to soft top	$236.75	3,786
RPO 426 Power Windows	$59.20	587
RPO 440 Two-tone Exterior Paint	$16.15	2,931
RPO 473 Hydraulic Folding Top	$139.90	661
RPO 469 245 hp engine w/2x4	$150.65	1,417
RPO 469C 270 hp engine w/2x4	$182.95	1,846
RPO 579A 250 hp engine w/FI & Manual	$484.20	141
RPO 579B 250 hp engine w/FI & Powerglide	$484.20	34
RPO 579D 290 hp engine w/FI	$484.20	745
RPO 675 Positraction Rear Axle	$48.45	4,170
RPO 684 Heavy Duty Brakes & Suspension	$425.05	142
RPO 685 4-Speed Transmission	$188.30	4,175
RPO 686 Metallic Brakes	$26.90	333

1959 Garage Watch

The 1959 wheel covers differ from those used in 1958 by virtue of the ventilation slots around their perimeter. The covers are polished stainless, while the two-ear spinners in the middle are chrome-plated castings. All cars came with blackwall tires as standard and whitewalls as an extra-cost option. The whitewall shown here, a 6.70x15 U.S. Royal Safety 8, is an actual original 1959 tire, not a reproduction.

The originality of its engine is important to the value of any vintage Corvette. When determining originality you should look at the engine stamping, which is located on the block's deck surface in a machined pad just forward of the passenger-side cylinder head. The stamping contains a two-letter application code and an assembly date. In the example shown here, CU denotes a 283/270 horsepower assembled on January 15th and coupled to a manual transmission.

In the course of determining whether a particular engine is correct for a given car, you should check the engine-block casting number. The casting number is located on the driver side of the flange at the back of the block, where it mates to the transmission or bellhousing. Early 1959 Corvette engines used block #3737739 or block #3756519, while later 1959s used block #3756519.

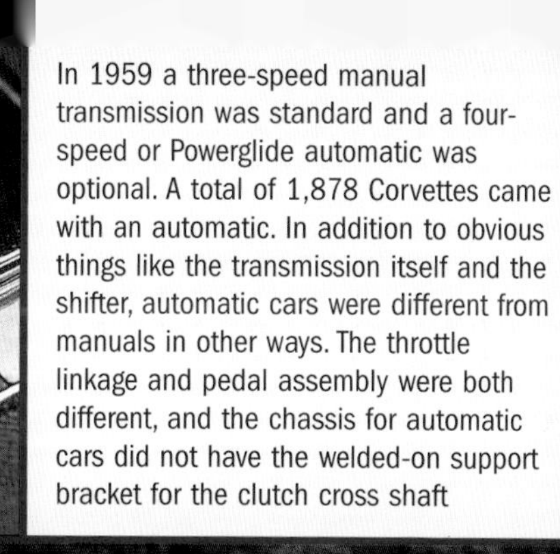

In 1959 a three-speed manual transmission was standard and a four-speed or Powerglide automatic was optional. A total of 1,878 Corvettes came with an automatic. In addition to obvious things like the transmission itself and the shifter, automatic cars were different from manuals in other ways. The throttle linkage and pedal assembly were both different, and the chassis for automatic cars did not have the welded-on support bracket for the clutch cross shaft

Factory dual Carter carburetor engines add interest and value to vintage Corvettes. Look carefully and you can see a small brass triangular tag attached to the top of each carburetor. Each tag contains the part number and assembly date for the carb.

1959

As shown here, original headlamp bulbs feature the "T-3" logo inside a clear triangle. Correct T-3 bulbs are currently being reproduced. Things like correct bulbs, hoses, hose clamps, belts, and the like are elements that separate good-quality cars from great ones.

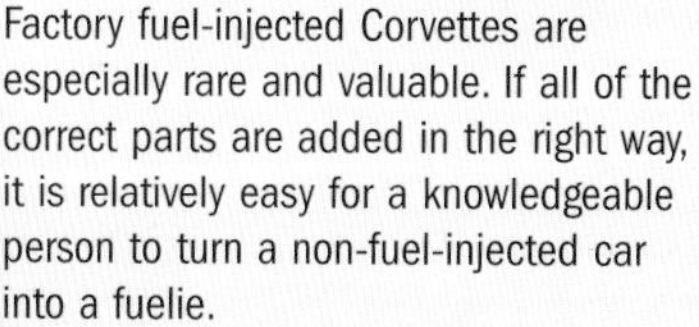

Factory fuel-injected Corvettes are especially rare and valuable. If all of the correct parts are added in the right way, it is relatively easy for a knowledgeable person to turn a non-fuel-injected car into a fuelie.

1959

1959 Corvette Replacement Costs for Common Parts

Convertible top	$230.00 (correct dated reproduction)
Windshield	$450.00 (correct dated reproduction)
Seat upholstery (per pair)	$190.00
Carpet	$400.00 (correct reproduction)
	$145.00 (functional replacement)
Door Panels (pair)	$150.00 (correct reproduction basic door panels minus all trim)
	$775.00 (correct reproduction door panels including all trim and sheet metal)
Hood	$700.00 (correct press-molded reproduction)
Hood surround panel	$900.00 (correct press-molded reproduction)
Wheel	$125.00 (used original)
Wheel cover	$200.00 (used original)
Front grille assembly (minus upper and lower moldings)	$500.00 (reproduction)
Front grille molding, upper and lower	$350.00 (reproduction)
Headlamp assembly (including bucket, cup, ring, adjusters, bezel mount kit, and bulb)	$50.00
Tail-lamp assembly (including housing, lens, gasket, and hardware)	$300.00
Exhaust system	$300.00
Front brake cylinders (pair)	$80.00
Rear brake cylinders (pair)	$60.00
Shock absorbers	$115.00 (replacement set of four)
Front wheel bearing	$60.00 (outer)
	$40.00 (inner)
Front springs (pair)	$90.00
Radiator	$325.00 (functional replacement)
Radiator support	$250.00 (reproduction)
Water pump	$50.00 (functional replacement), $85.00 (rebuilt original)
Ignition shielding	$300.00 (complete reproduction set)
Rear leaf springs (pair)	$200.00 (functional replacements)
Complete tune-up kit (ignition points, condenser, plugs, distributor cap, rotor, ignition wires)	$60.00
Fuel tank	$200.00 (reproduction)
Speedometer rebuild kit	$75.00

1959 Corvette Ratings Chart

Collectibility ★★★★
Smoothness of Ride ★★★
Reliability ★★★★
Comfort Cruising Speed: 65 miles per hour
Passenger Accommodations ★★★
Part/Service Availability ★★★★

The 1959 Corvettes have always been popular with collectors who appreciate their classic styling. They particularly appeal to those who enjoy the quad headlight design without the hybrid rear treatment introduced in 1961 or the gratuitous adornment found in 1958. In general, they are slightly less popular than similarly equipped 1956–1958 and 1961–1962 models and can therefore be bought for a little bit less money, with all else being equal.

Like all early Corvettes, 1959s contain plenty of chrome-plated trim items. Grille teeth, bumpers, and other chrome parts are expensive to restore if damaged or deteriorated.

Interiors were available in Blue, Black, Turquoise, and Red. 1959 Corvettes did not come with a trim tag (the factory began installing them in 1963) so it often takes some detective work to determine what the original color of a given interior was.

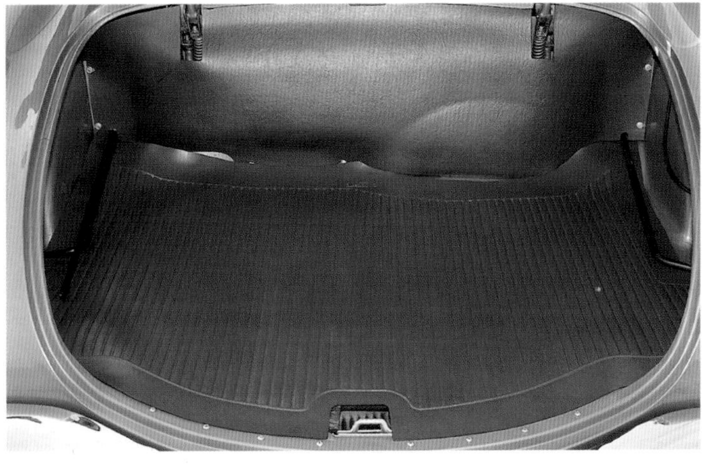

Trim items found in the trunk, including the cardboard at the rear and the vinyl mat, matched the car's interior color. The black tool on the left is for turning the jack while the one on the right is a lug wrench. The spare tire and jack are stowed beneath a plywood cover underneath the mat.

1959

All 1959 optional engines were fitted with aluminum valve covers, and all cars equipped with an optional Wonderbar radio received chrome ignition shielding over the distributor, ignition wires, and spark plugs.

Mileage is not normally a very important factor when considering an old Corvette for purchase. It is quite common that the mileage indicated is not the true mileage, for one reason or another. Of far greater importance, typically, is the condition, originality, and rarity of the car. There are, however, exceptions to this, such as this 1959, which had traveled only 2,846 miles when this photograph was recently taken.

The block casting date, located on the passenger side of the flange at the back of the block where it mates to the transmission bellhousing, needs to precede the car's final assembly date for the block to be correct. The date begins with a letter indicating the month ("A" represents January through "L" for December), followed by one or two numbers indicating the day, and either an "8" for 1958 or a "9" for 1959. This block was cast on January 14, 1959.

1959

What They Said in 1959

The appearance of the 1959 Corvette has been improved by the simple expedient of removing the phony hood louvers and the two useless chrome bars from the deck lid. Inside, the most significant change, and one of the only two that are noticeable, is in the seats. These have been redesigned and are among the most comfortable seats in any car, sports or otherwise.

With a combination of peak torque at 4,400 revolutions per minute and peak horsepower at 6,200 rpm, it does have a lag before the engine really gets to work. The 4-speed, all-synchromesh gearbox is still one of the smoothest-working units it has been our pleasure to use.

Taking everything into consideration, the Corvette is a pretty good car. It probably has more performance per dollar than anything you could buy, and parts are obtainable without sending to Italy, Germany, or England. —*Road & Track,* January 1959

With each annual change, Zora Arkus-Duntov, the Corvette's godfather, has emphasized performance improvements.

The washboardlike phony louvers on the hood and the Pontiac-like silver streaks on the trunk lid are now things of the past. Inside, there are recontoured seat cushions, a reverse lock on the four-speed's shift lever. . . . Also, the doorknob and armrest have been moved. Engineering changes at the rear include newly added longitudinal radius rods to prevent axle wind-up and rearranged and recalibrated shock absorbers.

With so much power so freely available, rapid cornering necessarily becomes a maneuver requiring careful control of all the elements involved.

The steering, stiff for parking, was fine for controlling incipient slides, but as before, we found the throttle linkage much too sensitive. As a result, the car again appears to have two personalities. Either you motor sedately (though deceptively quickly) through a corner, or pressing on somewhat, you're herding an untamed beast, one which responds more to the throttle than the wheel, and rather violently, at that.

That one Corvette is not the same as another is evident from the variety of options. What comes as a considerable surprise is the dualistic personality of the particular car tested. In the twinkling of a throttle linkage, it turns from a submissive sidewalk stalker to a fierce, roaring eater-upper of metallic monsters. Just as quickly, it reverts to silent smoothness, its exhaust murmuring, barely audibly, "Who, me?"

It's not a low-price car, and it's none too cheap to operate, but it goes well, it stops well, and with reservations, it corners well, too. For all-around performance per dollar, the Corvette is hard to beat. —*Sports Cars Illustrated,* March 1959

I Bought a 1959 Corvette

My car led a hard life, seeing action as a drag racer in the late 1960s, having a couple of accidents in the 1970s, and finally winding up in a salvage yard in 1979. Most of the good parts were picked off of it there and it would have undoubtedly wound up in the crusher if my cousin Teddy didn't step in and save it. He put a new nose on and fixed all of the stress cracks and painted it an original 1959 color called Crown Sapphire with white coves. The car was originally all white, including the coves, but he thought that was too boring a color scheme for such a sexy-shaped car.

After a new engine and interior were installed, the chrome was put back on, and a new top was fitted, the former junkyard heap got a second lease on life and looked like brand-new. Teddy kept the car for about two years and wound up selling it to one of his employees, who crashed it two days after he bought it! It wasn't hit very hard but there was still a lot of damage and he couldn't afford to fix it, so I bought it and had my cousin re-restore it.

After the car was finished it got its third lease on life and once again looked brand-new. The only changes I have made are to add a set of American Racing mags in place of the original style wheels and a Hurst shifter in place of the original one. I have kept the original hubcaps and shifter in case I (or a future owner) wants to put them back in.

I drive the car all the time on weekends and occasionally take it to work, where I have a safe parking spot for it. It has an LT1 engine but with all of the right valve covers, air cleaner, etc., on the outside, it looks like an original 1959 engine. With LT-1 power, a four-speed and 3.70 rear end it can keep up with just about anything out there but I enjoy mellow cruising more than anything else and don't feel the need for speed that I did when I was younger. *—Alan Bell*

When I was getting close to 40 years old I decided that I would buy myself a very special birthday present born the same year as I was—a 1959 Corvette! I've always thought the styling of Corvettes from the 1950s was truly beautiful and was attracted to the notion of owning a convertible, which is something I've never had before.

As strange as this sounds, I actually bought my car from a Ford dealership, where someone had traded it toward a new car. The engine is newer than 1959 so it's not a "matching numbers" car as far as that goes, but it runs beautifully.

The only thing that wasn't working when I bought the car was the power folding top. The dealership mechanics tried to get it working but weren't able to, so they lowered the price of the car a little bit from what we agreed on. I wound up having an independent shop that specializes in old cars get it working. It took almost four months between waiting for parts to arrive and refurbishing some of the original parts, but the wait was well worth it.

The longest trip I've taken in the car so far is round trip from Los Angeles to San Diego, which was a total of 268 miles. The car has a lot of power and I love the stick shift transmission. Gas mileage is surprisingly good at almost 20 on the freeway. The steering took some getting used to because no other car I've ever owned had non-power steering. But once I got used to it, it's not hard to steer. The same thing goes for the brakes, which also took some getting used to since they are not power.

For me, part of the fun of owning a car like this is seeing how surprised people are when they see that there's a woman at the wheel. They usually assume that I'm driving my husband's, brother's, or father's car! *—Eileen Gorman*

1960 was the final year to feature a rounded rear-body section and tail lamps formed into the body. Its elegant proportions and classic styling make it very popular with collectors today.

Chapter 8 1960

The 1960 Corvettes are very similar to 1959s in all respects. Exterior body contours are clean and purposeful and, as is typical of the era, there is plenty of chrome and polished stainless steel trim.

Eight exterior colors were offered in 1960, including Tuxedo Black, Ermine White, Roman Red, Sateen Silver, Horizon Blue, Tasco Turquoise, Cascade Green, and Honduras Maroon. As was the case with all 1953–1962 Corvettes, 1960s do not have a body data plate indicating the car's original color. With most cars, assembly line workers used a grease pencil to write the original color on the trunk side of the bulkhead separating the trunk area from the fuel tank. This was a quick way to indicate to the painters what color the body was supposed to be. This area of the bulkhead got painted over, but if you scrape the paint off (the edge of a coin works well for this) you can usually see the original color designation, which is often abbreviated. Abbreviations seen include "blk" for black, "mar" for maroon, and "sil" for silver.

As was the case since 1956, the body cove area could be painted a contrasting color for an additional charge. With a black or white exterior the cove would be painted silver, and with all other exterior colors it would be painted white.

The driver-side instrument cluster introduced in 1958 continued largely unchanged for 1960. It included a speedometer, tachometer, oil-pressure gauge, engine-temperature gauge, fuel-level gauge, and voltmeter.

The same design chassis that the Corvette was born with in 1953 continued in 1960, but certain changes to the suspension improved handling. At the rear, two trailing radius rods, each anchored at one end to a bracket on the axle and at the other end to a bracket on the chassis, did a great deal to suppress axle hop under hard acceleration. In addition, 1960 saw the addition of a rear anti-sway bar to supplement the front bar that had been standard since 1953. This had the effect of increasing roll resistance for flatter cornering.

Engine selection in 1960 remained virtually unchanged from the previous year. The base unit used a cast-iron intake, one four-barrel Carter carburetor, a mild camshaft, and hydraulic lifters to deliver 230 horsepower. The same basic engine fitted with an aluminum intake and two four-barrel Carter carburetors was rated at 245 horsepower. When equipped with Rochester mechanical fuel injection instead of carburetors, this same package delivered 250 horsepower.

For increased performance on the street and on the track, buyers had their choice of two high-output engines. A twin four-barrel version relied on high compression, solid lifters, and an aggressive camshaft profile to make 270 horsepower. For maximum power production, Chevrolet offered the same high-compression, solid-lifter engine with fuel injection. As in 1959 this option was rated at 290 horsepower.

You will sometimes see a reference to higher power ratings for 1960 fuel-injection engines, namely 275 horsepower for the milder version and 315 horsepower for the hotter version. These higher figures would have resulted from the aluminum cylinder heads that Chevrolet initially planned to install on 1960 Corvette engines, but quality-control problems with the castings prevented their use.

As in previous years a three-speed manual transmission was standard, regardless of which engine the car came equipped with. As extra-cost options the base engine and any of the optional engines could be ordered with a Borg-Warner four-speed manual transmission, and the base, 245- and 250-horsepower engines could be coupled to Chevy's two-speed automatic Powerglide.

All of the high performance options that first became available during the 1957 model year, including Positraction differential, wide wheels, and the heavy-duty suspension and brake package, were again offered in 1960.

The heavy-duty brake and suspension package, called RPO 684 in 1959, was changed to the heavy-duty brake and steering package and called RPO 687 in 1960. Unlike in 1957 through early 1959, when this rare option package included complex and somewhat exotic brake-cooling ductwork, 1960 Corvettes used much simpler scoops bolted to the back side of each wheel assembly.

In addition to the brake and steering package, Positraction differential, wide wheels and fuel injection, a 24-gallon fuel tank intended for serious endurance racing was also available in 1960. When equipped with this oversize tank the car had to be ordered with a hardtop only since the tank prevented a soft top from fitting in its folded-away position. Production figures are uncertain but it is likely that no more than two or three dozen 1960 Corvettes were originally built with the big tank.

As in previous years, a limited number of comfort and convenience options were offered to Corvette buyers in 1960. These included the complex hydraulic-assist power-top system, electric power windows, a vacuum-powered windshield washer system, and signal-seeking AM radio. Luxury options like AM/FM radio, air conditioning, power steering, and power brakes would not be offered for another three years.

As is always the case with Corvettes, originality and technical correctness of components is important to a 1960's value and desirability to collectors. Familiarize yourself with the correct location, appearance, and significance of the many casting numbers, casting dates, part numbers, and assembly codes that are found in most major components and assemblies. Especially important areas to evaluate include the VIN tag, the chassis number, which is typically stamped in two places on the top of the driver-side rail, and the engine numbers, which include the block casting number and date and the stamped-in assembly code.

Beginning early in the 1960 model year, each Corvette engine stamping includes two components. As before, it includes what's called an assembly code sequence, which reveals where the engine was manufactured, when it was manufactured, and what its horsepower rating and application were. And for the first time it also includes part of the serial number of the car that that engine was originally installed into. This makes it easier to determine whether a Corvette has its original engine.

The stamped-in assembly code and serial number should be located on the front of the passenger-side block deck surface, just forward of the cylinder head. Keep in mind that "restamping" or otherwise altering the engine stampings has been a common practice in the hobby and the originality of a stamping should be determined by a qualified expert if it is important to you.

To today's collectors 1960 Corvettes occupy a niche all their own. Their performance and various appointments are nearly identical to those of the years immediately before and after, so people's preferences are almost always based on aesthetics. Many enthusiasts prefer either the 1958s for their additional adornment or 1961–1962s because of the revised rear body design, but still others simply prefer the clean look and curvaceous lines seen in 1960 (and 1959).

When considering a 1960 for purchase you should be on the lookout for various problems that are commonly seen in first-generation Corvettes. Look for rust in the chassis, particularly in the rear cross member and the side rails where they connect to the rear cross member. Beware a damaged windshield, which cannot be replaced for anything near the cost of replacing the windshield in an ordinary car because of all the additional labor required with the Corvette. Try to ascertain the source for any play or irregularities in the feel of the front suspension and steering. Any parts that are broken or worn are available, but there will be a considerable difference between something as simple as wheel bearings in need of adjustment and a damaged steering box.

Interior colors included Blue, Black, Turquoise, and Red. Red was by far the most popular, finding its way into 4,920 cars.

1960 Corvette Specifications and Major Options

Specs

Base Price When New	$3,875.00
Production	10,261
Engine Type	V-8
Bore x Stroke (inches)	3.875x3.00
Displacement	283 cubic inches
Compression Ratio	9.5:1 (base engine)
Horsepower	230 (base engine)
Base Transmission	Three-speed manual
Wheelbase	102 inches
Overall width	70.5 inches
Overall height	51.9 inches
Overall length	168 inches
Track, front	57.0 inches
Track, rear	59.0 inches
Weight	2,900 pounds
Tires	6.70x15 bias ply
Suspension, front	Unequal-length control arms, kingpins, coil springs, telescoping shock absorbers
Suspension, rear	Semi-elliptic leaf springs, telescoping shock absorbers
Brakes	Bendix duo-servo hydraulic with 11.0-inch drums front and rear
Steering	Worm and ball-bearing roller, 16:1 ratio
0–60 mph	8.4 seconds (optional 283/270 horsepower engine, four-speed transmission, and 3.70:1 rear axle)
Standing 1/4-mile	16.1 seconds @ 89 mph (optional 283/270 horsepower engine, four-speed transmission, and 3.70:1 rear axle)
Top speed	130 mph (optional 283/270 horsepower engine, four-speed transmission, and 3.70:1 rear axle)

1960 Options

	Price	Quantity
FOA 101 Heater	$102.25	9,808
FOA 102 Wonderbar Radio	$137.75	8,166
FOA 107 Park Brake Alarm	$5.40	4,051
FOA 108 Courtesy Lamps	$6.50	6,774
FOA 109 Windshield Washer	$16.15	7,205
RPO 121 Clutch-type Radiator Fan	$21.55	2,711
RPO 261 Sunshades	$10.80	5,276
RPO 276 15x5-1/2K Wide Wheels	no chg.	246
RPO 290 6.70-15 Whitewall tires	$31.55	9,104
RPO 313 Powerglide Transmission	$199.10	1,766
RPO 419 Auxiliary Hardtop	$5,147.00	
In place of soft top	no chg.	1,641
In addition to soft top	$236.75	3,506
RPO 426 Power Windows	$59.20	544
RPO 440 Two-tone Exterior Paint	$16.15	3,309
RPO 473 Hydraulic Folding Top	$139.90	512
RPO 469 245 hp engine w/2x4	$150.65	1,211
RPO 469C 270 hp engine w/2x4	$182.95	2,364
RPO 579 250 hp engine w/FI	$484.20	100
RPO 579D 290 hp engine w/FI	$484.20	759
RPO 675 Positraction Rear Axle	$43.05	5,231
RPO 685 4-Speed Transmission	$188.30	5,328
RPO 686 Metallic Brakes	$26.90	920

1960 Garage Watch

In 1960 a three-speed manual transmission was standard, and a four-speed or Powerglide automatic was optional. All together, 1,766 Corvettes came with an automatic. In addition to obvious things like the transmission itself and the shifter, automatic cars were different from manuals in other ways. The throttle linkage and pedal assembly were both different, and the chassis for automatic cars did not have the welded-on support bracket for the clutch shaft.

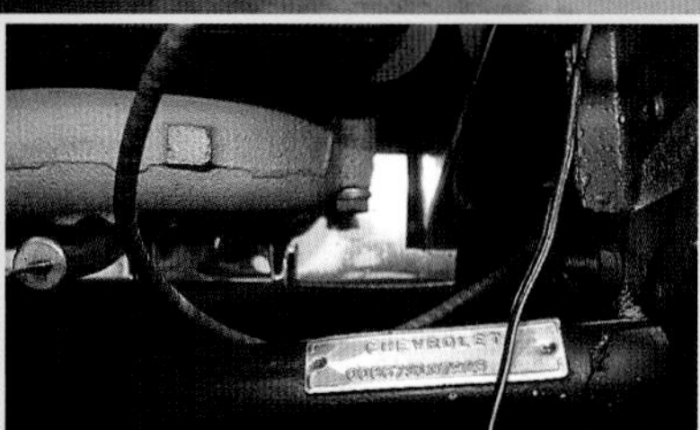

The 1960 Corvettes came with a serial number tag that was spot-welded to the steering column about 13 inches up from the steering box. It is not unheard of for the tag to fall off and get lost. Make sure the car you are considering for purchase has its tag.

A radio and heater were both extra cost options in 1960. Correct AM Wonderbar radios are difficult to find and quite expensive. They are also usually expensive to repair, so make sure you test its function in a car you are considering for purchase. Also test the function of the heater/defroster cables and switch.

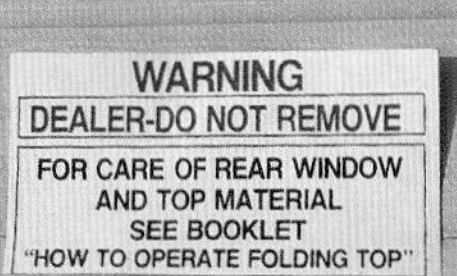

Original and correct reproduction soft tops contain manufacturing information heat-stamped into the rear window and an instructional tag sewn into the top material. As seen in the upper-right area of the heat stamp, this top is dated April 1960 ("4 0").

Since the dual exhaust exits through openings in the rear bumpers, the bumpers are more likely to be rusty around the exhaust pipes. This is because of the humidity and inherently corrosive nature of exhaust gas. Don't forget to evaluate the back side of the bumpers, which can be quite corroded even though the outsides look good.

1960

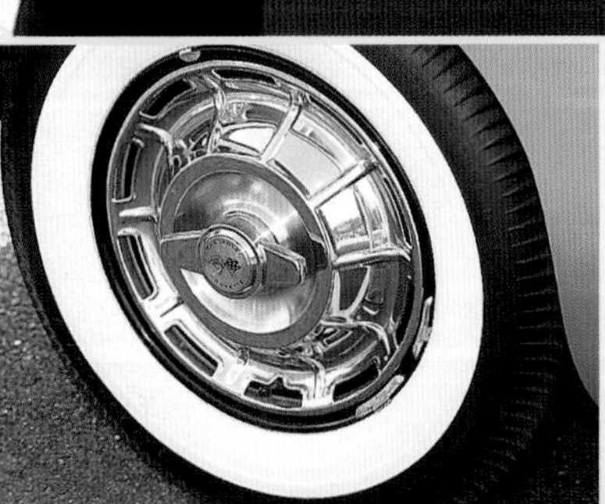

The standard wheel cover comprised a polished stainless-steel disc with a chrome-plated cast spinner in the middle. Cars fitted with optional wide wheels got small "dog dish" hubcaps instead of full wheel covers. Blackwall tires were standard and wide whitewall tires were an option. Beginning in 1960 wheels were normally painted the same color as the car's exterior, so this Horizon Blue car should have Horizon Blue wheels.

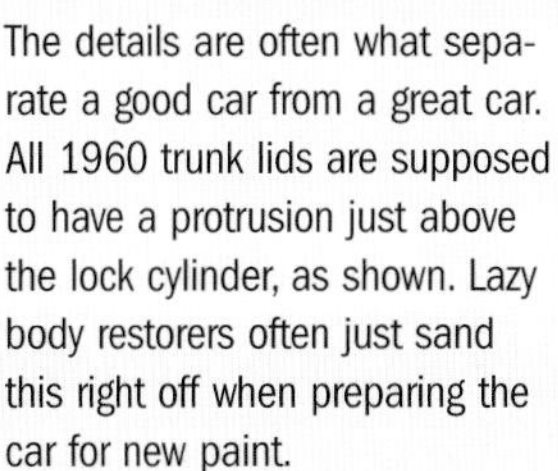

The details are often what separate a good car from a great car. All 1960 trunk lids are supposed to have a protrusion just above the lock cylinder, as shown. Lazy body restorers often just sand this right off when preparing the car for new paint.

1960

1960 Corvette Replacement Costs for Common Parts

Convertible top	$230.00 (correct dated reproduction)
Windshield	$450.00 (correct dated reproduction)
Seat upholstery (per pair)	$190.00
Carpet	$150.00 (reproduction)
Door Panels (pair)	$150.00 (correct reproduction basic door panels minus all trim)
	$800.00 (correct reproduction basic door panels including all trim and sheet metal)
Hood	$700.00 (correct press molded reproduction)
Hood surround panel	$900.00 (correct press molded reproduction)
Wheel	$125.00 (used original)
Wheel cover	$200.00 (used original)
Front grille assembly (minus upper and lower moldings)	$500.00 (reproduction)
Front grille molding, upper and lower	$350.00 (reproduction)
Headlamp assembly (including bucket, cup, ring, adjusters, bezel mount kit, and bulb)	$50.00
Tail-lamp assembly (including housing, lens, gasket, and hardware)	$300.00
Exhaust system	$300.00
Front brake cylinders (pair)	$80.00
Rear brake cylinders (pair)	$60.00
Shock absorbers	$115.00 (replacement set of four)
Front wheel bearing	$60.00 (outer) $40.00 (inner)
Front springs (pair)	$90.00
Radiator	$900.00 (correct reproduction), $325.00 (functional replacement)
Radiator support	$300.00 (reproduction)
Water pump	$50.00 (functional replacement), $85.00 (rebuilt original)
Ignition shielding	$300.00 (complete reproduction set)
Rear leaf springs (pair)	$200.00 (functional replacements)
Complete tune-up kit (ignition points, condenser, plugs, distributor cap, rotor, ignition wires)	$60.00
Fuel tank	$200.00 (reproduction)
Speedometer rebuild kit	$75.00

1960 Corvette Ratings Chart

Collectibility ★★★★
Smoothness of Ride ★★★
Reliability ★★★★

Comfort Cruising Speed: 65 miles per hour
Passenger Accommodations ★★★
Parts/Service Availability ★★★★

The 1960 Corvettes have always been popular with collectors who appreciate their classic styling. They particularly appeal to those who enjoy the quad headlight design without the hybrid rear treatment introduced in 1961 or the gratuitous adornment found in 1958. In general, they are slightly less popular than similarly equipped 1956–1958 and 1961–1962 models and can therefore be bought for a little bit less money with all else being equal.

The standard 230-horsepower engine was the only one to utilize painted steel valve covers and a painted cast-iron intake manifold. All optional engines used cast-aluminum covers and intake. All radio-equipped cars got chrome-plated ignition shielding over the distributor, ignition wires, and spark plugs.

Many engine compartment components, including the radiator, distributor, carburetor or fuel-injection unit, and generator shown here, have an identification tag affixed. The tag typically contains a part number and assembly-date code. This generator is part number 1102043 and it was assembled on March 29, 1960.

As with all 1953–1962 Corvettes, the rear chassis cross member is prone to rusting, so check it carefully. Also check the chassis side rails, particularly in the area around each rear wheel. It is usually helpful to jab the chassis in suspect areas with an ice pick or similar tool. If the chassis is sound this will have no effect, but if it is substantially weakened by corrosion on the inside, the pick will go through the metal.

Original headlamp bulbs feature the "T-3" logo inside a clear triangle. Correct T-3 bulbs are currently being reproduced. Things like correct bulbs, hoses, hose clamps, belts, and the like are elements that separate good-quality cars from great ones.

The originality of its engine is important to the value of any vintage Corvette. When determining the originality of an engine, evaluate the block casting number, the block casting date, and the engine stamping. Early 1960 engine stampings contain only assembly information, while later stampings also contain a portion of the serial number of the car that the engine was originally installed into.

A significant number of parts for 1960, including instruments, seat frames, and windshield frame, are not available new and are not being reproduced. Finding good used parts can be frustrating and costly, so you are much better off buying as complete a car as possible.

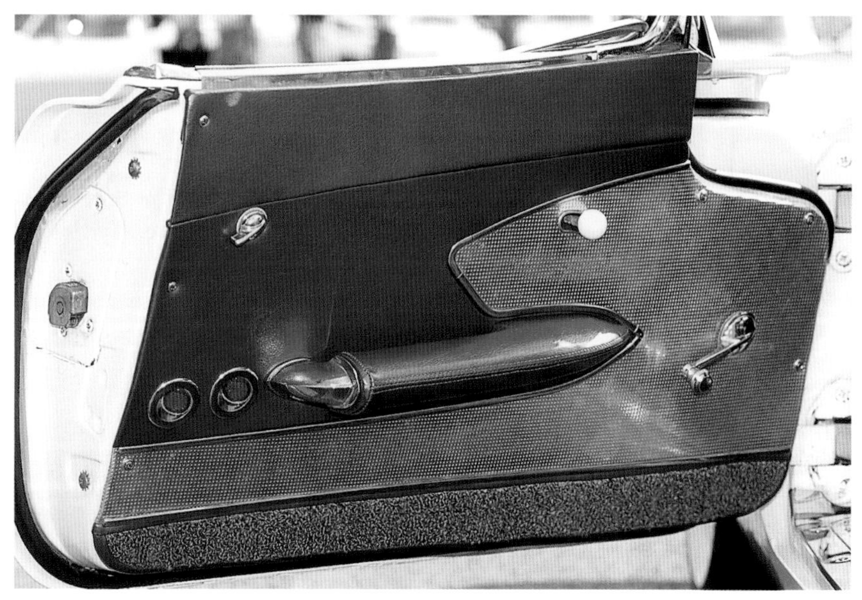

Door panels in early Corvettes were actually sculpted works of art comprising several distinct parts. Note the detailing seen in the latch area of this door. The unpainted top and bottom screws retain the rear window channel. The latch mechanism should be unpainted, but its three retaining screws should be body color. Weatherstrip should be unpainted, and the sloppy application of yellow glue holding it on is typical of factory appearance.

1960

What They Said in 1960

1960 will go down as the year of Speculation for Corvette, SCI not being the only magazine that was caught well off base on predictions of radically changed styling and construction. New-type Corvettes along the lines theorized had actually been proposed, but the terrific engineering concentration on the Corvair project literally left no time for other developments. From the exterior and in all important respects, then, the 1960 Corvette is identical to last year's.

Optional within the standard scheme of things are asbestos-based or sintered-iron brake linings, a third choice being the ceramic-metallic system available as a Regular Production Option. For 1960 there is no special handling kit, Zora Duntov feeling that some further mods to the standard chassis have made its handling good enough to do away with heavy-duty springs, etc. In addition to increasing rear suspension rebound travel by one inch, he has increased the diameter of the front anti-roll bar to 0.70 inch and has added a light-weight anti-roll bar to the rear suspension as well. By increasing roll resistance at the rear Duntov has brought the car closer to neutral steer feel on fast bends, where the Corvette now seems "lighter" on its feet and a shade more sensitive—not necessarily a good feel for racing use. The car can now be tossed around tight corners much more easily, but it must also be admitted that the larger rear roll couple tends to lift the inside rear wheel sooner than was the case before. —*Sports Cars Illustrated,* November 1959

Chassis improvements claimed by the manufacturer for the '60 Corvette are certainly true and welcome. We noticed much less body roll due chiefly to a new stabilizer bar that has been added behind the rear axle. Further stability comes from a front bar of thicker material and shallower bends to reduce twist load concentrations.

Brakes have been improved, but only slightly, by better leverage of pedal to reduce braking effort, and slightly larger diameter of front-wheel cylinders. The stock brakes are just not up to the potential of the car. The optional ceramic-metallic or sintered-iron options are certainly desirable for owners who like to drive Corvettes the way they were built to be driven.

It is not likely that the average person will ever wring his Corvette out on a road racing course, but with the power, speed and acceleration packaged into this sports machine, road racing conditions can unknowingly occur on any highway.

Over the long haul, Corvette comfort for its maximum two-passenger load and minimum of luggage is adequate for average-sized persons.

Heating and ventilation are good, but the most tiring thing on long trips with hard top on and windows open is wind buffeting the side of the face.

Corvette's all-synchro four-speed manual transmission is a joy to use, and shifting is often overdone, due mainly to the ease and convenient location of the short, positive lever. —*Motor Trend,* July 1960

I Bought a 1960 Corvette

1960

My 1960 was found at Pomona, a show with a lot of Corvettes and other types of sports cars. I bought it in 1984 after looking around at old Corvettes for just a couple of months. I started off specifically looking for a black 1954 as this was the car that my father had when I was a small boy but wound up buying a Maroon 1960 instead. The plan changed mid-stream because all 1954s came with two-speed automatics and six-cylinder engines, neither of which I really wanted. To me a classic sports car should always have a four speed and a car like a Corvette should have acceleration to match its reputation.

I have owned several other vintage sports cars including two Porsches and an Alfa Romeo. The Corvette's 283/270 horsepower dual quad engine is far more powerful than what was found in a Porsche, Alfa, or any foreign sports car of the time period, but at the same time a Corvette is considerably heavier than most sports cars. Even given its additional weight my Corvette is quite a bit faster than all of the other cars I've owned in a straight line. Both of the Porsches I had, one a 356B coupe and the other a 356B roadster, handled a little bit better than the Corvette, but the Corvette has a much more solid feel on the highway. The biggest improvement to the Corvette's handling and its ride came when I had Michelin radial tires installed.

After owning this 1960 for almost 18 years I don't think I'll ever sell it. Here in California it's a year-round car, and except for getting caught in the occasional rain during the "winter" a couple of times I never put the top up. When it gets unbearably hot in the summer I still enjoy the car, driving it along the coast where temperatures are typically 15 to 20 degrees cooler than inland. *—Gil Chapman*

I am particularly attracted to the clean, classic lines of a 1960. The elegance of double headlights and all the chrome combined with a rounded tail and Frenched-in tail lights really gives the car great balance and a unique design aesthetic. After looking diligently for more than a year, I finally found a Tasco Turquoise car with a matching turquoise interior. Since buying mine I have only seen two others with this color combination.

Over the course of the nine years I have owned the car, I have gotten everything to work as it was intended and have done minor cosmetic restoration both to the interior and exterior. The wiring system was particularly troublesome as quite a few modifications to it had been made over time to accommodate various alarm systems, radios, fog lights, and so on. I learned that it is far more economical in the long run to simply address the entire system at once.

I had all new wiring harnesses installed, which not only improved function and gave a greater measure of safety, but also enhanced appearance considerably. I also had the generator, voltage regulator, and starter motor professionally rebuilt. All of these components, as well as the engine and drive train, are originals.

While for me a 1960 Corvette is squarely among the most beautiful cars ever produced, it is definitely not among the best performing, at least not by the standards of today's vehicles. The ride is comparatively harsh and the car tends to wander as you drive along. It is susceptible to cross winds and any imperfections in the roadway. The brakes, which don't inspire great confidence under the best circumstances, get even more marginal in wet weather.

I try to exercise the car at least once a month and sometimes more often. I like the look of the body with the matching hardtop in place but generally do prefer open air driving whenever possible. Taking the hardtop off and putting it back on is definitely a two-person operation so I tend to leave it off in the spring, summer and fall and then put in on for the entire winter. When the weather is especially foul I forgo driving, but that doesn't generally detract from my enjoyment of the car because I get as much pleasure from owning and looking at the car as I do from driving it. *—Kenneth Lund*

1961s (and 1962s) were for the most part better than their predecessors in terms of quality control. Fit and finish of body panels and interior trim, as well as general drivability, were improved somewhat. Luxuries like air conditioning and power assists were still a couple of years away.

Chapter 9 1961

Corvettes underwent a fairly extensive exterior restyling in 1961. The chrome-toothed grille, which had been a Corvette trademark since the very beginning in 1953, was gone in favor of a cleaner, stamped-aluminum piece with a chrome center bar and surround. Also gone were chrome headlamp bezels, replaced instead with painted ones. The 1961 front end was further defined by the deletion of the large circular nose emblem seen in previous years and the inclusion of a simple crossed-flag emblem and the name "Corvette" spelled out in individual letters beneath it.

As had been the case since 1958, 1961s continued to feature three chrome-plated horizontal bars and stainless steel perimeter trim in the side-cove area. For $16.15 buyers could have the cove painted a contrasting color. Tuxedo Black and Ermine White cars got Sateen Silver Coves, while Roman Red, Sateen Silver, Jewel Blue, Fawn Beige, and Honduras Maroon cars all got Ermine White coves.

At the rear, 1961 styling was markedly changed. Foreshadowing what was to come with the 1963 Sting Ray, a sharply creased belt line and peaks replaced the rounded contours first seen in 1956. Also, four round tail lamps, which have been a Corvette tradition ever since, were first introduced in 1961.

Blackwall tires were standard fare in 1961 with wide whitewalls available as an extra-cost option. Full wheel covers, fashioned from stainless steel discs with a chrome-plated cast spinner, were included with all cars except those fitted with optional wide base wheels. Cars equipped with wide wheels, as they are called, came with small, rather plain hubcaps that covered the center portion of the wheels while leaving the outer few inches exposed.

Inside, 1961 Corvettes were little changed from their predecessor. The most notable change was increased interior room resulting from a decrease in transmission tunnel width. All cars came with vinyl seat covers and trim in either Fawn, Black, Red, or Blue.

A heater remained optional through 1961, and a relatively small number of cars were built without one. On those cars a simple steel-block off plate was installed on the firewall in place of the heater assembly. A signal-seeking AM radio was optional in 1961 and full instrumentation, including speedometer, tachometer, oil pressure, voltmeter, fuel, and coolant temperature gauges, was standard.

Corvette drive-line specifications, which had remained essentially unchanged since 1958, were updated in 1961. As in previous years a three-speed manual transmission was standard in 1961 with all engines, and a four-speed manual or two-speed automatic was optional. The four-speed could be ordered with any of the available engines, but the Powerglide automatic was available only with the lower horsepower, hydraulic-lifter engines.

Starting in 1961, the optional four-speed was built using an aluminum case. Prior to that the case was made from cast iron. As in previous years the Powerglide automatic case was made from cast iron.

The base engine in 1961 displaced 283 cubic inches and made 230 horsepower using a single Carter four-barrel carburetor, cast-iron intake manifold, relatively low compression, a mild camshaft profile, and hydraulic lifters. The same engine with optional aluminum intake and twin four-barrel carburetors was rated at 245 horsepower, and with Rochester mechanical fuel injection at 275 horsepower.

An optional high-compression, solid-lifter engine featuring an aggressive camshaft profile and two four-barrel Carter carburetors on an aluminum intake made 270 horsepower. The same basic engine package fitted with fuel injection instead of carburetors gave 315 horsepower.

The 1961 (and 1962) Corvettes tend to be the best built and most reliable of the first-generation Corvettes. Body construction methods and materials were continuously improved, and fit and finish of body panels is typically better than in previous years.

Chassis design for 1961 was essentially unchanged from previous years. Rear-trailing radius rods at each end of the axle housing, and a rear anti-sway bar in addition to the front one, help make handling somewhat better than in earlier years. As with all first-generation Corvettes, chassis rust is a problem, and the areas where the rear cross member and side rails connect should be carefully inspected.

The front of the chassis should also be inspected, not for rust but for collision damage. Though the chassis was heavy, it did not have nearly the same rigidity that later designs offered and would typically deform from a less severe collision.

Also look for major body repair, which obviously is indicative of collision damage. As is true both before and after, 1961 Corvette bodies were assembled from many separate panels bonded together with glued-on bonding strips behind each seam. Careful examination of the underside of the body will often reveal whether repair work has been performed or if a one-piece nose section has been substituted for the original multi-piece front end.

As is always the case with Corvettes, originality and technical correctness of components are important to the car's value and desirability to collectors. Familiarize yourself with the correct location, appearance, and significance of the many casting numbers, casting dates, part numbers, and assembly codes that are found in most major components and assemblies. Especially important areas to evaluate include the VIN tag, which in 1961 should be spot-welded to the steering column about 13 inches up from the steering box; the chassis number, which is typically stamped in two places on the top of the driver-side rail, and the engine numbers, which include the block casting number and date, the stamped-in assembly code, and the stamped-in serial number. The stamped-in assembly code and serial number should be located on the front of the passenger-side block deck surface, just forward of the cylinder head. Keep in mind that "restamping" or otherwise altering the engine stampings has been a common practice in the hobby, and a qualified expert should determine the originality of a stamping if it is important to you.

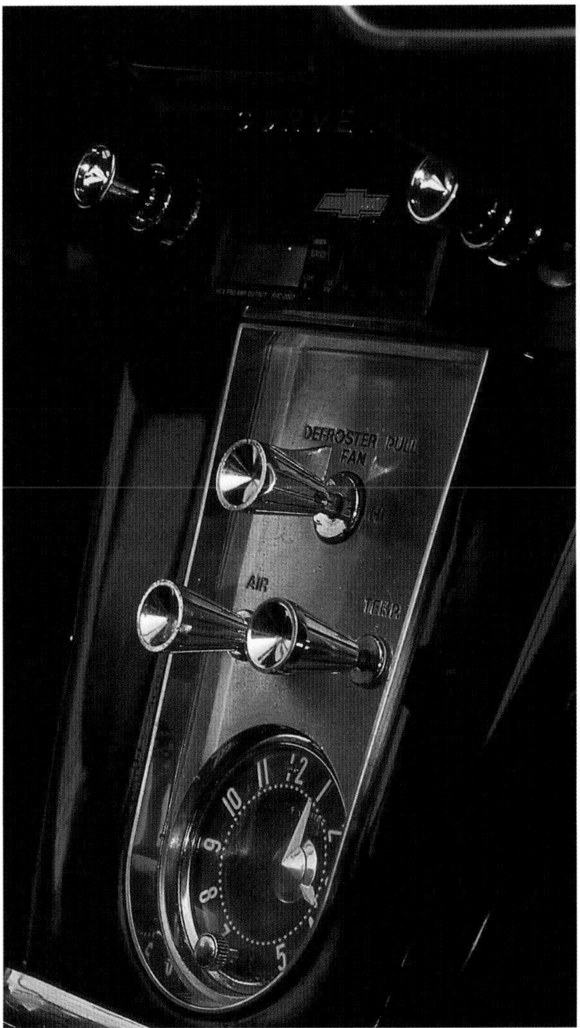

A number of different companies sell aftermarket stereos to fit into vintage Corvettes without making any modifications. They generally sound much better than original AM Wonderbar radios and are a less-expensive alternative to buying an original if it is missing. Do take the difference in value into consideration when evaluating a car equipped with a replacement radio.

1961 Corvette Specifications and Major Options

Specs

Base Price When New	$3,934.00
Production	10,939
Engine Type	V-8
Bore x Stroke (inches)	3.875x3.00
Displacement	283 cubic inches
Compression Ratio	9.5:1 (base engine)
Horsepower	230 (base engine)
Base Transmission	Three-speed manual
Wheelbase	102 inches
Overall width	70.5 inches
Overall height	51.9 inches
Overall length	168 inches
Track, front	57.0 inches
Track, rear	59.0 inches
Weight	3,080 pounds
Tires	6.70x15 bias ply
Suspension, front	Unequal-length control arms, kingpins, coil springs, telescoping shock absorbers
Suspension, rear	Semi-elliptic leaf springs, telescoping shock absorbers
Brakes	Bendix duo-servo hydraulic with 11.0-inch drums front and rear
Steering	Worm and ball-bearing roller, 16:1 ratio
0–60 mph	6.6 seconds (optional 283/315 horsepower engine, four-speed transmission, and 4.11:1 rear axle)
Standing 1/4-mile	14.2 seconds @ 98 mph (optional 283/315 horsepower engine, four-speed transmission, and 4.11:1 rear axle)
Top speed	128 mph (optional 283/315 horsepower engine, four-speed transmission, and 4.11:1 rear axle)

1961 Options

	Price	Quantity
FOA 101 Heater	$102.25	10,671
FOA 102 Wonderbar Radio	$137.75	9,316
RPO 276 15x5-1/2K Wide Wheels	no chg.	337
RPO 290 6.70-15 Whitewall tires	$31.55	9,780
RPO 313 Powerglide Transmission	$199.10	1,458
RPO 353 275 hp engine w/FI	$484.20	118
RPO 354 315 hp engine w/FI	$484.20	1,462
RPO 419 Auxiliary Hardtop		5,680
In place of soft top	no chg.	2,285
In addition to soft top	$236.75	3,395
RPO 426 Power Windows	$59.20	698
RPO 440 Two-tone Exterior Paint	$16.15	3,368
RPO 468 270 hp engine w/2x4	$182.95	2,827
RPO 469 245 hp engine w/2x4	$150.65	1,175
RPO 473 Hydraulic Folding Top	$161.40	422
RPO 675 Positraction Rear Axle	$43.05	6,915
RPO 685 4-Speed Transmission	$188.30	7,013
RPO 686 Metallic Brakes	$37.70	1,402
RPO 687 Heavy-Duty Brakes & Suspension	$333.60	233
LPO 1408 6.70-15 Nylon blackwall tires	$15.75	n/a
LPO 1625 24-gallon fuel tank	$161.40	n/a

1961 Garage Watch

Even though Corvette's trademark chrome-plated grille teeth were replaced in 1961 by a one-piece bright anodized aluminum grille, there is still no shortage of chrome on these cars. Chrome plating is a significant portion of a restoration budget, so carefully evaluate the condition of bumpers and other bright trim when considering a car for purchase. cross shaft.

The 1961 Corvettes came with a serial-number tag that was spot-welded to the steering column about 13 inches up from the steering box. It is not unheard of for the tag to fall off and get lost. Make sure the car you are considering for purchase has its tag.

As with all 1953–1962 Corvettes, the windshield assembly in 1961 is a complex affair requiring quite a bit of skilled labor to service. Factor this in when considering a car with a damaged windshield.

The front upper-body panel extends from the front of the car to the instrument cluster, comprising the top surface of the dash. This is true for all 1956–1962 Corvettes. Beware of poor collision repairs wherein only a portion of this panel was replaced and there is a seam between the old and new. Scrutinize the underside of the panel from underneath the dash area and underneath the area forward of the firewall.

To determine engine originality, evaluate the engine stamping, which is located on the block's deck surface in a machined pad just forward of the passenger-side cylinder head. One section of the stamping contains part of the serial number of the car the engine was originally installed into. Another section contains a two letter application code and an assembly date. Here, CU denotes a 283/270 horsepower engine assembled on April 18 and coupled to a manual transmission.

In the course of determining whether a particular engine is correct for a given car, you should check the engine-block casting number. The casting number is located on the driver side of the flange at the back of the block, where it mates to the transmission or bellhousing. Most 1961 Corvettes used block #3756519, though very late cars may have used block #3789935.

1961 Corvette Replacement Costs for Common Parts

Convertible top	$230.00 (correct dated reproduction)
Windshield	$450.00 (correct dated reproduction)
Seat upholstery (per pair)	$190.00 (reproduction)
Carpet	$145.00 (reproduction)
Door Panels (pair)	$150.00 (reproduction basic door panels minus all trim)
	$775.00 (reproduction basic door panels including all trim and sheet metal)
Hood	$700.00 (correct press-molded reproduction)
Hood surround panel	$900.00 (correct press-molded reproduction)
Wheel	$125.00 (used original)
Wheel cover	$200.00 (used original)
Front grille bar	$110.00 (reproduction)
Front grille molding, upper and lower	$350.00 (reproduction)
Headlamp assembly (including bucket, cup, ring, adjusters, bezel mount kit, and bulb)	$50.00
Tail-lamp assembly (including housing, lens, gasket, and hardware)	$100.00
Exhaust system	$300.00
Front brake cylinders (pair)	$80.00
Rear brake cylinders (pair)	$60.00
Shock absorbers	$115.00 (replacement set of four)
Front wheel bearing	$60.00 (outer)
	$40.00 (inner)
Front springs (pair)	$90.00
Radiator	$800.00 (correct reproduction)
	$325.00 (functional replacement)
Radiator support	$300.00 (reproduction)
Water pump	$50.00 (functional replacement)
	$85.00 (rebuilt original)
Ignition shielding	$300.00 (complete reproduction set)
Rear leaf springs (pair)	$200.00 (functional replacements)
Complete tune-up kit (ignition points, condenser, plugs, distributor cap, rotor, ignition wires)	$60.00
Fuel tank	$200.00 (reproduction)
Speedometer rebuild kit	$75.00

1961 Corvette Ratings Chart

Collectibility ★★★★
Smoothness of Ride ★★★
Reliability ★★★★
Comfort Cruising Speed: 65 miles per hour
Passenger Accommodations ★★★
Part/Service Availability ★★★★

The 1961 Corvettes have always been popular with collectors, though 1962s generally enjoy a slight edge because they are the last of the first-generation Corvettes as well as the first year for 327 engines. The 1961s offer better performance and build quality than all of the earlier Corvettes. Like their predecessors, however, they offer little in the way of creature comforts. Features like air conditioning, power steering, and power brakes would not be offered until 1963 with the introduction of the Sting Ray model.

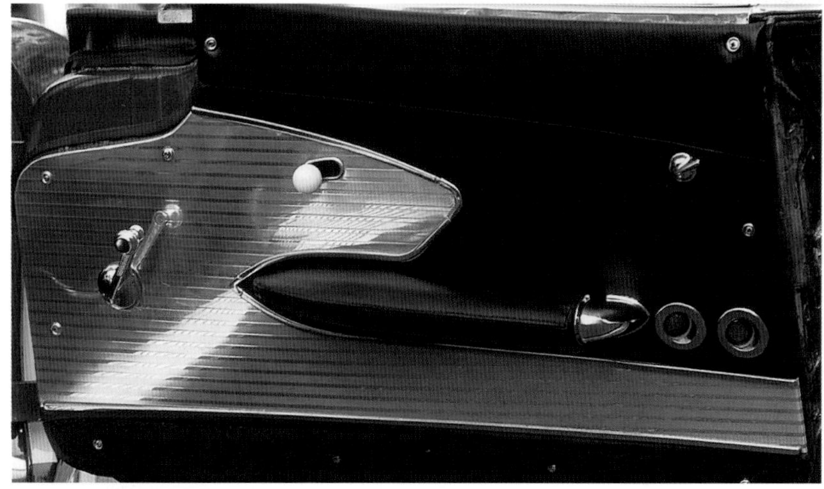

Door panels in early Corvettes were complex affairs consisting of a combination vinyl-covered parts, trim pieces, and a large metal panel. The vinyl is relatively inexpensive to replace, but the trim and metal panel are not.

Beginning early in the 1961 model year, Corvettes were equipped with an aluminum coolant overflow tank. All tanks had a manufacturing logo and date stamped in. This example was made in January 1961.

The trunk area is trimmed with a vinyl mat and molded cardboard shield at the rear. The cardboard in this car should be red, not black. The jack and spare tire are stowed under a plywood covering beneath the mat.

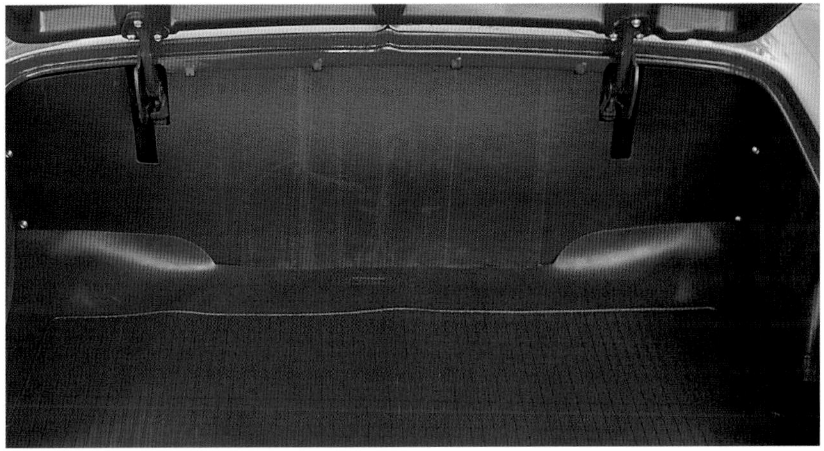

Gauges for early Corvettes are not being reproduced and can be difficult to find and expensive to buy. Check the function of all gauges when evaluating a car for purchase. Note the 6,500 rpm tachometer redline in this 1961, which correlates to either a 270- or 315-horsepower engine. Lower horsepower engines used a lower redline.

The most pronounced changes to styling are seen in the 1961 rear. Its sharp fender arches and beltway crease, along with four tail lamps, foreshadowed the complete redesign that would come in 1963.

Corvette underwent a fairly extensive restyling in 1961, but underneath the new look was essentially the identical car as before.

The 1961 interior continued the early jet age-inspired design theme introduced in 1958. The functional center console features heater and defroster controls, radio, and clock.

As with all early Corvette engine compartments, 1961's was beautiful as well as functional. Chrome ignition shielding was installed on all radio-equipped cars, and a dual quad air cleaner was used on 245 and 270 horsepower engines.

1961

What They Said in 1961

Dealing first with the tame version of the Corvette, our figures show it to be a very lively performer despite its modest 230 bhp and automatic slush-pump.

In summary, the 230-bhp Corvette with Powerglide is a very relaxing, comfortable car to drive, particularly in heavy traffic. And it romps from a standstill to 100 honest mph in 24.0 seconds, a very respectable time.

Our next test Corvette had a 4-speed transmission, the standard (for 4-speed jobs) 3.70 axle ratio and a more exotic 270-bhp engine. We chose this model for test No. 2 in order to see what carburetors lose over the more expensive fuel injection. Unfortunately, the fuel-injection car had a 4.10 axle ratio, but even so we can conclude that the carburetors show no loss in low-speed performance and very little depreciation at the top end. In fact our crew, after driving the cars and studying the mass of accumulated data, began to wonder "why fuel injection?" The 2x4 carburetor job was smooth, flexible and free from carburetion flat-spots. Our conclusions were that the carburetors give more real torque in a usable speed range than fuel injection, and are almost as good as f.i. up to around 100 mph. Above that speed the extra power makes itself felt, and the only real advantage of fuel injection is for competition and, in particular, freedom from c.s.c. (carburetor starvation on corners).

The third test car was the "super" Corvette . . . with fuel injection this sensational engine develops well over one horsepower per cubic inch. Some people claim that this true competition Corvette is too hot for street driving. We do not agree at all. It is extremely easy to drive under any condition of traffic, and the engine is so flexible that it doesn't seem to make any difference which of the 4 gears you happen to choose.

This engine makes a little more noise than the 230-bhp job—around town. The mechanical tappets can be heard and the exhaust note rumbles. When you really get on it, the noise increases considerably, and at 6500 rpm it literally shrieks. But all this performance and crescendo is completely driver-controlled—you can have it if you want it, or not. —*Car Life,* September 1961

It matters not whether someone wants a two-seater merely for transportation, or an all-out racing machine—there is a Corvette to fit his desires, no matter how extreme.

Seated in the cockpit, a 1961 underbody contour change becomes apparent—the transmission hump has been narrowed so that the driver's right leg and throttle foot don't appear to be as cramped.

The instrument panel is still one of the very few that contain a full complement of instruments. The only warning lights that appear are for the hand brake and high beam of the headlights.

Driving both Corvettes (a 230-hp and a 315-hp version) definitely demonstrated that their character is very much the sports variety, even though they are very plush vehicles. Tufted carpeting and considerable use of chrome trim . . . create an air of luxury. When you grasp the steering wheel and negotiate a turn at high speed, and when you shift the four-speed gearbox, you completely lose sight of your luxurious environment and realize that you are driving a true sports car.

No matter what you pay for a sports car . . . there is none that shifts more easily and more consistently than the Corvette four-speed box.

The Corvette's cornering ability is definitely in the superior category, and for many reasons. The car has a fairly low center of gravity, moderately stiff suspension and a stiff front stabilizer bar. Engineering wisely sacrificed softness of ride for safety in this machine. —*Motor Trend,* September 1961

1961

I Bought a 1961 Corvette

I guess it would be correct to say that every young guy or girl dreams of owning a Corvette. In April of 1967 my dream came true with the purchase of a 1961 for $900.00, which at the time did not seem too unreasonable. The car was originally black with a red interior and white soft top. It came with a 283/245 horsepower engine, automatic transmission, and power windows and had about 39,000 miles when I bought it.

I used the car for an everyday driver, and then in the spring of 1968 I did an engine and transmission swap, substituting a new 283 and three-speed manual transmission for the original 283 and automatic. Not knowing about the original engine and transmission, I gave them to a friend.

Late in the summer of 1968 the car was painted the beautiful red it is now. About two months after that it was stolen. A friend from work drove me home and I called my wife at her job to tell her what had happened. She mentioned the incident to one of the girls in her office. Fortunately for me, that girl's husband, while on his way to work, subsequently spotted the car about 10 miles from where it had been stolen. Much to my surprise the only damage was to the ignition switch and the trunk lock, and the gas tank was empty.

Since then I have added a four-speed and rebuilt the 283 twice. When the engine was apart for the second rebuild I upgraded it with some performance parts.

I like to refer to my Corvette as a "Heinz Car — 57 Varieties" because of the non-matching parts in it. But after owning a 41-year-old car for 35 years, I think it still looks great and can run with the best of them. *—Larry Lukash*

I purchased my 1961 from a well-known Corvette dealer. My desire to own this particular vehicle goes back to my childhood, when I thought the style and design of the 1961 Corvette was the ultimate of any car on the road. I still feel the same way today. I love the two-tone paint, the ducktail back, and everything else about the car.

There are numerous updates and improvement modifications you can make to these cars, but I had it rebuilt exclusively to factory specifications as if it were built in 1961. I find that almost everything written about driving the car in review articles is true. You are constantly shifting, the steering is less than great, the braking by today's standards is real poor, but I can tell you, it's a lot of fun to drive and I wouldn't change a thing about the car.

As far as performance and power are concerned, the car with its high compression engines really gets up and goes. The performance diminishes with an adult passenger on board, but it still goes pretty good with the added weight. I've noticed that I can chirp the rear tires in first, second, and third gears when I'm alone in the car.

When I purchased the car, the body and interior, while not perfect, were in excellent condition. However the frame, suspension, and entire drive train were another story altogether. I think because of my relative lack of knowledge I paid too much for the car to begin with, considering all of the work it needed to not only make it correct, but also to make it safe. After restoring the frame, suspension, engine, transmission, and rear end, I just about doubled the amount of money I had into the car. I can honestly say that aside from the aggravation in the early stages of owning the car and getting past the feeling of being taken advantage of by the selling dealer, the car, to me, is worth every dollar I have into it now that I know it is safe and reliable. *—Thomas Riccinto*

1962 marked the final year for the first-generation Corvette design. Body panel fit and finish was relatively good, especially when compared with earlier Corvettes. Poorly aligned doors, irregular hood and trunk gaps, and misalignment between adjacent panels are usually indicative of collision damage and poor quality repairs.

Chapter 10 1962

Corvette's fairly extensive exterior restyling, first seen in 1961, continued into 1962 with some minor tweaking. As in 1961, it featured a stamped aluminum grille with a chrome center bar and surround. For 1962, however, the grille was anodized black rather than silver. The 1962 front end was further defined by its unique nose emblem, which featured crossed flags within a chrome circle. The name "Corvette" was spelled out in individual chrome-plated letters beneath it.

In 1962 the previously used three horizontal side-cove bars were replaced with a simulated grille made from a ribbed casting painted flat black between chrome ridges. The side cove's stainless perimeter trim was dropped altogether in 1962, as was the optional contrasting cove color.

At the rear, 1962 styling mirrored the design first seen in 1961. Foreshadowing what was to come with the all-new 1963 Sting Ray, a sharply creased belt line and peaks replaced the rounded contours first seen in 1956. Also, four round tail lamps, which have been a Corvette tradition for decades, were used in 1962.

Blackwall tires were standard fare in 1962 with narrow whitewalls available as an extra-cost option. The 1962 Corvettes were the first to come with rocker molding. They were made from one-piece, stamped aluminum featuring horizontal ribs and bright anodizing. Up until about serial number 6,000 they were unpainted, and thereafter they had flat black paint between their horizontal ribs.

Inside, 1962 Corvettes were little changed from their predecessors. All cars came with vinyl seat covers and trim in either Fawn, Black, or Red.

A passenger heater, which was previously available as an option, became standard in 1962. Some 1962s were built without one, though, either under RPO 610 (which was for export cars) or via special order arrangements with Chevrolet's Central Office. A signal-seeking AM radio was optional in 1962, and full instrumentation, including speedometer, tachometer, oil pressure, voltmeter, fuel, and coolant-temperature gauges, was standard.

Corvette driveline specifications were significantly updated in 1962. As in previous years a three-speed manual transmission was standard with all engines, and a four-speed manual or two-speed automatic was optional. The four-speed could be ordered with any of the available engines, but the automatic was only available with the lower horsepower, hydraulic-lifter engines.

As was true the previous year, the optional four-speed was built using an aluminum case. Unlike in the past, however, 1962 saw the first use of an aluminum case for the Powerglide two-speed automatic.

Corvette's basic engine design was unchanged for 1962 but displacement was increased to 327 cubic inches from the previously used 283 cubic inches. The standard engine, which relied on a single Carter four-barrel carburetor atop a cast-iron intake, a mild hydraulic-lifter camshaft, and relatively low compression, delivered 250 horsepower.

The dual four-barrel carburetor options, which had been offered since 1956, were dropped altogether in 1962. Optional engines started with a 300-horsepower version that was similar to the base engine but used different cylinder heads and a different carburetor. Moving up the scale, a-340 horsepower engine could be ordered. It had higher compression, a more aggressive solid-lifter camshaft, and an aluminum intake manifold. For 1962 the milder version of the fuel-injection option was discontinued, leaving the high-compression, solid-lifter, high-output version as the only available choice. This formidable power plant was rated at 360 horsepower.

The 1962s tend to be the best built and most reliable of the first-generation Corvettes. Body construction methods and materials were continuously improved, and fit and finish of body panels is typically better than in previous years.

Chassis design for 1962 was essentially unchanged from previous years. Rear-trailing radius rods at each end of the axle housing and a rear anti-sway bar in addition to the front one help make handling somewhat better than in earlier years. As with all first-generation Corvettes, chassis rust is a problem and the areas where the rear cross member and side rails connect should be carefully inspected.

The front of the chassis should also be inspected, not for rust but for collision damage. Though the chassis was heavy, it did not have nearly the same rigidity that later designs offered and would typically deform from a less severe collision.

Also look for major body repair, which obviously is indicative of collision damage. As was the case both before and after, 1962 Corvette bodies were assembled from many separate panels bonded together with glued-on bonding strips behind each seam. Careful examination of the underside of the body will often reveal whether repair work has been performed or if a one-piece nose section has been substituted for the original multi-piece front end.

As is always the case with Corvettes, originality and technical correctness of components is important to the car's value and desirability to collectors. Familiarize yourself with the correct location, appearance, and significance of the many casting numbers, casting dates, part numbers, and assembly codes that are found in most major components and assemblies. Especially important areas to evaluate include the VIN tag, which in 1962 should be spot-welded to the steering column about 13 inches up from the steering box; the chassis number, which is typically stamped in two places on the top of the driver-side rail; and the engine numbers, which include the block casting number and date, the stamped-in assembly code, and the stamped-in serial number. The stamped-in assembly code and serial number should be located on the front of the passenger-side block deck surface, just forward of the cylinder head. Keep in mind that "restamping" or otherwise altering the engine stampings has been a common practice in the hobby, and a qualified expert should determine the originality of a stamping if it is important to you.

When evaluating a car for purchase, look for problems commonly seen in the interior, including rusty seat frames and steering wheel cracks where the spokes meet the outer rim. Also, check the function of all gauges, wipers, turn signals, lights, horns, radio, and heater.

1962 Corvette Specifications and Major Options

Specs

Base Price When New	$4,038.00
Production	14,531
Engine Type	V-8
Bore x Stroke (inches)	4.00x3.25
Displacement	327 cubic inches
Compression Ratio	10.5:1 (base engine)
Horsepower	250 (base engine)
Base Transmission	Three-speed manual
Wheelbase	102 inches
Overall width	70.5 inches
Overall height	51.9 inches
Overall length	168 inches
Track, front	57.0 inches
Track, rear	59.0 inches
Weight	3,080 pounds
Tires	6.70x15 bias ply
Suspension, front	Unequal-length control arms, kingpins, coil springs, telescoping shock absorbers
Suspension, rear	Semi-elliptic leaf springs, telescoping shock absorbers
Brakes	Bendix duo-servo hydraulic with 11.0-inch drums front and rear
Steering	Worm and ball-bearing roller, 16:1 ratio
0–60 mph	5.9 seconds (optional 327/360 horsepower engine, four-speed transmission, and 4.11:1 rear axle)
Standing 1/4-mile	14.9 seconds @ 102.5 mph (optional 315/360 horsepower engine, four-speed transmission, and 4.11:1 rear axle)
Top speed	132 mph (optional 315/360 horsepower engine, four-speed transmission, and 4.11:1 rear axle)

1962 Options

	Price	Quantity
FOA 102 Wonderbar Radio	$137.75	13,076
RPO 242 Crankcase Vent (California)	$5.40	n/a
RPO 276 15x5-1/2K Wide Wheels	no chg.	561
RPO 313 Powerglide Transmission	$199.10	1,532
RPO 396 340 hp engine	$107.60	4,412
RPO 419 Auxiliary Hardtop		8,074
In place of soft top	no chg.	3,179
In addition to soft top	$236.75	4,895
RPO 426 Power Windows	$59.20	995
RPO 473 Hydraulic Folding Top	$139.90	350
RPO 582 360 hp engine w/FI	$484.20	1,918
RPO 583 300 hp engine	$53.80	3,294
RPO 675 Positraction Rear Axle	$43.05	14,232
RPO 685 4-Speed Transmission	$188.30	11,318
RPO 686 Metallic Brakes	$37.70	2,799
RPO 687 Heavy Duty Brakes & Suspension	$333.60	246
RPO 1832 6.70-15 Whitewall tires	$31.55	n/a
RPO 1833 6.70-15 Nylon blackwall tires	$15.70	n/a

1962 Garage Watch

All 1962 Corvettes used the cross-flow design aluminum radiator introduced early in the 1961 model year. A blue and silver metal tag screwed to the top of the radiator contains a part number and manufacturing date. This tag was used through approximately mid-1961, after which the part number and date were stamped directly into the top of the radiator. Correct radiators are being reproduced but are not inexpensive at about $1,400.

Check the engine-block casting number when determining originality of an engine. This is located on the driver-side flange at the back of the block, where it mates to the bellhousing. All 1962 Corvettes used block #3782870. Also look at the engine stamping, located on the block's deck surface, forward of the passenger-side cylinder head, and the block casting date, located opposite the casting number on the passenger-side flange.

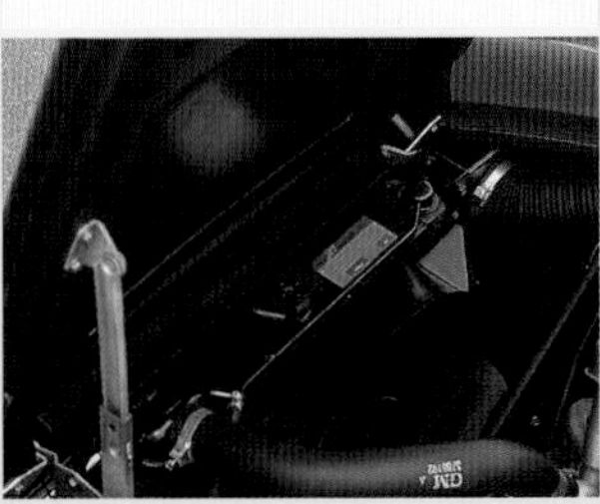

Though in 1962 headlamp bezels are painted and the grille is anodized, there is still no shortage of chrome. Quality chrome plating is expensive, a fact that should be kept in mind when evaluating any vintage Corvette for purchase.

Contrasting cove colors were no longer an option beginning in 1962. One-piece cast-metal black and silver cover insert, absence of stainless trim between the cove and rest of the body, rocker-panel moldings, and relatively thin whitewall tires were all changes introduced in 1962.

Check the engine-block casting number when determining originality of an engine. This is located on the driver-side flange at the back of the block, where it mates to the bellhousing. All 1962 Corvettes used block #3782870. Also look at the engine stamping, located on the block's deck surface, forward of the passenger-side cylinder head, and the block casting date, located opposite the casting number on the passenger-side flange.

As with all 1953–1962 Corvettes, the rear-chassis cross member is prone to rusting, so check it carefully. Also check the chassis side rails, particularly in the area around each rear wheel. It is usually helpful to jab the chassis in suspect areas with an ice pick or similar tool. If the chassis is sound, this will have no effect, but if it is substantially weakened by corrosion on the inside, the pick will go through the metal.

As with all vintage Corvettes, 1962 bodies are assembled from numerous panels bonded together with reinforcing strips behind each seam. This paintless body shows the light color of the raw fiberglass and the dark color of bonding adhesive between adjacent panels. Any deviation from this pattern normally indicates repair work was performed. When evaluating a car, scrutinize the underside of the body, which for the most part should be raw, unpainted fiberglass, for any evidence of damage or repairs.

1962

1962 Corvette Replacement Costs for Common Parts

Convertible top	$230.00 (correct dated reproduction)
Windshield	$450.00 (correct dated reproduction)
Seat upholstery (per pair)	$190.00 (reproduction)
Carpet	$145.00 (reproduction)
Door Panels (pair)	$150.00 (reproduction basic door panels minus all trim)
	$525.00 (reproduction basic door panels including all trim and sheet metal)
Hood	$700.00 (correct press-molded reproduction)
Hood surround panel	$900.00 (correct press-molded reproduction)
Wheel	$125.00 (used original)
Wheel cover	$200.00 (used original)
Front grille bar	$110.00 (reproduction)
Front grille molding, upper and lower	$350.00 (reproduction)
Headlamp assembly (including bucket, cup, ring, adjusters, bezel mount kit, and bulb)	$50.00
Tail-lamp assembly (including housing, lens, gasket, and hardware)	$100.00
Exhaust system	$300.00
Front brake cylinders (pair)	$80.00
Rear brake cylinders (pair)	$60.00
Shock absorbers	$115.00 (replacement set of four)
Front wheel bearing	$60.00 (outer)
	$40.00 (inner)
Front springs (pair)	$90.00
Radiator	$800.00 (correct reproduction)
$325.00 (functional replacement)	
Radiator support	$300.00 (reproduction)
Water pump	$50.00 (functional replacement)
$85.00 (rebuilt original)	
Ignition shielding	$300.00 (complete reproduction set)
Rear leaf springs (pair)	$200.00 (functional replacements)
Complete tune-up kit (ignition points, condenser, plugs, distributor cap, rotor, ignition wires)	$60.00
Fuel tank	$200.00 (reproduction)
Speedometer rebuild kit	$75.00

1962 Corvette Ratings Chart

Collectibility ★★★★
Smoothness of Ride ★★★
Reliability ★★★★
Comfort Cruising Speed: 65 miles per hour
Passenger Accommodations ★★★
Part/Service Availability ★

The 1962 Corvettes have always been popular with collectors. They are the last of the first-generation Corvettes, as well as the first year for 327 engines, and they offer the best performance and build quality among first-generation Corvettes. Like their predecessors, however, they offer little in the way of creature comforts. Features like air conditioning, power steering, and power brakes would not be offered until the following year with the introduction of the Sting Ray model.

Vintage Corvettes with authentic, documented race history are of great interest to collectors. The Dallas Chevrolet dealer and well-known competitor Delmo Johnson raced this 1962 from new. Johnson and his usual codriver, Dave Morgan, were extremely successful road racing Corvettes at places like Sebring and Daytona.

Check the way the side windows mate to the convertible top frame. Early Corvette top frames often get distorted in this area and can be expensive and time consuming to fix properly.

The front header bow on convertible top frames in all vintage Corvettes is prone to rusting. Check the bow carefully and squeeze it along where the top material and weatherstrip cover areas that you can't see, listening for the telltale "crunch" that indicates corrosion underneath.

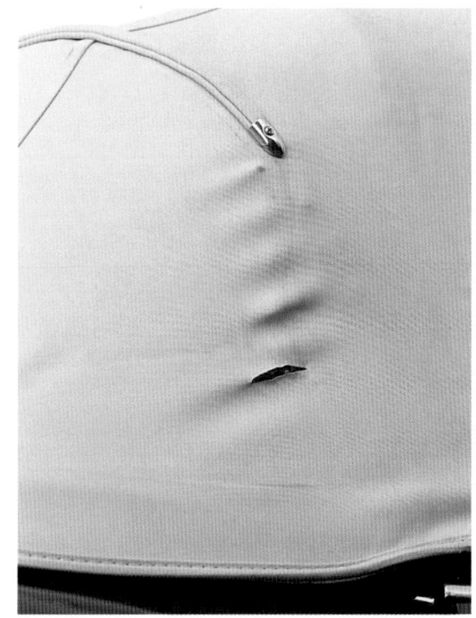

Since very few vintage Corvettes get used in inclement weather anymore, it is not uncommon for convertible tops to be left in the stowed position. This often causes tears in the top material and creases in the back window. It also usually causes the top material to shrink substantially, thus preventing the top from going into its up position. A correct reproduction top, with new pads, typically costs about $700.

Corvettes have inspired customizers to do their own thing since the very beginning. Generally speaking, most people prefer, and will pay more for, unaltered cars. Simple bolt-on items like the custom wheels seen here don't usually alter value beyond the cost to replace them with stock wheels and wheel covers. These Cragars give the car a real "period" look and add to the owner's enjoyment of his car, which is what the ol' Corvette hobby is all about.

Refinishing vintage Corvettes differs from refinishing metal body cars in numerous ways. If you buy a car that needs paint work, seek out an experienced pro who specializes in Corvettes.

Most Corvettes raced in the 1950s and early 1960s, like this 1962 originally owned by noted driver Delmo Johnson, relied on optional fuel injection for competitive power. Factory fuel-injected Corvettes are particularly popular with collectors today.

What They Said in 1962

Big news for the '62 Corvette is mainly concentrated in the engine compartment. The engine has been enlarged from 283 to 327 cubic inches. . . . The first thing we noticed when driving the '62 360-horsepower Corvette was the increased low-speed torque that accompanied the increased displacement.

The vertical steering wheel close to the driver and little room between lap and wheel always gives us fits for the first few days. . . . The vinyl-covered bucket seats are very comfortable and seat adjustment is ample even for the driver with very long legs. Clutch, brake, and throttle action is smooth and the shift lever for the four-speed transmission in our test car was in a perfect position.

The '62 Corvette does not lean on corners but maintains very good balance up to the point where the wheels start to slide. With the limited-slip differential, medium speeds through tight corners produced heavy steering and the front end "pushed," but if enough power was used to get the rear wheels "loose," front wheels tracked much better and the car could be directed through a corner by the throttle. Acceleration off the corners was a real thrill and plenty of speed could be attained in a short stretch before braking and downshifting for the next corner.

As the only sports car manufactured in volume in this country, the Corvette is a tremendous package. It costs much less than foreign cars of comparable performance, is a snap to service, and is not temperamental in traffic. If you wish, you can order options to go racing or if you are a little old lady from Pasadena, you can order one with Powerglide to get you to and from the knitting shop. —*Hot Rod,* January 1962

America's only true production sports car is still going strong after eight years on the market and shows no signs of letting up.

A wide variety of power trains is available, and with a little thought, a prospective owner can order just about any combination to meet any condition imaginable.

The stock 6.70x15 boots aren't the answer for traction. No amount of experimenting off the line could keep the tires from smoking, clear to second gear. Several top-end runs produced an honest 132 mph long before the end of the Riverside straight.

The stock brakes worked well, but after the high-speed runs they needed a 10-minute break because they were all through. If you can stand a little squealing and don't mind the heavier pedal pressures, RPO 686 gives more stopping power with sintered iron brake linings. For all-out competition, choose RPO 687. We had the car long enough to put over 1,000 miles on the odometer, and one trip to the high desert exposed the car to temperatures that ranged from a low of 35 degrees to a high of 93, and the Rochester fuel-injection unit worked perfectly. It was very responsive at any rpm in any gear.

The stock suspension feels just about right—a trifle on the hard side, but we, personally, wouldn't want it any softer. We had it up on our favorite mountain road and found we had no trouble negotiating the curves 20 to 25 mph faster than we've been taking them in sedans. The 'Vette is rock-steady and dead-flat in the corners. Understeer is slight, with the front end pushing only on the tightest corners.

The steering wheel is a beautiful thing, with its three drilled, engine-turned spokes, but its location leaves much to be desired. It is mounted in a vertical position and most drivers will find it too close. This, and the miserably mounted throttle pedal (it kept falling off) are the only real beefs we have with this otherwise completely satisfying car. This is an exciting high-performance automobile with real hair on its chest—the type of car that only the true enthusiasts will appreciate. —*Motor Trend,* August 1962

1962

I Bought a 1962 Corvette

I found my 1962 through an ad in the local newspaper in the spring of 1991. At that time the car had been sitting for more than 10 years, having been last registered all the way back in 1980.

The owner whom I bought it from had gotten it running just enough for me to limp home and into my garage with it. Once there, I put the car up on jack stands and completely removed the front end and all of the brake components.

My son Michael, who was 13 at the time, wire brushed the entire frame while the car was raised up and partially disassembled. After all of the dirt, grease, and surface rust was cleaned off the frame, we painted it semi-flat black.

Next we turned our attention to the suspension and brakes. The front end was completely rebuilt, and at the rear we installed new springs and spring shackles. We replaced all of the brake lines on the chassis, rebuilt the brake cylinders at each wheel, and rebuilt the brake master cylinder.

With the brakes and suspension finished, we next pulled the engine and transmission. The engine was brought to Piston Racing Engines in Farmingdale, New York, to be rebuilt. While the engine work was being done, I stripped the entire body and removed all of the interior items.

I also stripped and cleaned the engine compartment while the engine was out. After repainting the engine compartment semi-flat black, I reinstalled the newly rebuilt engine and all other underhood components.

I then brought the car, without any exterior chrome or paint on the body, to the painter, Gaspar. He did a beautiful job making needed body repairs and painting it in black urethane. The exterior part of the restoration was completed with rechromed front and rear bumpers and new tail lights.

I redyed the original dash pad, which had faded somewhat over the years. I also repainted the gauge cluster housing and various other interior parts before reassembling the interior.

After the restoration was completed I drove the car for a couple of years and enjoyed it very much. Then I decided to change the appearance of the car to give it a little bit of a vintage hot-rod look. I added an L-88-style hood and chrome Cragar SS mags. At that time I also added a front disc-brake conversion kit. The disc brakes and dual master cylinder let me drive the car with peace of mind, knowing that no matter what, it will stop.

I really love the way the car looks and am very happy with all of the restoration and modifications I've done to it over the years. But the best part of owning this 1962 is putting the top down and just driving it along the beach. *—Paul Pergamo*

The Sting Ray body, introduced in 1963, is considered by many to be a landmark in automotive styling. The split in the rear window was eliminated in 1964, making 1963 the only year for what collectors call the "split window." 1963s originally equipped with blackwall tires, including the one shown here, were equipped with stainless steel disc/ chrome spinner hubcaps on 15x5.5-inch steel rims painted to match body color. Cars equipped with optional whitewall tires received steel rims painted gloss black.

Chapter 11 1963

A nearly all-new Corvette, featuring styling based on the highly praised 1959 Sting Ray racer, was introduced in 1963. For the first time in the marque's history, both a coupe and convertible version were offered. Also for the first time, a trim tag was affixed to the car. Located next to the serial number tag on a steel support beneath the glove box assembly, the metal trim tag contains stamped-in number and letter codes that indicate original exterior and interior colors, whether the seat covers were vinyl or leather, body build date, and to a limited extent, what options the car came with.

Beneath the highly sculpted 1963 Sting Ray body was a completely revised chassis layout. Gone were the outdated kingpin front end, third-arm-bearing steering system, and solid-rear-axle arrangement. The new chassis featured a ball joint front end, recirculating ball steering, and four-wheel independent suspension. These features gave the new Corvette a more comfortable ride as well as improved handling.

In keeping with a trend that had begun several years before, the list of comfort and convenience features and options grew considerably in 1963. Power steering and brakes, AM-FM radio, and air conditioning all became available. Leather seats were also offered for the first time, though in 1963 they were available in Saddle Tan only.

Air conditioning became available in mid-April of 1963 (at approximately serial number 13,000), and according to Chevrolet records only 274 1963 Corvettes came with it. Today, factory air-conditioned 1963s command a considerable premium, and buyers are cautioned to watch out for retro-fitted systems being represented as factory installations. Original paperwork for the car, such as the window sticker and dealer invoice, as well as the correctness of the many unique components that constitute the 1963 air-conditioning system, are excellent evidence of its authenticity. Air conditioning could not be ordered with the optional carbureted 340-horsepower or fuel-injected 360-horsepower engines in 1963.

At the same time it offered more in the way of luxury, Corvette continued to be a performance leader in 1963. As before, a 327/250 horsepower engine and three-speed manual transmission were standard. Performance engine options included 300- and 340-horsepower carbureted engines and a 360-horsepower fuel-injected engine.

A four-speed manual transmission, Positraction limited-slip differential in ratios ranging from 3.08:1 to 4.56:1, and metallic brake linings were offered for those interested in spirited street driving and limited competition events. Buyers desiring to go racing for real were well advised to choose the heavy-duty racing brake and suspension package that was offered as option Z06.

Z06 equipped Corvettes were formidable road racers in their day and remain extremely popular with collectors today. All Z06 Corvettes were coupes and all were fitted with fuel injection, four-speed, Positraction, heavy-duty springs and shocks, a thicker anti-sway bar, and a heavy-duty brake system.

Since it's the first year of an extensive redesign, the 1963s have quite a few unique components. On the exterior these include split back-window glass and their moldings, simulated hood grille inserts, fiberglass (as opposed to the later pot metal) headlamp buckets, and a "roller" style gas-fill door that was used through approximately serial number 16,000.

Unique components inside include a plastic glove box door, a leather-grained, color-coordinated plastic-rimmed steering wheel, and a three-piece aluminum center-console assembly. Almost all of the components unique to 1963 are available as new reproductions, but their limited application causes them to be quite expensive. Take this into consideration when evaluating a car for purchase.

As with all Corvettes, 1963 bodies are made from fiberglass and are thus immune to corrosion. The chassis and the body's supporting substructure are, however, made from steel and as such are susceptible to rust. The most rust-prone areas are the chassis' boxed side rails, which hold water and dirt when their inadequate drain holes get clogged. Look at the areas toward the rearward end of the chassis side rails beneath the backs of the doors. Even if these areas of the chassis look solid, tap them along their bottoms with a hammer or a sharp implement such as an ice pick. This will reveal whether the steel is weakened by corrosion eating its way through from the inside out.

Any car being considered for purchase should be driven, if possible. This will allow you to determine whether everything functions properly. One area to pay particular attention to is the function of the Positraction differential. Problems with the unit most frequently manifest themselves when the differential is hot and you make a sharp turn after coming to a complete stop. A series of bangs or chattering from the differential usually indicates worn Positraction clutches. If you are lucky, a fluid change will cure or at least reduce the problem, but if not a complete rebuild is called for.

Besides evaluating the functionality of a prospective purchase you should also investigate the originality and technical correctness of the car's components. Familiarize yourself with the correct location, appearance, and significance of the many casting numbers, casting dates, part numbers, and assembly codes that are found in most major components and assemblies. Especially important areas to evaluate include the VIN tag, trim tag, chassis number, and engine numbers. Keep in mind that "restamping" or otherwise altering the engine numbers has been a common practice in the hobby and the originality of a stamping should be determined by a qualified expert if it is important to you.

The split-window design found only in 1963 has made this year a favorite with collectors, but it also can make 1963s more costly to restore. Since rear window glass and stainless trim were only used for one year, they are expensive.

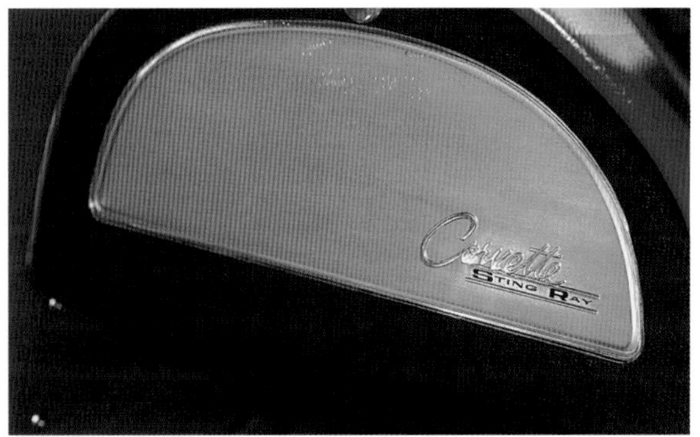

1963s use a unique glove box door constructed entirely from plastic. The doors are prone to cracking and though reproductions are available, they are quite expensive.

1963 Corvette Specifications and Major Options

Specs

Base Price When New	$4,257.00 (coupe)
	$4,037.00 (convertible)
Production	10,594 (coupe)
	10,919 (convertible)
Engine	V-8
Bore x Stroke (inches)	4.00x3.25
Displacement	327 cubic inches
Compression Ratio	10.5:1 (base engine)
Horsepower	250 (base engine)
Transmission	Three-speed manual standard, four-speed manual and two-speed automatic optional
Wheelbase	98 inches
Overall width	69.6 inches
Overall height	49.8 inches
Overall length	175.3 inches
Track, front	56.3 inches
Track, rear	57.0 inches
Weight	3,050 pounds
Tires	6.70x15 bias ply
Front suspension	Independent unequal-length wishbones and coil springs, anti-sway bar, telescopic shock absorbers.
Rear suspension	Independent radius arms, transverse leaf spring, half-shafts acting as upper locating members, lower transverse rods, telescopic shock absorbers
Steering	Recirculating ball
Brakes	Four-wheel drum, ll.0-inch drums front and rear, 328 square inches swept area.
0-60 mph	6.2 seconds (327/300 with 3.36:1 axle and four-speed manual transmission), 5.8 seconds (327/360 with 3.70:1 axle and four-speed manual transmission)
Standing 1/4-mile	14.8 seconds @ 98 mph (327/300 with 3.36:1 axle and four-speed manual transmission), 14.5 @ 102 mph (327/360 with 3.70:1 axle and four-speed manual transmission)
Top speed	120 mph (327/300 with 3.36:1 axle and four-speed manual transmission), 130 mph (327/360 with 3.70:1 axle and four-speed manual transmission)

1963 Options

	Price	Quantity
898 Saddle leather seat trim	$80.70	1,114
941 Sebring Silver exterior paint	$80.70	n/a
A01 Soft-Ray tinted glass	$16.15	629
A02 Soft-Ray tinted windshield	$10.80	470
A31 Power Windows	$59.20	3,742
C05 White folding top (in place of black)	no chg.	5,728
Beige folding top (in place of black)	no chg.	444
C07 Auxiliary Hardtop		5,739
In place of soft top	no chg.	1,099
In addition to soft top	$236.75	4,640
C48 Heater delete (credit)	-$100.00	124
C60 Air conditioning	$421.80	274
G81 Positraction rear axle	$43.05	17,554
G91 3.08:1 non-Posi rear axle	$2.20	211
J50 Power brakes	$43.05	3,336
J65 Metallic brakes	$37.70	5,310
L75 300 hp engine	$53.80	8,033
L76 340 hp engine	$107.60	6,978
L84 360 hp engine w/FI	$430.40	2,610
M20 4-Speed transmission	$188.30	17,973
Wide ratio w/250 hp and 300hp		8,444
Close ratio w/340 hp and 360 hp		9,529
M35 Powerglide transmission	$199.10	2,621
N03 36-gallon fuel tank	$202.30	63
N11 Off-road exhaust system	$37.70	n/a
N34 Simulated wood steering wheel	$16.15	130
N40 Power steering	$75.35	3,063
P48 Knock-off wheels	$322.80	n/a
P91 6.70-15 Nylon blackwall tires	$15.70	412
P92 6.70-15 Rayon whitewall tires	$31.55	n/a
T86 Back-up lamps	$10.80	318
U65 AM Wonderbar radio	$137.75	11,368
U69 AM-FM radio	$174.35	9,178
Z06 Special performance package*	$1,293.35	199

*Z06 special performance package initially included P48 knock-off wheels and N03 36-gallon fuel tank and was priced at $1,818.45. The price was reduced to $1,293.35 when P48 and N03 were deleted from the package.

1963 Garage Watch

Corvettes first carried trim tags, held on by Pop rivets, in 1963. Here, G4 indicates a body build date of March 4 ("A" represents the first month of production, which for 1963 was September 1962, and so on). The style, 63 837, indicates 1963 coupe ("63 867" would denote a 1963 convertible). BLK trim indicates black vinyl interior, and 900A indicates a Tuxedo Black exterior. The body numbers were sequenced with production but do not match the car's serial number.

All 1963s came with a serial-number tag spot-welded to a steel brace beneath the glove box area. All 1963 coupes started as 30837S1, while all convertibles read 30867S1. The final five digits of the sequence indicate the serial number of the particular car. This is the 1,182nd Corvette built in 1963.

Check the engine-block casting number when determining originality of an engine. This is located on the driver-side flange at the back of the block, where it mates to the bellhousing. All 1963 Corvettes used block #3782870. Also look at the engine stamping, which is located on the block's deck surface, forward of the passenger-side cylinder head, and the block casting date, which is located opposite the casting number on the passenger-side flange.

The Z06 option in 1963 and the J56 option in 1964 both used this very unusual master cylinder. This component is not being reproduced and was probably not used on any other types of cars or trucks, making it extremely rare. Restorable examples will typically sell for at least $3,000.

This original 1963 master cylinder is called a "thumbscrew" master because of the type of screw used to hold its lid on. Though dual-reservoir master cylinders weren't mandatory until 1967, it is usually a good idea to install one to all but eliminate the possibility of total brake failure. If you do replace the original master cylinder with a more modern unit, be sure to save the original one.

Beginning in 1963 front suspension utilized ball joints instead of kingpins Ball joints were originally riveted to the control arms (although replacements are usually bolted on). This level of chassis restoration, with features such as riveted ball joints and correct-paint finishes on different components, adds significant value to a vintage Corvette. The Corvette here is a Z06, which further enhances its value. Special Z06 components visible in this photo include the finned brake drum and ventilated backing plate. Partially visible is one of the vent-opening covers, held on with three bolts.

1963

1963 Corvette Replacement Costs for Common Parts

Convertible top	$175.00
Windshield	$450.00 (correct reproduction)
Seat upholstery (per pair)	$190.00 (correct vinyl reproductions)
	$400.00 (correct leather reproductions)
Carpet	$275.00
Door Panels (pair)	$155.00 (reproduction without upper metal supports installed)
	$650.00 (reproduction with upper metal supports, window felts, and all trim installed)
Headliner	$210.00 (correct reproduction)
Hood	$850.00 (correct press-molded reproduction)
Front fender	$195.00 (correct press-molded reproduction)
Wheel	$125.00
Wheel cover	$150.00 (good used)
Front grille	$245.00 (correct reproduction)
Headlamp assembly (including bucket, cup, ring, adjusters, bezel mount kit, and bulb)	$50.00
Tail-lamp assembly	$75.00
Exhaust system	$275.00
Shock absorbers	$75.00
Front wheel bearing	$15.00
Front springs (pair)	$175.00
Brake master cylinder	$100.00 (functional replacement)
Front brake cylinders (pair)	$40.00
Rear brake cylinders (pair)	$30.00
Radiator	$800.00 (correct dated reproduction)
Radiator support	$350.00
Water pump	$75.00 (rebuilt original)
Ignition shielding	$360.00
Cylinder head (pair)	$300.00 (rebuildable originals)
Rear leaf spring	$110.00 (functional replacement)
Complete tune-up kit (ignition points, condenser, plugs, distributor cap, rotor, ignition wires)	$60.00
Fuel tank	$200.00

1963 Corvette Ratings Chart

Collectibility ★★★★★
Smoothness of Ride ★★★★
Reliability ★★★★
Comfort Cruising Speed: 75 miles per hour
Passenger Accommodations ★★★★
Part/Service Availability ★★★★★

The "mid-year" Corvettes (those made 1963–1967) have always been extremely popular with collectors. The 1963s are especially sought after because they are the first of the series and because they are the only year to feature the well-known body split in the middle of the rear window on coupes. As a result of this, 1963 is probably the only year in which coupes may be even more popular than convertibles. As with all years, 1963 models featuring desirable options such as fuel injection, full power, or air conditioning are most sought after. Though knock-off wheels are listed as an available option, it is believed that no 1963s were delivered to retail customers with them. Manufacturing problems with the wheels delayed availability until 1964, when they were installed on 806 cars.

The hideaway headlamps used from 1963 through 1967 rely on ball-in-socket pivots and electric motors, both of which are susceptible to failure over time. Watch out for buckets that are lazy or refuse to open. A stripped motor-driven gear and pivots frozen by corrosion are often to blame. Early 1963 buckets were made of fiberglass, while 1964 through 1967 were metal castings. Fiberglass buckets are difficult to find and expensive. 1963 grilles feature separate bright trim pieces around the perimeter, with numerous attachment points along the perimeter that are easily broken. Look at the attachment tabs on the body for evidence of collision damage.

1963 interiors feature a number of one-year-only items, including the gauge faces, three-piece shifter console, color-matched steering wheel, shifter, and radio. This makes it especially important to buy as complete a car as you possibly can to begin with. Note that the car shown has power windows, with the switches located toward the rear of the shifter console.

Option N03, a 36-gallon fiberglass tank, was available 1963–1967 in coupes only. It actually was located in the passenger compartment behind the seats and used the uncarpeted fiberglass cover shown here. Most "big tank" Corvettes were equipped with a high-horsepower engine and other performance options, but there are documented examples with base engines and even air conditioning.

1963 saw the introduction of four-wheel independent suspension, recirculating ball steering, and luxuries like power steering, power brakes, and air conditioning. Air conditioning became available only after the middle of the year and with rare exceptions was not installed in cars having a serial number under 13,000. Though few people rely on second-generation Corvettes for everyday transportation, they are relatively easy and convenient to drive regularly. This convertible has had the same owner since 1968 and has traveled more than 400,000 miles!

Fuel-injected 1963 Corvettes were among the fastest production cars of their era. The fuelie engine compartment is as beautiful to look at as it is functional.

1963

Many engine compartment components, including the block, heads, manifolds, radiator, distributor, carburetor or fuel-injection unit, and alternator, contain a part number and manufacturing date. Some parts have this information in a separate tag that is affixed, while others, like the alternator shown here, have the information stamped in. This alternator was assembled on "3B13," which translates to March 13, 1963. For any component to be correct for a given car it must have the right part number and a date code that precedes the final assembly of the car by no more than about six months.

The Corvette interior was completely revised for 1963 and demonstrates aerospace influence in its design. Available colors included Black, Red, Saddle, and Dark Blue. Genuine leather seats were available only in Saddle.

1963

What They Said in 1963

One glance at the new Corvette tells you that it is faster and sportier than its predecessors. And when you drive a Corvette Sting Ray, either the convertible or the fastback Sport Coupe, you find that the excitement is far more than skin-deep. Hiding independent rear suspension under its sculptured tail, the Corvette is now second to no other production sports car in road-holding and is still the most powerful.

Thanks to the improved geometry and the rearward relocation of the center of gravity for 1963, steering effort is very low, and the car inspires a high degree of confidence, which continues to grow with closer acquaintance. Cornering behavior is extremely stable, and the car has the added advantage of a power reserve that a high-speed drift can be entered and maintained even by moderately skilled drivers.

One of the necessary luxuries, and therefore one of the most appreciated, is the introduction of fully adjustable seats. . . . The pedals are extremely well placed. . . . Considerable effort has been made to enrich the interior of the Corvette. The 1963 models have all-vinyl interiors, and Chevrolet plans to offer genuine leather upholstery later in the year. The floor covering is a deep twist carpet, which is also used in the luggage space behind the passenger compartment. The deep twin windows give a good rear view.

Prices of the two Corvette Sting Ray models have not yet been announced, but Chevrolet spokesmen have indicated that no appreciable increase is expected. If this is true, they offer fantastic value for money, whether you want to race or drive fast over long distances in comfort, or merely need a smart-looking car to use around town. —*Car and Driver,* October 1962

A true sports car (even purists now admit it), the Corvette enjoys a reputation unmatched by any other U.S.-built automobile and surpassed by only a few foreign-built ones.

The razzle-dazzle performance of the fuel-injected, 4-speed Corvette far overshadows that of the model Car Life has selected for its road test; however, we feel that the version we've tested here [327/300 with Powerglide] may become by far the most popular with the general public. Driving such a Corvette is sheer delight. Despite its deceptive smoothness, it's a lusty performer only 2.8 seconds slower to 80 mph than the fuel-injected 4-speed convertible tested by *Road & Track.*

Tricky, twisting roads are this Corvette's meat. With its new suspension it seems to lock onto them, going precisely where directed and sticking to the tightest corners without the shadow of a doubt. . . . This suspension is the best thing since gumdrops! Indeed, we found very little to criticize in either version of the Corvette. Our two main objections centered on design features of the coupe a) the bar down the center of the rear window makes it all but impossible to see out via the rearview mirror; and, b) getting luggage in and out of the adequate-sized compartment is difficult because . . . there's no trunk opening. —*Car Life,* December 1962

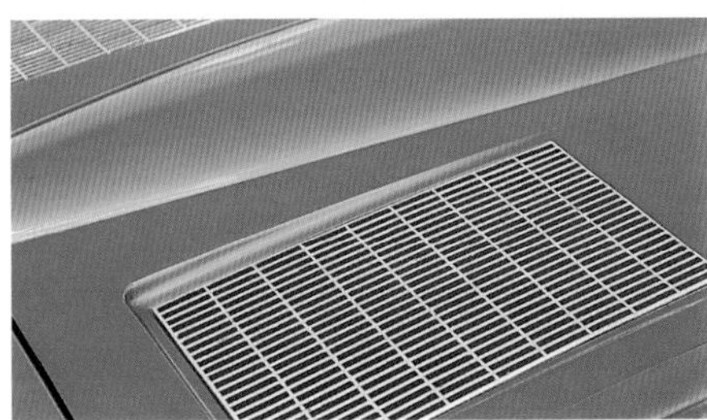

The 1963s use a unique hood that can be expensive to replace. It has recesses that hold simulated vents made from cast metal. The vents are available as reproductions for about $300 per pair.

I Bought a 1963 Corvette

I set my sights on purchasing a used Corvette when I came of driving age. I located a 1963 coupe with only 36,000 miles. It was Sebring Silver with a dark blue interior and was powered by a 327/250 horsepower engine.

A few years after earning a mechanical engineering degree, I was fortunate enough to secure employment with General Motors, starting a career that has resulted in the best job I could dream of, working on the Corvette Engineering Team.

In the meantime, a few more Corvettes have passed through my hands, but in 1981, as my dad had retired, he agreed to apply his years of automotive knowledge in helping me restore the 1963. We worked side by side for three winters to accomplish a National Corvette Restorers Society Top Flight award-winning body-off-the-frame restoration.

Today, my daughter and I use the 1963 for occasional cruises, and I continue to enjoy it as if it were a new car each spring. *—Bill Nichols*

For my generation a 1963 "Split Window" is the consummate Corvette. It was the first really modern Corvette when it first came out, and though the mechanical aspects are obviously far outdated by today's standards, the styling is still fresh and inspiring.

I have owned the car since 1984 and over the years have done just about everything except take the body off the frame. The 340-horsepower 327 engine has been bulletproof in the years I've owned the car. It was rebuilt after 164,000 miles and I've put 40,000 on since then.

There were only two areas where I had ongoing problems—the radio and the brakes. The radio worked when I bought the car, but not very well. I had it in and out three times before it would finally work and sound decent for what quality it could be expected to produce.

The brakes felt fine for a while but then started pulling to one side, so thinking it was a simple situation, I had the drums machined and new shoes and wheel cylinders installed. After that it worked perfectly for a little while but then a new problem erupted. It would pull to one side, and then the next time I stopped it might pull to the other side. Needless to say, this took the fun out of driving the car. I had the hoses and steel brake lines replaced and then had the master cylinder rebuilt with a sleeve. Since that was essentially everything in the whole brake system, I was sure the problem would be fixed—but it wasn't. After a lot of head scratching, we finally realized that three of the four drums were horribly warped and out of round. They were too thin from having been machined many times, and because of the excessive thinness they warped. Four new drums solved the problem and now the brakes feel like those of a new car.

I put about 5,000 miles on the clock each year and don't hesitate to take the car out unless it's raining or extremely hot. Over the coming winter I am going to install an aftermarket air-conditioning system so the car will be usable even in very hot weather. *—Robert McCann*

1964s have always been an in-between year for collectors. For many, they don't offer the appeal of 1963s, which were the first of the new series, or of 1965s, which feature four-wheel disc brakes and mark the introduction of big-block power. All else being equal, this has made 1964s the most affordable of the 1963–1967 "midyear" series.

Chapter 12 1964

A nearly all-new Corvette, featuring styling based on the highly praised 1959 Sting Ray racer and chassis design modeled after the Corvette SS Racer, CERV I, and other experimental vehicles, was introduced in 1963. Not surprisingly, changes to the Corvette in 1964, while numerous, were confined to details rather than anything major.

Changes in styling details are immediately noticeable on the exterior of both coupes and convertibles. With coupes, the controversial split rear window that was lauded by some as a beautiful design feature, but decried by others as a safety hazard because it restricted rearward visibility, was replaced with a more conventional one-piece window.

Gone from both coupes and convertibles were the two simulated hood vents introduced in 1963. Though the vents were eliminated for 1964 the recesses in the hood that they sat in remained. The recesses were eliminated in 1965, making 1963 hoods with the recesses and the vents, and 1964 hoods with the recesses but without the vents, both one-year-only items.

The 1964 Corvettes were fitted with a redesigned hubcap as standard equipment. As was typical of the era, they featured a chrome spinner mounted to a stainless steel disc. The hubcaps mounted to gloss black painted steel wheels measuring 15 x 5.5 inches.

Early in 1964 cast aluminum knock-off wheels became available as an extra-cost option. The outer edges of each knock-off's 36 radial ribs as well as the outer edge of the rim were polished, while the areas between the ribs were left in their raw, "as cast" condition. Later versions of the knock-off wheel were painted between the ribs.

The 1964 seats look similar to those used in 1963 but have thicker backs that taper less toward the top. All 1964s came with a simulated-walnut plastic-rimmed steering wheel. This wheel was an option in 1963 but standard in 1964–1967.

As in 1963, the 1964 chassis utilizes a ball joint front end, recirculating ball steering, and four-wheel independent suspension. These features provide a more comfortable ride as well as improved handling when compared with pre-1963 Corvettes.

In keeping with Corvette's continuing evolution into a personal luxury car as well as a capable sports car, numerous comfort and convenience options were offered in 1964. Power steering, brakes, and windows, AM-FM radio, and air conditioning were all available at extra cost.

Leather seats were also offered as an option in 1964. Unlike the previous year, however, leather could be had in any of the available interior colors.

At the same time it offered plenty in the way of luxury, Corvette continued to be a performance leader in 1964. As before, a 327/250 horsepower engine and three-speed manual transmission were standard. Performance engine options included 300- and 365-horsepower carbureted engines and a 375-horsepower fuel-injected engine. A four-speed manual transmission, Positraction limited-slip differential in ratios ranging from 3.08:1 to 4.56:1, and heavy-duty racing brake and suspension packages were offered in 1964.

The racing suspension package included heavy-duty springs and shocks and a thicker front anti-sway bar. The racing brake package featured a number of unique components, including a dual reservoir master cylinder, ventilated brake backing plates, larger than normal cast-iron drums with radial fins to help dissipate heat, and hub-mounted, stamped steel fans to move cooling air through the brake assemblies.

Once again a 36-gallon fiberglass fuel tank was available as an extra-cost option in coupes only. The "big tank," as it is frequently called by collectors, could be ordered with or without the other racing-oriented options.

As with all Corvettes, 1964 bodies are made from fiberglass and are thus immune to corrosion. The chassis and the body's supporting substructure, however, are made from steel and as such are susceptible to rust. The most rust-prone areas are the chassis' boxed side rails, which hold water and dirt when their inadequate drain holes get clogged. Look at the chassis side rails in the areas beneath the backs of the doors. Even if these areas look solid, tap them with a hammer or a sharp implement such as an ice pick. This will reveal whether the steel is weakened by corrosion eating its way through from the inside out.

Any car being considered for purchase should be driven, if possible. This will allow you to determine whether everything functions properly. Areas that are sometimes problematic in 1964 Corvettes include the Positraction differential and rearwheel bearing assemblies. Problems with the Positraction most frequently manifest themselves when the differential is hot and you make a sharp turn after coming to a complete stop. A series of bangs or chattering from the differential usually indicates worn Posi clutches.

Rear-wheel bearing assemblies can be checked for excessive end play or side-to-side wobble, either of which indicates a problem. Squealing, groaning, or other noises emanating from a bearing assembly are also strongly indicative of a failure.

Besides evaluating the functionality of a prospective purchase you should also investigate the originality and technical correctness of the car's components. Familiarize yourself with the correct location, appearance, and significance of the many casting numbers, casting dates, part numbers, and assembly codes that are found in most major components and assemblies. Especially important areas to evaluate include the VIN tag, trim tag, chassis number, and engine numbers. Keep in mind that "restamping" or otherwise altering the engine numbers has been a common practice in the hobby, and the originality of a stamping should be determined by a qualified expert if it is important to you.

1964 Corvettes were equipped with an aluminum coolant-overflow tank that had a manufacturing logo and date stamped in. This example was made in October 1963. Note also the correct logos on the overflow tank's hose and the correct reproduction Tar Top Delco battery beneath the tank.

As with all 1963–1967 Corvettes, 1964s use a fiberglass tub and lid assembly for spare tire stowage. Don't forget to make sure the assembly and the spare are present. Also check to make sure the jack and lug wrench, which should be stored in the tool well behind the seats, are present.

1964 Corvette Specifications and Major Options

Specs

Base Price When New	$4,252.00 (coupe) $4,037.00 (convertible)
Production	8,304 (coupe) 13,925 (convertible)
Engine	V-8
Bore x Stroke (inches)	4.00x3.25
Displacement	327 cubic inches
Compression Ratio	10.5:1 (base engine)
Horsepower	250 (base engine)
Transmission	Three-speed manual standard, four-speed manual and two-speed automatic optional
Wheelbase	98 inches
Overall width	69.6 inches
Overall height	49.8 inches
Overall length	175.3 inches
Track, front	56.3 inches
Track, rear	57.0 inches
Weight	3,050 pounds
Tires	6.70x15 bias ply
Front suspension	Independent unequal-length wishbones and coil springs, anti-sway bar, telescopic shock absorbers
Rear suspension	Independent radius arms, transverse leaf spring, half-shafts acting as upper locating members, lower transverse rods, telescopic shock absorbers
Steering	Recirculating ball
Brakes	Four-wheel drum, ll.0-inch drums front and rear, 328 square inches swept area
0–60 mph	8.0 seconds (327/300 with 3.36:1 axle and Powerglide automatic transmission), 6.0 seconds (327/360 with 3.70:1 axle and four-speed manual transmission)
Standing 1/4-mile	15.2 seconds @ 85 mph (327/300 with 3.36:1 axle and Powerglide automatic transmission), 14.5 @ 103 mph (327/360 with 3.70:1 axle and four-speed manual transmission)
Top speed	130 mph (327/300 with 3.36:1 axle and Powerglide automatic transmission), 148 mph (327/360 with 3.70:1 axle and four-speed manual transmission)

1964 Options

		Price	Quantity
n/a	Genuine leather seats	$80.70	1,334
A01	Soft-Ray tinted glass	$16.15	6,031
A02	Soft-Ray tinted windshield	$10.80	6,387
A31	Power Windows	$59.20	3,706
C05	White folding top (in place of black)	no chg.	4,843
	Beige folding top (in place of black)	no chg.	591
C07	Auxiliary Hardtop		7,023
	In place of soft top	no chg.	1,220
	In addition to soft top	$236.75	5,803
C48	Heater delete (credit)	$100.00	60
C60	Air conditioning	$421.80	1,988
F40	Special suspension	$37.70	82
G81	Positraction rear axle	$43.05	18,279
G91	3.08:1 non-Posi rear axle	$2.20	2,310
J50	Power brakes	$43.05	2,270
J56	Special brake system	$629.50	29
J65	Metallic brakes	$53.80	4,780
K66	Transistor ignition	$75.35	552
L75	300 hp engine	$53.80	10,471
L76	365 hp engine	$107.60	7,171
L84	360 hp engine w/FI	$538.00	1,325
M20	4-Speed transmission	$188.30	19,034
	Wide ratio w/250 hp and 300 hp		10,538
	Close ratio w/340 hp and 360 hp		8,496
M35	Powerglide transmission	$199.10	2,480
N03	36-gallon fuel tank	$202.30	38
N11	Off-road exhaust system	$37.70	1,953
N40	Power steering	$75.35	3,126
P48	Knock-off wheels	$322.80	806
P91	6.70-15 Nylon blackwall tires	$15.70	372
P92	6.70-15 Rayon whitewall tires	$31.85	19,977
T86	Back-up lamps	$10.80	11,085
U69	AM-FM radio	$176.50	20,934

1964 Garage Watch

Attention to detail is what separates good vintage Corvettes from great ones. Items normally considered perishable, including the battery, hoses, belts, and spark plug wires, are being reproduced with original finishes, textures, logos, and date codes. These are reproduction spark plug wires dated "1-Q-64," which translates to the first quarter of 1964.

Many engine compartment components, including the block, heads, manifolds, radiator, distributor, carburetor or fuel-injection unit, and alternator, contain a part number and manufacturing date. Some parts have this information in a separate tag that is affixed, some have the numbers cast into the part when it is made, and still others, like the alternator shown here, have the information stamped in. This alternator was assembled on "3H19," which translates to August 19, 1963.

All 1964s came with a Harrison aluminum cross-flow-type radiator. The part number and manufacturing date code should be stamped into the top of the radiator. This example was made in October 1963. As with all components, the manufacturing date of the radiator should precede the assembly date of the car by no more than six months.

This level of chassis restoration and detailing takes a great deal of time and money to accomplish. Expect to pay a premium for a car with a chassis like this. Note the finned brake drum, ventilated brake backing plate, brake cooling scoop (often referred to as an "elephant ear"), and thick anti-sway bar, all part of this car's J56 Special Brake System option.

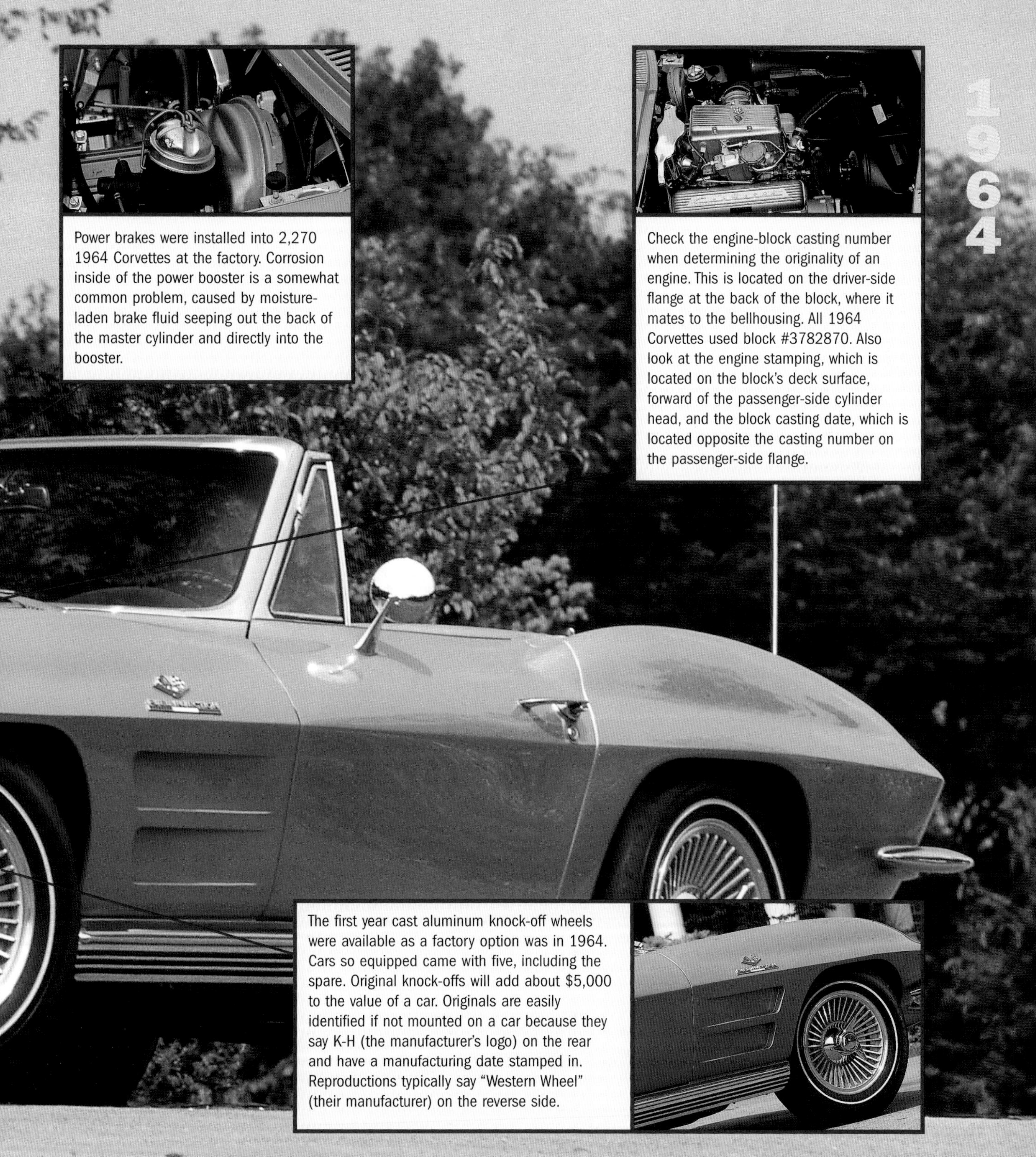

Power brakes were installed into 2,270 1964 Corvettes at the factory. Corrosion inside of the power booster is a somewhat common problem, caused by moisture-laden brake fluid seeping out the back of the master cylinder and directly into the booster.

Check the engine-block casting number when determining the originality of an engine. This is located on the driver-side flange at the back of the block, where it mates to the bellhousing. All 1964 Corvettes used block #3782870. Also look at the engine stamping, which is located on the block's deck surface, forward of the passenger-side cylinder head, and the block casting date, which is located opposite the casting number on the passenger-side flange.

The first year cast aluminum knock-off wheels were available as a factory option was in 1964. Cars so equipped came with five, including the spare. Original knock-offs will add about $5,000 to the value of a car. Originals are easily identified if not mounted on a car because they say K-H (the manufacturer's logo) on the rear and have a manufacturing date stamped in. Reproductions typically say "Western Wheel" (their manufacturer) on the reverse side.

1964

1964 Corvette Replacement Costs for Common Parts

Convertible top	$175.00
Windshield	$450.00 (correct reproduction)
Seat upholstery (per pair)	$190.00 (correct vinyl reproductions)
	$400.00 (correct leather reproductions)
Carpet	$275.00
Door Panels (pair)	$155.00 (reproduction without upper metal supports installed)
	$650.00 (reproduction with upper metal supports, window felts, and all trim installed)
Headliner	$210.00 (correct reproduction)
Hood	$850.00 (correct press-molded reproduction)
Front fender	$195.00 (correct press-molded reproduction)
Wheel	$125.00
Wheel cover	$150.00 (good used)
Front grille	$245.00 (correct reproduction)
Headlamp assembly (including bucket, cup, ring, adjusters, bezel mount kit, and bulb)	$50.00
Tail-lamp assembly	$75.00
Exhaust system	$275.00
Shock absorbers	$75.00
Front wheel bearing	$15.00
Front springs (pair)	$150.00
Brake master cylinder	$100.00 (functional replacement)
Front brake cylinders (pair)	$40.00
Rear brake cylinders (pair)	$30.00
Radiator	$800.00 (correct dated reproduction)
Radiator support	$350.00
Water pump	$75.00 (rebuilt original)
Ignition shielding	$360.00
Cylinder head (pair)	$300.00 (rebuildable originals)
Rear leaf spring	$110.00 (functional replacement)
Complete tune-up kit (ignition points, condenser, plugs, distributor cap, rotor, ignition wires)	$60.00
Fuel tank	$200.00

1964 Corvette Ratings Chart

Collectibility ★★★★
Smoothness of Ride ★★★
Reliability ★★★★
Comfort Cruising Speed: 65 miles per hour
Passenger Accommodations ★★★
Part/Service Availability ★★★★

The 1960 Corvettes have always been popular with collectors who appreciate their classic styling. They particularly appeal to those who enjoy the quad headlight design without the hybrid rear treatment introduced in 1961 or the gratuitous adornment found in 1958. In general, they are slightly less popular than similarly equipped 1956–1958 and 1961–1962 models and can therefore be bought for a little bit less money with all else being equal.

1964 interiors were offered in Black, Red, Silver, Saddle, and White. Two-tone interiors were also available, including Black/Silver, Dark Blue/Silver, Black/White, Dark Blue/White, Red/White, and Saddle/White. Leather seat covers were an extra-cost option and could be combined with any interior color.

1964 was the first year a simulated walnut-grain plastic steering wheel was standard. This wheel was optional in 1963. Color-keyed seat belts were standard in all 1964s. The yellow tag hanging from the radio knob contains tuning instructions. Clear ribbed floor mats were standard equipment, as was the electric clock. Switches for optional power windows are toward the rear of the shifter console.

1964 instruments are unique in featuring conical recesses like 1963s but having flat black coloring like 1965–1967s. When evaluating a car for purchase, remember to check the function of everything, including all gauges, radio, turn signals, windshield wipers, lights, horns, and so on.

As with all vintage Corvettes, 1964s featuring factory-installed fuel injection are highly desirable to collectors. They combine exceptional performance with beautiful appearance. The super-rare dual-reservoir master cylinder in this car is part of the J56 Special Brake System option.

As with all 1957–1965 Corvettes, 1964s that came from the factory with fuel injection are quite valuable and fakes are not uncommon. Unfortunately, there is nothing in the car's serial number that identifies those that originally came with fuel injection, making it fairly easy to transform a carbureted car into a fuel-injected one and claim it's an original. Look for components unique to fuelies to help authenticate the option, including a radiator support with provision for the fuel-injection air intake and riveted steel plates on the inner fender wells that receive the fuelie air cleaner attaching bolts.

1964

What They Said in 1964

Reference to the Sting Ray usually brings to mind visions of a 375-bhp engine, fuel injection, a four-speed transmission, and all the accoutrements of a competition sports car. However, this car can be obtained in much more docile forms that make it an ideal fast tourer for those not interested in the ultimate in performance.

There was some criticism of the quality of the fiberglass body when the Sting Ray first appeared, but we were unable to find any ripples or other faults on our test car.

The interior is very pleasing and well finished, and is laid out in the best sports car tradition. Bucket seats are provided for driver and passenger and there is considerable luggage space behind the seats. However, access to this space is through the doors alone, which is extremely awkward when bulky items are concerned, and if the rear window could be hinged in Aston Martin style it would be a great improvement.

In keeping with the other automatic features, the car was equipped with power steering, which we believe to be almost unnecessary on a Sting Ray, but was one of the best we have ever encountered. It was not noticeable at speed, but gave considerable assistance when parking.

One of the most interesting features of the car is the independent rear suspension, which is a very successful layout and also a big step forward for General Motors.

The result leaves little to be desired because there are none of those qualities, such as a tendency toward rear-wheel steering, which one normally associates with independent rear suspension . . . the handling of the car remains completely predictable.

To match the performance of the car, the brakes are adequate for normal fast driving but they will definitely fade and become uneven when used to the limit. When one considers both the weight and speed of the Sting Ray, it would appear to be an excellent car for a disc brake system, and it is surprising that General Motors has not yet adopted discs for this model. —*Road & Track*, March 1964

The first car we tested was the Chevy Sting Ray, a red Sports Coupe. The car was equipped with a four-speed stick shift, power brakes, and windows. There was an excellent AM-FM radio, a great big heater, which was more than welcome in the 20-degree cold weather, large clear and well-lighted dials, a clock with a second hand that could be seen without hunting all about the dash. We could see how fast we were going, how quickly the engine was turning over, if the generator was charging, for there was a good ammeter, and just how high the oil pressure was. No blinking light, no guesswork.

In checking the gas tank we noticed that the filler cap was large and easily accessible. . . . The bucket seats most certainly were the most comfortable we ever experienced. . . . The doors, which curve into the roof, fitted flush and accurately with the body sides, assuring draught-free rides. This also made for easy access. Steering was light, sure, and positive. Shifting by hand was quick. The safety release on the shift allowed for no mistakes. The shift knob was round, large, and afforded a positive grip.

Clutch motion was easy and sure. Brakes responded excellently. They did not lock or pull. You always had complete control. At no time did the machine "wallow." It did not drive you, you drove it. Good control, good seating, and certainly big-car comfort was found inside the Corvette.

To sum up our experience with the Corvette Sting Ray, we must say that it was a delightful one. We were pleased with the car and found it lives up to all its vaunted capabilities plus the outstanding and much-overlooked fact that it is an excellent car for family use. The wife can use it on her daily shopping trips, visiting friends, and the man of the house can use it on the private roads of his Sports Car club. This is one car that can really serve the entire family with the greatest safety measures available today. —*Motor Car Illustrated*, May 1964

I Bought a 1964 Corvette

My story starts in 1975 when I purchased my first Corvette, a 1969 T-top with 350/350 horsepower engine, four speed, and air conditioning. From that day on I was hooked, and after owning a total of 14 Corvettes in the intervening years, I now have the one I always wanted. That car is a 1964 factory fuel-injected coupe. One of the things that attracted me to the car was the fact that it was totally original and had never been taken apart.

In the first year of ownership my six-year-old son Michael and I attended local car shows and cruise nights. Then in the fall of 1999 my car went to Unique Motorsports in Connecticut for a body-off-the-frame restoration. Since the car had never been disassembled previously we took extensive, detailed notes and photographs to document the restoration. Most of the original parts were simply cleaned and put back on the car. The restoration was to National Corvette Restorers Society standards.

This 1964 is the best-performing, best-appearing Corvette I've ever had and I'm very proud to own this beautiful car. I look forward to enjoying it with my son at shows and on the road in the years to come. *—Mike Lombardi*

I acquired my 1964 in a rather strange way. I was actually asked to sell it for the owner. He had purchased it sight unseen after being told it was a rare, one-of-a-kind Corvette. But when the car was delivered he was quite disappointed, as it was basically apart with the chassis partially restored. The owner decided he did not want to undertake a restoration, and I was called to sell it for him due to my resources in the Corvette hobby. I made some calls and came up empty. Even though it was the only known documented 1964 convertible with heavy-duty suspension, heavy-duty brakes, and fuel injection, most collectors and restorers shy away when a restoration has been started and the car is already disassembled.

With no takers I made the owner an offer myself and he accepted. I was thrilled because I knew once the restoration was complete, not only would I have a beautiful mid-year roadster, but also the rarest one in existence.

Being in the hobby for over 25 years, I'm always looking for the rare find. I happened upon this by pure accident, but was very glad I did. After showing the car for five years and accomplishing everything I set out to do, I decided to sell it and another private collector in the Detroit area now owns it.

The only disappointment that I had while I owned it was that the car earned so much respect as a rolling chassis with its fuel injection, heavy-duty suspension parts, and big brakes staring back at you. It offered excellent power and handling back in the days when it was so uncommon to have both. But then a year later the chassis was paired up with its Silver Blue convertible body and it seemed to disappear into the common. But even with the rare chassis parts covered by the body the educated eye still recognizes it as the rarest of the rare. I do miss the car but fortunately have the opportunity to visit it often. *—Greg Ornazian*

1963–1967s consistently rank among the most collectible cars of all time. Viewed from virtually any angle they look like rolling works of sculptural art.

Chapter 13 1965

The 1965 was important in the evolution of Corvette because it's the year that heralded the arrival of numerous innovations, including Chevrolet's famous big-block engine option, factory-installed side exhaust, and four-wheel disc brakes.

The highly popular Sting Ray body style, introduced in 1963, continued in 1965 with minor revisions. The most noticeable of these were new front fender vents. They were vertical in orientation rather than horizontal and, unlike 1963–1964 vents, they were functional in exhausting hot engine compartment air.

The 1965 coupes had vents on the roof pillar behind the doors that were part of an interior ventilation system. All small-block engine cars got a flat hood featuring a single wind split up the middle. Big-block cars got a different hood that utilized a "power bulge" with functional air vents. Wheel covers were completely redesigned in 1965. As before, aluminum knock-off wheels were available at extra cost.

The same basic chassis design introduced in 1963 continued in 1965. The biggest news was the installation of disc brakes as standard equipment. The long-awaited disc-brake system utilized four-piston calipers acting on very large 11.75-inch-diameter rotors. It was incredibly effective under the most demanding racing conditions yet was entirely suitable for everyday driving around town. Four-wheel drum brakes were still offered in the beginning of 1965, and 316 cars were so equipped, earning their buyers a $64.50 credit.

The standard engine displaced 327 cubic inches and produced 250 horsepower. It relied on a mild, hydraulic-lifter camshaft, single four-barrel carburetor bolted to a cast-iron intake manifold, and a 10.5:1 compression ratio.

The 1965s had the greatest range of optional engines in Corvette history. The 327s could be had in carbureted versions giving 300, 350, and 365 horsepower and in a fuel-injected version that made 375 horsepower. Beginning in mid-March 1965, buyers could also opt for the remarkable new 396-cubic-inch big block, which was rated at a whopping 425 horsepower.

The 1965 396 had to be ordered with option K66 transistor ignition and a four-speed transmission. The big engine could not be had with air conditioning. All big-block-equipped cars had suspension and drive-train revisions to handle the extra weight and power. These included heavier front coil springs, a thicker front stabilizer bar, a rear stabilizer bar (the rear stabilizer bar was also fitted in small-block cars equipped with the optional F40 heavy-duty suspension package), and heavier attaching hardware for the axle shafts.

The 1965 396 cars also had special radiators to handle the tremendous heat the big blocks would generate. Like their small-block counterparts, these radiators were made from aluminum but they were larger in cross section. In addition to 1965 396 cars these special radiators were used again only in 1967–1969 L88 and 1970–1972 ZR1/ZR2-optioned Corvettes, making them very rare.

Other very rare, and hence very expensive, parts originally found on 1965 396 Corvettes include their exhaust manifolds, carburetor, starter motor, cylinder heads, and engine block.

In addition to the new big-block engine, transistor ignition, and heavy-duty suspension package, other performance options offered in 1965 include off-road exhaust (which included large-diameter pipes and low-restriction mufflers), side-mount exhaust, and a 36-gallon fuel tank. A heavy-duty transmission, nicknamed "the rock crusher" because of its noisy operation, was also offered.

Contrasting with the performance choices offered at extra cost was an increasingly long list of comfort and convenience options available in 1965. Power steering, windows, and brakes, air conditioning, telescopic steering column, teakwood steering wheel, leather seats, and headrests were among the more popular offerings.

The same basic interior layout seen in 1963–1964 was again used in 1965. Significant changes included revised instruments with flat rather than conical faces and new control knobs. Other changes included a new seat upholstery pattern, new door panel design, and new carpet configuration.

The 1965 Corvettes have remained extremely popular with collectors for many years. They offer the stunning good looks that have made the midyear series (1963–1967) genuine classics in combination with either luxury or performance features that few cars of the era could approach.

At one end of the spectrum was the 1965 396/425, a vehicle whose performance ranks it among the fastest production cars ever built. At the other end one could have a luxurious, long-distance touring sports car in the form of a two-top convertible with air conditioning, full power, leather headrest seats, automatic transmission, and a host of other desirable options.

Even after more than 40 years' worth of Corvettes had rolled off the assembly line, legendary retired Corvette chief engineer Zora Duntov still considered 1965 the best all-around car made. In that year one could combine the potent and high revving fuel-injected small block, four-wheel disc brakes, beautiful side-mount exhaust, aluminum knock-off wheels, and a host of other wonderful features.

In spite of all they had to offer, however, 1965 Corvettes were of course not perfect. As with all midyears they are prone to chassis rust, particularly in the side rails beneath the rear areas of the doors. They also tend to run too hot, particularly air-conditioned cars and big blocks.

As is always the case with Corvettes, originality and technical correctness of components is important to the value and desirability of any 1965. Familiarize yourself with the correct location, appearance and significance of the many casting numbers, casting dates, part numbers, and assembly codes that are found in most major components and assemblies. Especially important areas to evaluate include the VIN tag, which in 1966 should be riveted to the brace beneath the glove box door, the chassis number, which is typically stamped in two places on the top of the driver-side chassis rail, and the engine numbers, which include the block casting number and date, the stamped-in assembly code, and the stamped-in serial number. The stamped-in assembly code and serial number should be located on the front of the passenger-side block deck surface, just forward of the cylinder head. Keep in mind that "restamping" or otherwise altering the engine stampings has been a common practice in the hobby, and the originality of a stamping should be determined by a qualified expert if it is important to you.

1965 Corvettes are easily identified by their distinct wheel covers. In keeping with the movement away from non-functional adornment, gone were the simulated hood and fender vents seen in 1963–1964. Fender vents in 1965 were functional, as were hood vents in big-block hoods. Small-block hoods did not have any vents at all.

1965 Corvette Specifications and Major Options

Specs

Base Price When New	$4,321.00 (coupe) $4,106.00 (convertible)
Production	8,186 (coupe) 15,376 (convertible)
Engine	V-8
Bore x Stroke (small block, in inches)	4.00x3.25
Displacement (small block)	327 cubic inches
Bore x Stroke (big block, in inches)	4.094x3.76
Displacement (big block)	396 cubic inches
Compression Ratio	10.5:1 (base engine)
Horsepower	250 (base engine)
Transmission	Three-speed manual standard, four-speed manual and two-speed automatic optional
Wheelbase	98 inches
Overall width	69.6 inches
Overall height	49.8 inches
Overall length	175.1 inches
Track, front	56.8 inches
Track, rear	57.6 inches
Weight	3,260 pounds
Tires	7.75x15 bias ply
Front suspension	Independent unequal-length wishbones and coil springs, anti-sway bar, telescopic shock absorbers
Rear suspension	Independent radius arms, transverse leaf spring, half-shafts acting as upper locating members, lower transverse rods, telescopic shock absorbers
Steering	Recirculating ball
Brakes	Four-wheel disc, four-piston calipers, 11.75-inch rotors front and rear, 461.2-square-inches swept area
0–60 mph	5.7 seconds (396/425 with 3.70:1 axle and close-ratio four-speed transmission)
Standing 1/4-mile	14.1 @ 103 mph (396/425 with 3.70:1 axle and close-ratio four-speed transmission)
Top speed	136 mph (396/425 with 3.70:1 axle and close-ratio four-speed)

1965 Options

		Price	Quantity
n/a	Genuine leather seats	$80.70	2,128
A01	Soft-Ray tinted glass	$16.15	8,752
A02	Soft-Ray tinted windshield	$10.80	7,624
A31	Power Windows	$59.20	3,809
C07	Auxiliary Hardtop	$236.75	7,787
C48	Heater and defroster delete (credit)	$100.00	39
C60	Air conditioning	$421.80	2,423
F40	Special suspension	$37.70	975
G81	Positraction rear axle	$43.05	19,965
G91	3.08:1 non-Posi rear axle	$2.20	1,886
J50	Power brakes	$43.05	4,044
J61	Drum Brakes (substitution credit)	$64.50	316
K66	Transistor ignition	$75.35	3,686
L75	327 cid, 300 hp engine	$53.80	8,358
L76	327 cid, 365 hp engine	$129.15	5,011
L78	396 cid, 425 hp engine	$292.70	2,157
L79	327 cid, 350 hp engine	$107.60	4,716
L84	327 cid, 375 hp engine w/FI	$538.00	771
M20	4-Speed transmission	$188.30	21,107
M35	Powerglide transmission	$199.10	2,021
N03	36-gallon fuel tank	$202.30	41
N11	Off-road exhaust system	$37.70	2,468
N14	Side mount exhaust system	$134.50	759
N32	Teakwood steering wheel	$48.45	2,259
N36	Telescopic steering column	$43.05	3,917
N40	Power steering	$96.85	3,236
P48	Knock-off wheels	$322.80	1,116
P91	7.75-15 nylon blackwall tires	$15.70	168
P92	7.75-15 rayon whitewall tires	$31.85	19,300
T01	7.75-15 nylon goldwall tires	$50.05	989
U69	AM-FM radio	$203.40	22,113
Z01	Comfort and convenience group	$16.15	15,397

1965 Garage Watch

This unusual dual-reservoir master cylinder was only used with power brakes. The master used on 1966 Corvettes with power brakes looks identical but is different in that it has larger outlet holes. Options like power brakes, steering, and windows add value to a vintage Corvette and, for many people, make it more enjoyable to drive.

The originality of its engine is important to the value of any vintage Corvette. When determining the originality of an engine evaluate the block casting number, the assembly and serial-number stampings, and the block casting date.

The first year Corvettes came with four-wheel disc brakes as standard equipment was 1965. The brake calipers are prone to leaking, especially when the car is used infrequently. Fluid stains like this on the inside of a tire are a sure sign of leakage.

All 1965s equipped with a small-block engine used this Harrison aluminum cross flow-type radiator, part number 3155316. As with many parts under the hood, radiators were stamped with the manufacture date, a date code that contains two numbers for the year and a single letter for the month, with "A" representing January, and so on. This example's date code of 64M translates to December 1964. Note the "16 CT" inspection stamp on the radiator and original style GM upper-radiator hose and hose clamp.

Factory original 1965 396 cars are especially valuable and therefore especially susceptible to counterfeiting. An unusual feature of original 396 cars is relocation of the battery from the passenger side to the driver side with access via a bolted-on trap door in the wheel well. Air-conditioned cars shared this same feature. Components specific to the 396 engine include the radiator, alternator, exhaust manifolds, and carburetor. Original, correctly dated examples of these parts are difficult to find, and expensive when you do find them.

The rear anti-sway bar was part of option F40, called Special Suspension. It was also used on all cars equipped with the 396 engine.

The front anti-sway bar in cars equipped with the 396 engine was thicker than the standard bar. The front chassis extension that the anti-sway bar mounts to on each side of the car is usually bent after a front-end collision. Inspect this area for irregularities, the presence of which indicates previous collision damage.

1965

1965 Corvette Replacement Costs for Common Parts

Convertible top	$175.00
Windshield	$450.00 (correct reproduction)
Seat upholstery (per pair)	$190.00 (correct vinyl reproductions), $400.00 (correct leather reproductions)
Carpet	$275.00
Door Panels (pair)	$350.00 (reproduction with upper metal supports and window felts installed)
	$630.00 (reproduction with upper metal supports, window felts, and all trim installed)
Headliner	$210.00 (correct reproduction)
Hood	$850.00 (correct press-molded reproduction)
Front fender	$195.00 (correct press-molded reproduction)
Wheel	$125.00
Wheel cover	$250.00 (good used)
Front grille	$375.00 (correct reproduction)
Headlamp assembly (including bucket, cup, ring, adjusters, bezel mount kit, and bulb)	$50.00
Tail-lamp assembly	$75.00
Exhaust system	$275.00
Shock absorbers	$75.00
Front wheel bearing	$15.00
Front springs (pair)	$150.00
Brake master cylinder	$100.00 (functional replacement)
Front brake cylinders (pair)	$40.00
Rear brake cylinders (pair)	$30.00
Radiator	$800.00 (correct dated reproduction for small block)
Radiator support	$350.00
Water pump	$75.00 (rebuilt original)
Ignition shielding	$360.00
Cylinder head (pair)	$300.00 (small block rebuildable originals)
Rear leaf spring	$110.00 (functional replacement)
Complete tune-up kit (ignition points, condenser, plugs, distributor cap, rotor, ignition wires)	$60.00
Fuel tank	$200.00

1965 Corvette Ratings Chart

Collectibility ★★★★★
Smoothness of Ride ★★★★
Reliability ★★★★
Comfort Cruising Speed: 80 miles per hour
Passenger Accommodations ★★★★
Part/Service Availability ★★★★★

The 1965 Corvettes are among the most popular Corvettes ever made. As usual, highly optioned and big block-equipped cars are the most valuable. If you are paying a premium for a rare specimen, do your homework or enlist the services of an expert because deceitful practices like altering engine numbers, converting small blocks to big blocks, and adding rare options to cars that did not originally come with them is not uncommon.

All glass originally installed into vintage Corvettes was marked with a manufacturer's logo, a date code, and various items of technical information. All glass was supplied by Libby Owens Ford and should have its LOF logo. This example is dated JJ, which correlates to May 1965.

This is the back side of a front fender. The U-shaped channel running along adjacent to the fender lip is a bonding strip. Like all early Corvette bodies, those used in 1965 comprise numerous panels glued together. There are bonding strips glued on behind each seam to reinforce it. By looking at the underside of the body panels and the bonding strips, you can almost always determine where repairs have been made.

Interior colors included Black, Red, Blue, Saddle, Silver, Green, and Maroon. In addition, two-tone interiors could be had in White/Black, White/Red, and White/Blue. Standard seats were vinyl, but leather was available at extra cost. Standard steering wheel was simulated walnut-grained plastic. A genuine Teakwood wheel was optional.

1965 Corvettes featured a choice of five different optional engines ranging from a relatively mild 300-horsepower 327 all the way up to a pavement-scorching 425-horsepower 396. The car shown has under 10,000 original miles and is completely unrestored under the hood.

Detail items such as the coolant warning sticker on the fan shroud and correct hoses, hose clamps, and belts separate great quality from very good quality.

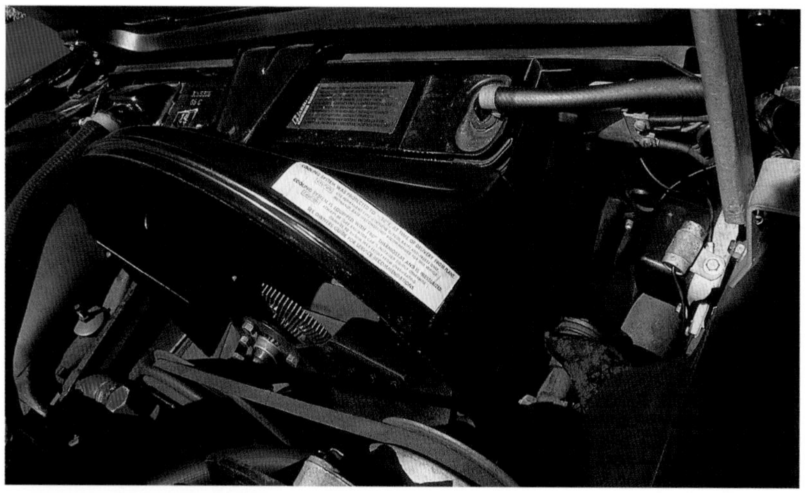

In addition to checking key-component part numbers and date codes, don't overlook checking the mechanical function of any vintage Corvette you are considering for purchase. The steering box is somewhat problematic because during decades of use the lubricant tends to leak out the bottom seal and few people bother to refill it. Parts to rebuild the box are available but doing so is typically quite costly.

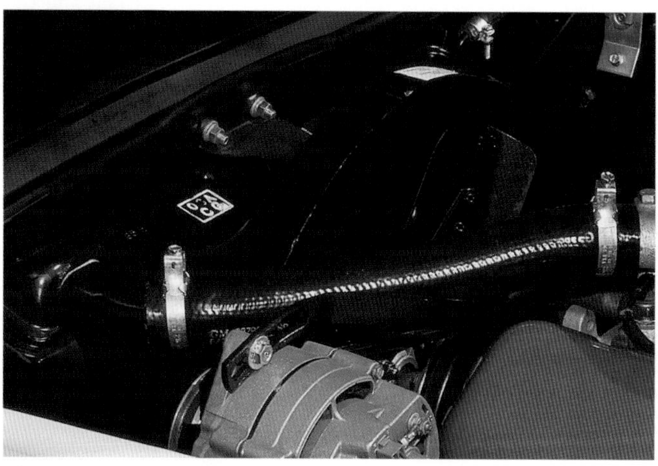

All 1965 396 Corvettes were fitted with this larger-than-normal radiator. This unusual radiator is one component among several that can help confirm or refute whether the big-block engine is a factory installation. As with all Harrison aluminum radiators, the part number (3007436) and manufacturing date code are stamped into the top. The date in this example is 65E, which translates to May 1965.

What They Said in 1965

It has the performance, polish, and pizzazz to suit almost any situation. Ten years ago, who could have guessed that the 1965 Corvette would have fuel injection, 4-speed manual transmission, limited-slip differential, all independent suspension and, wonder of wonders, disc brakes? The Corvette has become a car that any manufacturer would be proud to produce, and a far, far cry from the 6-cyl phut-phut with 2-speed automatic transmission that was standard in the first model to bear the Corvette name.

In many ways the Corvette is the original "build to suit" sports car. There is a complete range of options that make it possible to satisfy almost any driver who might consider buying such a car.

Anyone who has driven a Sting Ray will feel right at home in the 1965 Corvette. The new seats are firm but comfortable, the driving position is improved by the telescopically adjustable steering column and the complete instrumentation is a pleasure to contemplate, though the reflection from the glass makes them hard to read about half the time. The engine whumps into life with a mean rumble at the twist of the key, the clutch is deceptively easy in operation yet positive in action, the stubby gearshift lever moves into place with a crispness that is pure sensual pleasure. On the negative side, we aren't altogether pleased with the vision to the rear of the coupe. The combination of inside and outside mirrors work pretty well, but looking back over your shoulder . . . there is a blind spot that could hide a Cadillac.

Making a fast start, thanks to good weight distribution, independent rear suspension and Positraction, the big machine simply squats and squirts. Oh yes, it is possible to apply black stripes of rubber in whatever lengths you like, but it doesn't require a drag race expert to get good clean, fast starts time after time.

But it was the brakes of the '65 Corvette that pleased us most of all. Long ago we gave up (read chickened out) on doing stomp-down, all-out panic stops in American cars, but the Corvette restored our faith to such an extent that we did 0–80–0–80–0 time after time and grew bored, almost, with the ease and lack of fuss with which the car stopped straight and true. —*Road & Track,* December 1964

The arrival of the 396-cu-in., 425-bhp engine in the Corvette has been eagerly anticipated ever since word of its eventual coming leaked out when the 1965 Sting Ray was introduced last fall.

Known as the "Turbo-Jet 396," the new V-8 is a thoroughly up-to-date production version of the "Porcupine" head engine, which made a brief but spectacular appearance at Daytona three years ago. It replaces the "Turbo-Fire 409" throughout the Chevrolet line and though there are some points of similarity between the two engines, none of the parts are actually interchangeable.

Our test car was a convertible and it was a pleasure to make its acquaintance again. The cloth top, which is easily and conveniently stowed under the panel behind the seats, is the very model of what a convertible (or roadster) top ought to be—including admirable weather tightness when that is needed.

The 4-speed all-synchro gearbox, the same as before, is about as near faultless as any we've ever encountered.

It is difficult to describe precisely the 425-bhp Corvette's place in the automotive scheme of things. It's an interesting technical exercise, building a nice big engine like the 396 and putting it in a good chassis like the Corvette, but it honestly isn't a very satisfactory car for driving in everyday traffic. It's too much of a brute for that. And with all that power, any manner in which it is driven on anything except dead dry paving, the car is going to be a very large handful. It is not a car for the inexpert or the inattentive—two blinks of the eye and a careless poke of the toe and you could be in serious trouble. —*Road & Track,* August 1965

I Bought a 1965 Corvette

My interest was always in solid-axle Corvettes, primarily 1956s and 1957s. What really induced me to buy this 1965 was the fact that it's a red fuelie convertible. I already owned a red 1957 fuelie, which, of course, was a convertible, and I thought it would be pretty neat to own the first and last years for fuel injection, both in red.

After buying the 1965 I have to admit that it has grown on me a lot. The styling is almost as unique and beautiful to me as the 1957, and the ride is much better. I am a strong believer in driving all of my cars, and the 1965 has a solid feel and a quietness to it that the older Corvettes don't seem to have.

Four-wheel disc brakes and power brakes give the 1965 stopping power that inspires confidence as if it were a new car. My car also has optional factory side pipes, which give it a muscular sound to match its performance. The side pipes also dress up the car a lot, giving it a very classy look without being too flashy.

Another thing I really like about my 1965—and all older Corvettes—is how much they make you feel connected when you go for a drive. I can't knock the ride of a new Corvette, but with the old ones you really feel the road—every little bump and imperfection. When you put the shifter into a different gear, you can actually feel the parts inside the transmission meshing together. When you press on the gas pedal, you can feel the linkage engage and then you can envision the injectors feeding the fuel into the engine. It's a much more personal experience and for me that makes driving the 1965 all the more fun.

As with all of my cars I take certain liberties to improve performance and safety. For example, with the 1956s and 1957s I add seat belts, because they didn't originally come with them. With the 1965 I added high-performance gas shocks and installed speed-rated Goodyear radials. The radials give a quieter, softer ride but at the same time improve cornering, high speed stability, and wet traction.

I only bought the 1965 to round out my collection, but it wound up opening a new area of interest to me. Because it's actually a better riding and handling car than the solid axles, I actually drive that car the most. *—Peter Sheridan*

After searching the local newspaper classified ads for only a few weeks, I found what sounded like the perfect car for me. It was a 1965 coupe with the 365-horsepower engine, four-speed close ratio, and 370:1 Posi rear end. It had no power assist or air conditioning, which would have raised the price and were of little interest to a 22-year-old anyway.

The car turned out to be every bit as clean as the ad had said, not surprising given that it was only about two years old and had less than 14,000 miles. After some intense haggling a deal was struck and the dream car was mine.

The car remained in use on a daily basis from the time I bought it until 1978, which is when a growing family, as well as the advancing age of the Sting Ray, dictated the purchase of a new, larger car. Naturally, that meant another Chevrolet!

Following the purchase of the new Chevy, the Corvette served as a second car and a weekend "fun car" for the next nine years, at which time it went into a prolonged stretch of storage that lasted from 1987 to 1994. Even though the insurance and registration weren't kept current during that time period, the car was run with some regularity and kept more or less roadworthy.

In 1994, at the suggestion of a co-worker who knew I had the car, I got involved with a local Corvette club. That, along with the growing interest of my two sons, encouraged me to do some restoration work and get the Corvette back into like-new condition. *—Carl Munich*

1966 offered something for everyone. At one end of the spectrum were Corvettes fitted with 427/425 engines. These were arguably the fastest production cars of their era. At the other end, one could have a stunning long-distance luxury touring car, a two-top convertible with air conditioning, full power, leather headrest seats, automatic transmission, and a host of other desirable options.

Chapter 14 1966

Nineteen sixty-six was by all measures a great year for Corvette. The highly acclaimed Sting Ray body style first introduced in 1963 continued with minor revisions from the previous year. Gone were the vents located on the pillars in back of each side window. Hoods were fitted with a "Corvette" emblem in the front, driver-side corner. A new silver and chrome "egg-crate" style cast grille replaced the black horizontal bar design used in 1965 and hubcap design was revised somewhat.

Nineteen sixty-six was the final year for the cast-aluminum knock-off wheel option. As in previous years, in addition to the four road wheels the spare tire was also mounted on a knock-off. All knock-off-equipped cars came with a special lead hammer for loosening and tightening the three-eared spinners. Original knock-off wheels were manufactured by Kelsey-Hayes and bear that company's logo (K-H) as well as a manufacturing date code stamped on the reverse side.

All small-block engine cars got a flat hood featuring a single wind split up the middle. Big-block cars got a special hood that featured a "power bulge" with functional air vents on either side.

In addition to the special hood, big-block cars were also distinguished by a number of other features. Rather than U-bolts and nuts, heavy-duty caps and bolts held axle-shaft U-joints to the differential yokes. A large copper radiator instead of the small block's aluminum unit handled engine-cooling chores. Big-block cars did not come with the aluminum radiator-expansion tank found in small blocks. The fuel line from the tank to the fuel pump was 3/8-inch diameter instead of the small block's 5/16-inch. All big blocks (as well as small-block cars equipped with the optional heavy-duty suspension package) were fitted with a rear stabilizer bar.

The same basic ladder-type chassis design introduced in 1963 continued in 1966. As in 1965, four-wheel disc brakes were standard equipment. The "Special Heavy-Duty Brakes" option included a proportioning valve mounted beneath the master cylinder, dual-pin front brake calipers, an extra support for each front caliper, heat insulators on the caliper pistons, and pads featuring semi-metallic linings bonded to heavier backings.

J56 Special Heavy-Duty Brakes included vacuum power assist, which was also available as a separate option with the standard brake system. Whether as part of the heavy-duty brake option or by themselves, vacuum power brakes included a unique master cylinder. Rather than the non-power-brake master, which was a single reservoir unit, the power-brake master had separate reservoirs for the front and rear calipers.

The standard engine in 1966 displaced 327 cubic inches and relied on a mild, hydraulic-lifter camshaft, single four-barrel carburetor bolted to a cast-iron intake manifold, and a 10.5:1 compression ratio. It was rated at 300 horsepower.

Optional engine choices diminished in 1966 compared with the previous year, but there was still something for just about everyone. In addition to the base 300-horsepower small block, a 350-horsepower version was available. Its extra power came from domed, 11.0:1 compression pistons, larger valves, and a more aggressive camshaft profile.

The big block was enlarged in 1966 to a hefty 427 cubic inches and offered in two different states of tune. The mild version used a hydraulic-lifter camshaft, relatively low 10.25:1 compression, and a cast-iron intake to produce 390 horsepower. The wild version was fitted with an aggressive solid-lifter camshaft, large-valve rectangular-port cylinder heads, a 11.0:1 compression ratio, a larger Holley four-barrel, and a high-rise aluminum intake manifold. This 427 was initially rated at 450 horsepower, but that was changed to 425 early in the model year, likely in response to criticism from the insurance industry and highway safety groups.

The 1966 427/425 had to be ordered with option K66 transistor ignition and Positraction rear axle, and could not be had with air conditioning, the optional Powerglide automatic transmission, or the standard three-speed manual transmission.

In addition to the new big-block engines and transistor ignition, other performance options offered in 1966 include off-road exhaust (which included larger-diameter pipes and low-restriction mufflers), side-mount exhaust, a 36-gallon fuel tank, and a heavy-duty suspension package.

The 36-gallon fuel tank, called option N03, was available in coupes only. Made from fiberglass with internal steel baffles, the oversize tank mounted in the passenger compartment behind the seats. "Big tank cars," as they are called, were intended for serious endurance racing and that is how most were used. A number of documented examples wound up in cars otherwise not equipped for serious competition. Some of these were ordered by traveling salesman who drove long stretches where fuel was difficult to come by, while others were ordered for no logical reason whatsoever. Only 66 1966 Corvettes were built with a big tank, making cars so equipped quite rare and extremely valuable.

The high-performance suspension package, dubbed "F41 Special Front and Rear Suspension," included stiffer front coil springs, a stiffer rear spring made from seven rather than nine leaves, a rear stabilizer bar, a thicker-diameter front stabilizer bar, and special shock absorbers.

Contrasting with the performance choices offered at extra cost was an increasingly long list of comfort and convenience options available in 1966. Power steering, windows, and brakes, air conditioning, telescopic steering column, teakwood steering wheel, leather seats, and headrests were among the more popular offerings.

The same basic interior layout introduced in 1963 was again employed in 1966. Revisions can be seen in the dash control knobs, seat upholstery pattern, and seat-belt configuration. Early 1966 belt buckles are identical to the 1965 design, while later buckles are the same as those used in 1967.

The 1966 Corvettes have remained among the most popular with collectors for many years. They offer the stunning good looks that have made the midyear series (1963–1967) genuine classics in combination with either luxury or performance features that few cars of the era could even approach.

In spite of all they had to offer, however, 1966 Corvettes were far from perfect. As with all midyears they are prone to chassis rust, particularly in the side rails beneath the rear areas of the doors. They are also susceptible to rust in the bottom of the radiator support, in the rear trailing arms, and in the support bar riveted and bonded to the underside of the nose between the headlamp buckets. Like all Corvettes of the era, 1966s tend to run too hot, particularly air-conditioned cars and big blocks.

Coupes provide a quieter, tighter ride than do convertibles, but of course, you can't put the top down with a coupe. The owner of this car keeps radial tires and reproduction knock-off wheels on it for driving, but also has original tires and knock-offs for show. Substituting modern radials for original-type bias-ply tires dramatically improves the ride quality and performance.

1966 Corvette Specifications and Major Options

1966

Specs

Base Price When New	$4,295.00 (coupe)	
	$4,084.00 (convertible)	
Production	9,958 (coupe)	
	17,762 (convertible)	
Engine	V-8	
Bore x Stroke (small block, in inches)		4.00x3.25
Displacement (small block)		327 cubic inches
Bore x Stroke (big block, in inches)		4.25x3.76
Displacement (big block)	427 cubic inches	
Compression Ratio	10.5:1 (base engine)	
Horsepower	300 (base engine)	
Transmission	Three-speed manual standard, four-speed manual and two-speed automatic optional	
Wheelbase	98 inches	
Overall width	69.6 inches	
Overall height	49.8 inches	
Overall length	175.1 inches	
Track, front	56.8 inches	
Track, rear	57.6 inches	
Weight	3,260 pounds	
Tires	7.75x15 bias ply	
Front suspension	Independent unequal-length wish bones and coil springs, anti-sway bar, telescopic shock absorbers	
Rear suspension	Independent radius arms, transverse leaf spring, half-shafts acting as upper locating members, lower transverse rods, telescopic shock absorbers	
Steering	Recirculating ball	
Brakes	Four-wheel disc, four-piston calipers, II.75-inch rotors front and rear, 461.2 square inches swept area	
0–60 mph	8.3 seconds (327/300 with 3.36:1 axle and Powerglide automatic transmission), 4.8 seconds (427/425 with 4.11:1 axle and four-speed manual transmission)	
Standing 1/4-mile	15.7 seconds @ 86 mph, (327/300 with 3.36:1 axle and Powerglide automatic transmission), 13.4 seconds @ 105 mph (427/425 with 4.11:1 axle and four-speed manual transmission)	
Top speed	115 mph (327/300 with 3.36:1 axle and Powerglide automatic transmission), 140 mph (427/425 with 4.11:1 axle and four-speed manual transmission)	

1966 Options

		Price	Quantity
n/a	Genuine leather seats	$79.00	2,002
A01	Soft-Ray tinted glass	$15.80	11,859
A02	Soft-Ray tinted windshield	$10.55	9,270
A31	Power Windows	$59.20	4,562
A82	Headrests	$42.15	1,033
A85	Shoulder belts	$26.35	37
C07	Auxiliary Hardtop	$231.75	8,463
C48	Heater and defroster delete (credit)	$97.85	54
C60	Air conditioning	$412.90	3,520
F41	Special suspension	$36.90	2,705
G81	Positraction rear axle	$42.15	24,056
J50	Power brakes	$42.15	5,464
J56	Special heavy duty brakes	342.30	382
K19	Air injection reactor	$44.75	2,380
K66	Transistor ignition	$73.75	7,146
L36	427 cid, 390 hp engine	$181.20	5,116
L72	427 cid, 425 hp engine	$312.85	5,258
L79	327 cid, 350 hp engine	$105.35	7,591
M20	4-Speed transmission	$184.35	10,837
M21	4-Speed close ratio transmission	$184.35	13,903
M22	4-Speed close ratio, heavy duty	$237.00	15
M35	Powerglide transmission	$194.85	2,401
N03	36-gallon fuel tank	$198.05	66
N11	Off-road exhaust system	$36.90	2,795
N14	Side mount exhaust system	$131.65	3,617
N32	Teakwood steering wheel	$47.40	3,941
N36	Telescopic steering column	$42.15	3,670
N40	Power steering	$94.80	5,611
P48	Knock-off wheels	$316.00	1,194
P92	7.75-15 rayon whitewall tires	$31.30	17,969
T01	7.75-15 nylon goldwall tires	$46.55	5,557
U69	AM-FM radio	$199.10	26,363
V74	Traffic hazard lamp switch	$11.60	5,764

1966 Garage Watch

This special dual-reservoir master was used only on 1965–1966 Corvettes and is entirely different from the units used on Corvettes and other GM vehicles from 1967 forward. As such, it's relatively rare, with rebuildable examples worth at least $500. It is worthwhile to note that 1965 and 1966 master cylinders used the same casting but were not identical. The earlier masters were machined for smaller brake lines than were the later ones.

The correct carburetor increases the collector value of a vintage Corvette and usually helps it to perform better as well. All 1966s came originally with a Holley carburetor. The carburetor's part number and manufacturing date were stamped into the front portion of the air horn.

The originality of its engine is important to the value of any vintage Corvette. When determining the originality of an engine, evaluate the block casting number, the assembly and serial-number stampings, and the block casting date.

1966

Though 1963-1967 Corvette bodies are made from corrosion-resistant fiberglass, the chassis is steel and susceptible to rust. Especially vulnerable areas include the side rails below and toward the rear of each door, all the way back to the side-rail end plates shown here. In addition to examining the chassis for rust, look at the front header bar, which is found beneath the fiberglass.

The year 1966 marks the second and final year a genuine Teakwood steering wheel was offered as an option. The better-quality reproduction Teak wheels sell for about $800, and a mint original can bring at least 50 percent more. Note the ribbed chrome ring between the horn button and steering wheel. This ring tightened and loosened the optional telescopic steering column.

Factory original 427 cars are especially valuable and therefore especially susceptible to counterfeiting. All factory-built big-block cars share a number of special features, including a different radiator, radiator support, differential, fuel line, hood, suspension components, and axle-shaft mounts. As shown here, the axle-shaft mounts for big-block cars are machined caps held by bolts rather than U-bolts and nuts.

1
9
6
6

1966 Corvette Replacement Costs for Common Parts

Convertible top	$175.00
Windshield	$450.00 (correct reproduction)
Seat upholstery (per pair)	$190.00 (correct vinyl reproductions), $400.00 (correct leather reproductions)
Carpet	$275.00
Door Panels (pair)	$350.00 (reproduction with upper metal supports and window felts installed)
	$630.00 (reproduction with upper metal supports, window felts, and all trim installed)
Headliner	$210.00 (correct reproduction)
Hood	$850.00 (correct press-molded reproduction)
Front fender	$195.00 (correct press-molded reproduction)
Wheel	$125.00
Wheel cover	$150.00 (good used)
Front grille	$375.00 (correct reproduction)
Headlamp assembly (including bucket, cup, ring, adjusters, bezel mount kit, and bulb)	$50.00
Tail-lamp assembly	$75.00
Exhaust system	$275.00
Shock absorbers	$75.00
Front wheel bearing	$15.00
Front springs (pair)	$150.00
Brake master cylinder	$100.00 (functional replacement)
Front brake cylinders (pair)	$40.00
Rear brake cylinders (pair)	$30.00
Radiator	$800.00 (correct dated reproduction for small block)
Radiator support	$350.00
Water pump	$75.00 (rebuilt original)
Ignition shielding	$360.00
Cylinder head (pair)	$300.00 (small block rebuildable originals)
Rear leaf spring	$110.00 (functional replacement)
Complete tune-up kit (ignition points, condenser, plugs, distributor cap, rotor, ignition wires)	$60.00
Fuel tank	$200.00

1966 Corvette Ratings Chart

Collectibility ★★★★★
Smoothness of Ride ★★★★
Reliability ★★★★
Comfort Cruising Speed: 80 miles per hour
Passenger Accommodations ★★★★
Part/Service Availability ★★★★★

The 1966 models are among the most popular Corvettes ever made. As usual, highly optioned and big-block-equipped cars are the most valuable. If you are paying a premium for a rare specimen, do your homework or enlist the services of an expert because deceitful practices like altering engine numbers, converting small blocks to big blocks, and adding rare options to cars that did not originally come with them are not uncommon.

1966 interiors were available in Black, Red, Silver, Green, Bright Blue, Saddle, Dark Blue, and two-tone Blue/White. Standard seat covers were vinyl, with leather available at extra cost.

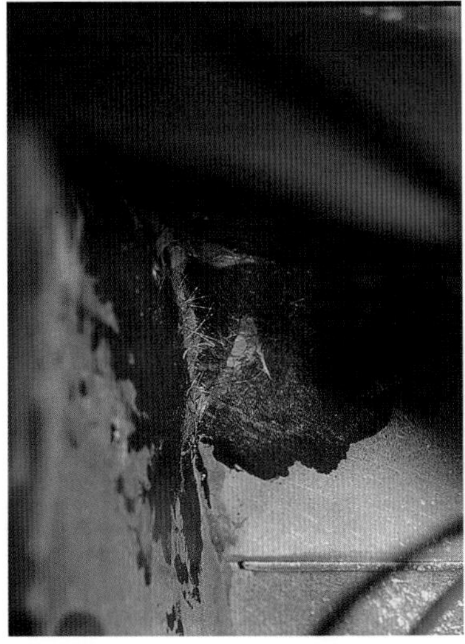

It is often difficult to tell whether and how much body damage a Corvette has suffered just by looking at the topside. Examining the underside of the body will often reveal far more. Sloppy fiberglass work such as this is a sure sign of a repair.

Don't forget to check the function of all mechanical and electrical components when evaluating a prospective purchase. Items that often don't function include the clock, odometer, and radio. Anything missing can be replaced and anything broken can be fixed, but just about nothing found inside, outside, or underneath a vintage Corvette is inexpensive, so take any missing or non-functioning items into consideration when formulating an offer.

The front anti-sway bar in big-block cars is thicker than the standard bar. The front chassis extension that the anti-sway bar mounts to on each side of the car is usually bent after a front-end collision. Inspect this area for irregularities, the presence of which indicates previous collision damage. The four grease pencil slashes on the side of the chassis denote the number of shims between the chassis and bottom of the radiator support on this side. Each body mount point on the chassis also originally had marks correlating to the number of shims needed.

If you are considering a high-end vintage Corvette for purchase, you should go to the extra trouble to check transmission and differential numbers. This example is coded "AO," which means it is a 3.70:1 Positraction unit. The assembly date is "10 4 65," which is October 4, 1965.

As is always the case with Corvettes, originality and technical correctness of components is important to the value and desirability of any 1966. Familiarize yourself with the correct location, appearance, and significance of the many casting numbers, casting dates, part numbers, and assembly codes that are found in most major components and assemblies. Especially important areas to evaluate include the VIN tag, which in a 1966 should be riveted to the brace beneath the glove box door; the chassis number, which is typically stamped in two places on the top of the driver-side rail; and the engine numbers.

As with all desirable options, 1966s that originally came with knock-off wheels are more valuable than those that had the wheels added later. Original knock-off wheel cars came with longer bolts for the spare tire tray to accommodate the increased width of the knock-off. They also came with a special jacking-instruction sticker on the underside of the jack compartment cover. And as shown here, original knock-offs will be dated correctly for the car. Original wheels have a manufacturing date stamped into the reverse side. This example was made on July 15, 1965.

Side exhaust pipes, Goldstripe tires, and knock-off wheels were some of the many options available in 1966. Highly optioned cars are more desirable to collectors and hence more valuable.

1966

What They Said in 1966

Son of a Gun—just what the Corvette needed, more power! Last year's 396 "porcupine head" Corvette was cranking out quite a bit more than its advertised 425 bhp, and with 427 cu. in., the gap between advertised and actual becomes even broader. However, Chevrolet insists that there are only 425 horses in there, and we'll just have to take their word for it. Though we feel compelled to point out that these are 425 horses of a size and strength never before seen by man. . . .

Last month we said that the most dominant feature of any Ferrari was its engine. Well the same thing is true of this big 427 Sting Ray, except that we'd go one step farther and say that it's the power, more than the engine, that overwhelms every other sensation. There's power literally everywhere, great gobs of steam-locomotive, earth-moving torque.

The interior appearance has no significant changes either. It is still roomy, comfortable, and very well sealed against wind and weather. The seats have a broad range of adjustment, and though they're not the super-buckets of a Ferrari GTB, they are pleasant to sit in for long drives.

The driving controls and small switches are just fine. . . . Our test car had power brakes and power steering, and we were grateful for both. The power brakes are . . . smooth, free from any grabbiness or directional instability, and they do get it stopped! Even bringing it down from speeds in the 130–140 bracket without any sweat.

Driving the car on an unrestricted proving ground road is a memorable experience. It accelerates from zero to 100 in less than eleven seconds—faster than a lot of very acceptable cars can get to 60—and is so smooth and controllable in the three-figure speed ranges that it all becomes sort of unreal. In fact, in those circumstances it's pretty hard to tell anything about the car at all, except that it goes like bloody hell and stops and steers without scaring you. —*Car & Driver,* November 1965

We once tried a young neighbor's motorized skateboard and found that it had two qualities in common with the 427 Corvette: They both go very fast, and both require a considerable measure of driving expertise.

Our test Corvette was equipped with the most brutish version of the biggest engine offered by a company that disclaims any interest in racing. It coyly rates it at 425 hp, but we think an extra two teams of Borax mules lie hidden behind the barn door.

The 427 has the kind of torque that made World War II fighter planes try to wrap themselves around their propeller on takeoff.

For drivers who have the guts and skill to master it—and the maturity to recognize it for what it is and handle it accordingly—the 427 Turbo-Jet Corvette is a road king.

On wet pavement, the power goes to the standard whitewalls but not to the road. Even though the steering will lose its ease, we don't think we'd own this car without changing over to Cinturato of Michelin-X (or their equivalent) tires, along with the optional 6-inch-rim aluminum wheels—anything to further a closer association between the 'Vette and the road, wet or dry.

In other respects, our convertible was at home in the rain. Unlike earlier models, it was completely weatherproof with a top that may be easily flicked up or down with one hand.

For those rare individuals who want, and can handle, its potential, the 427 Turbo-Jet is a red-hot machine, but if it gets away from you, don't say we didn't warn you. —*Motor Trend,* March 1966

I Bought a 1966 Corvette

I had previously sold a 1967 427/400 roadster considered a "driver" and was in the market for a restored midyear to round out my collection. At the time I had four Corvettes (1955, 1958, 1970, and 1978) in my collection along with my first collectible car, the well-recognized 1957 Thunderbird. The midyears are often considered as the most desirable of the vintage Corvettes, especially the "big blocks" (1965–1967) and my own preference was initially a 1967, often considered the midyear of choice.

I was told of a collector who was liquidating his collection that included a 1966 427/425 Coupe that had been featured in an article in a major Corvette publication. The car had undergone a "state-of-the-art" restoration, including a blueprinted rebuild of its original 427/425 engine. The aim of the article, titled "King vs. Kong," was to determine which was the faster big block, the 1967 427/435 L71 or the 1966 427/425 L72. To accomplish this, a best-of-five drag race shootout was conducted with the 1966 winning with a best quarter-mile time of 13.102 seconds @ 107.14 mph. Considering that the drag racing took place in Florida during the summer with an ambient air temperature of 94 degrees, that is quite a fast time.

A friend who had seen the 1966 informed me of its quality and I contacted its owner. We agreed on a trade of my 1957 Thunderbird plus some money for the 1966 Coupe. Upon delivery of the car he stated, "You now own the fastest Corvette in the country." I'm sure he didn't consider L88s or L89s! If it wasn't the fastest, it was certainly one of the most striking looking and one of the best restorations to its original factory condition. The car has achieved Bloomington Gold, NCRS National Top Flight and the prestigious Duntov Award. When the 1966 model year reached its 25th anniversary, a major publication commissioned a well-known artist to do a rendering for its centerfold tribute, and this 1966 was the choice.

Other features of this car include Laguna Blue paint, unique to 1966, leather interior, teakwood steering wheel, close-ratio four speed and original knock-off wheels with original blackwall non-DOT tires. It has often been said that the car has a mean and intimidating look. I maintain a second set of wheels and tires (reproduction knock-offs and modern radials) that allow me to periodically test drive the car at reasonably fast but safe speeds on the local expressway service roads. It possesses raw power and handles with firmness and stability. It no doubt lives up to its reputation for speed, and its single four-barrel carburetion is less temperamental than the 1967 400HP & 435 HP tri-power setups. It seems significantly more powerful than the 1967 427/400 L68 and the 1970 454/390 LS5 that I had owned, and the 1972 454/270 LS5 that I presently own.

The 1966 portrays "pure muscle" as compared to my "gentle" 1955, "elegant" 1958, "racy" 1972 and "flashy" 1978 Indy Pace Car. I have had numerous offers to purchase the car, as people in the market are impressed by its good looks and quality. I have declined all offers, as the 1966 has become my midyear of choice. —*Terry Strassberg*

This is one of only 20 authentic factory 1967 L88s. All 1967 L88s came with F41 special front and rear suspension, K66 transistor ignition, M22 heavy-duty transmission, and J50/J56 power assist "special heavy-duty brakes." L88s could not be ordered with air conditioning, a heater or defroster, or a radio.

Chapter 15 1967

Chevrolet's radically redesigned third-generation Corvette was supposed to make its debut in 1967, but a host of persistent problems led to its delay until the following year. With no time to make substantial changes, engineers and designers were given the task of mildly massaging the 1966 into the 1967 model. It is one of the great ironies in Corvette history that the 1967, which wasn't even supposed to exist, is by many accounts the single most collectible of all years.

The fact that it is the last of the ever popular "midyear" series contributes to the appeal of the 1967 model. Its clean exterior is another factor. Front fender vents were revised slightly from the 1965–1966 style but remained fully functional, and front fender and hood emblems used in previous years were eliminated.

Also gone were the full wheel covers that had been used, in various configurations, since 1953. The standard treatment in 1967 was a silver Rally Wheel wearing a small chrome center cap and polished stainless beauty ring on the perimeter. Knock-off wheels were discontinued as an option because of safety regulations forbidding the use of wheel spinners that protruded. In their place Chevrolet offered a very handsome aluminum "bolt-on" wheel.

Inside, the only major changes were a different upholstery pattern, different control knobs, and repositioning of the park brake handle from under the dash to the center console area.

Underneath the car virtually nothing changed in 1967. Four-wheel disc brakes were again standard, as was four-wheel independent suspension. Big-block-equipped cars, as well as those fitted with optional F41 special front and rear suspension, got a rear anti-sway bar in addition to the standard front bar. Big blocks also got a larger diameter fuel line, 3/8 inch instead of 5/16 inch, and heavy-duty retaining caps and bolts to hold the rear-axle shaft U-joints to the differential yokes instead of the standard U-bolts and nuts.

The standard engine in 1967 displaced 327 cubic inches and relied on a mild, hydraulic-lifter camshaft, single four-barrel carburetor bolted to a cast-iron intake manifold, and 10.5:1 compression ratio. It was rated at a respectable 300 horsepower. For $105.35 extra buyers could choose the optional 327-cubic-inch, 350-horsepower engine. The extra horsepower came from 11.0:1 compression, larger valves, and a more aggressive camshaft.

While small-block engine choices were limited to only two, there were no fewer than five different 427-cubic-inch engines to pick from. A handsome new hood design featuring a contrasting color on the "power bulge" denoted the presence of a big block.

The tamest 427 used hydraulic lifters, relatively low compression, and a single Holley four-barrel atop a cast-iron intake to produce 390 horsepower. The same engine fitted with an aluminum intake and three two-barrel Holleys was rated at 400 horsepower. The extra 10 horsepower was hardly worth the additional money, but the appearance of the exotic-looking three-carburetor setup (commonly called "tri-power") and its triangular, chrome-plated air cleaner definitely was.

Tri-power could be had on a more potent 427. Benefiting from large-valve cylinder heads, 11.0:1 compression, a racy camshaft, and solid lifters, it generated 435 horsepower. That same engine could be ordered with an additional option, aluminum cylinder heads. The horsepower rating didn't change, but the weight savings afforded by the light alloy heads undoubtedly made cars so equipped even faster. The price of the aluminum heads was a steep $368.65 on top of the $437.10 it cost for the tri-power 427/435 horsepower engine, for a grand total of $805.75! It is not surprising that only 16 examples of the aluminum-headed engine, called option L89, were sold.

The final engine option offered in 1967 was called L88. It was officially rated at 430 horsepower and cost a titanic $947.90. The 430-horsepower rating was intended to discourage anyone except serious racers from buying an L88, and actual output was near 600 horsepower! The L88 engine was in essence an all-out race engine that squarely places Corvettes so equipped among the fastest production cars ever made.

Only 20 L88 Corvettes were built in 1967, and the few documented survivors are easily the most valuable production Corvettes ever made.

At the other end of the spectrum from an L88, buyers could outfit their 1967 Corvette from a long list of comfort and convenience options. Power steering, windows, and brakes, air conditioning, AM-FM radio, telescopic steering column, leather seats, speed warning indicator, cast-aluminum "bolt-on" wheels, and headrests were among the more popular options.

As in previous years, 1967 Corvettes came standard with a three-speed manual transmission. Only 424 cars were so equipped and many of those have been converted to four-speeds or automatics in the intervening years, making three-speed cars quite rare today. As with other unusual configurations, however (such as drum brakes on a 1965), this is a situation where rarity does not equate to desirability or value.

The vast majority of 1967s were originally built with one of three different optional four-speeds that were available. For 2,324 buyers not interested in rowing the gears themselves, Chevrolet's Powerglide transmission was specified. This two-speed automatic could be coupled to a 300, 390, or 400 horsepower engine only.

Corvettes have inspired customizers to do their own thing since the very beginning. Generally speaking, most people prefer, and will pay more for, unaltered cars. Simple bolt-on items like the custom wheels seen here don't usually alter value beyond the cost to replace them with stock wheels and wheel covers. These give the car a real "period" look and add to the owner's enjoyment of his car, which is what the old Corvette hobby is all about.

The L88 engine made its power by virtue of 12.5:1 compression, a full race camshaft, a huge Holley four-barrel atop an open plenum aluminum intake, and a long list of severe-duty internal parts. Fewer than a dozen authentic 1967 L88 Corvettes still exist, and they sell in the high six-figure range. There are numerous bogus L88s floating around, so perform thorough research and enlist the services of a reputable expert before purchasing one.

Cast-aluminum bolt-on wheels found their way onto only 720 new Corvettes in 1967. This low number was undoubtedly the result of the option's $263.30 price tag. High then, but a bargain compared to today, when excellent original bolt-ons typically sell for at least $1,500 each. Reproductions cost about $1,500 for a set of four.

1967 Corvette Specifications and Major Options

Specs

Base Price When New	$4,388.75 (coupe) $4,240.75 (convertible)
Production	8,504 (coupe) 14,436(convertible)
Engine	V-8
Bore x Stroke (small block, in inches)	4.00x3.25
Displacement (small block)	327 cubic inches
Bore x Stroke (big block, in inches)	4.25x3.76
Displacement (big block)	427 cubic inches
Compression Ratio	10.5:1 (base engine)
Horsepower	300 (base engine)
Transmission	Three-speed manual standard, four-speed manual and two-speed automatic optional
Wheelbase	98 inches
Overall width	69.6 inches
Overall height	49.8 inches
Overall length	175.1 inches
Track, front	56.8 inches
Track, rear	57.6 inches
Weight	3,260 pounds
Tires	7.75x15 bias ply
Front suspension	Independent unequal-length wishbones and coil springs, anti-sway bar, telescopic shock absorbers
Rear suspension	Independent radius arms, transverse leaf spring, half-shafts acting as upper locating members, lower transverse rods, telescopic shock absorbers
Steering	Recirculating ball
Brakes	Four-wheel disc, four-piston calipers, II.75-inch rotors front and rear, 461.2-square-inches swept area
0–60 mph	7.8 seconds (327/300 with 3.36:1 axle and four-speed manual transmission), 5.0 seconds (427/435 with 3.55:1 axle and four-speed manual transmission)
Standing 1/4-mile	16.0 seconds @ 86.5 mph (327/300 with .36:1 axle and four-speed manual transmission), 12.90 seconds @ 111 mph (427/435 with 3.55:1 axle and four-speed manual transmission)
Top speed	121 mph (327/300 with 3.36:1 axle and four-speed manual transmission), 150 mph (427/435 with 3.55:1 axle and four-speed manual transmission)

1967 Options

		Price	Quantity
n/a	Genuine leather seats	$79.00	1,601
A01	Soft-Ray tinted glass	$15.80	11,331
A02	Soft-Ray tinted windshield	$10.55	6,558
A31	Power Windows	$57.95	4,036
A82	Headrests	$42.15	1,762
A85	Shoulder belts	$26.35	1,426
C07	Auxiliary Hardtop	$231.75	6,880
C08	Vinyl covering for auxiliary hardtop	$52.70	1,996
C48	Heater and defroster delete (credit)	$97.85	35
C60	Air conditioning	$412.90	3,788
F41	Special suspension	$36.90	2,198
G81	Positraction rear axle	$42.15	20,308
J50	Power brakes	$42.15	4,766
J56	Special heavy-duty brakes	342.30	267
K19	Air injection reactor	$44.75	2,573
K66	Transistor ignition	$73.75	5,759
L36	427 cid, 390 hp engine	$200.15	3,832
L68	427 cid, 400 hp engine	$305.50	2,101
L71	427 cid, 435 hp engine	$437.10	3,754
L79	327 cid, 350 hp engine	$105.35	6,375
L88	427 cid, 430 hp engine	$947.90	20
L89	Aluminum cylinder heads for L71	$368.65	16
M20	4-Speed transmission	$184.35	9,157
M21	4-Speed close ratio transmission	$184.35	11,015
M22	4-Speed close ratio, heavy duty	$237.00	20
M35	Powerglide transmission	$194.35	2,324
N03	36-gallon fuel tank	$198.05	2
N11	Off-road exhaust system	$36.90	2,326
N14	Side mount exhaust system	$131.65	4,209
N36	Telescopic steering column	$42.15	2,415
N40	Power steering	$94.80	5,747
N89	Cast aluminum bolt-on wheels	$263.30	720
P92	7.75-15 rayon whitewall tires	$31.35	13,445
QB1	7.75-15 Redline tires	$46.65	4,230
U15	Speed warning indicator	$10.55	2,108
U69	AM-FM radio	$172.75	22,193

1967 Garage Watch

This is the transmission's serial-number stamping. This transmission was originally installed into the 19,738th Corvette built in 1967. This stamping is typically located in the rear edge of the transmission's main case, on the driver side. The identification code and assembly-date stamping is typically in the rear edge of the main case on the passenger side.

Original 1967 Corvette transmission cases contain two stampings. One contains the latter part of the serial number for the car the unit was originally installed into, and the other contains an identification code and an assembly date. The stamping shown here, "P7E22," translates to a four-speed manual transmission built at the Muncie plant on May 22, 1967.

Check the engine-block casting number and casting date. The date, which should precede the car's final assembly date by no more than about six months, begins with a letter indicating the month ("A" for January through "L" for December), followed by one or two numbers indicating the day, and either a "6" for 1966 or a "7" for 1967. This big-block example, which reads upside down, is "D 18 7" for April 18, 1967.

The 1967 Corvettes came with a trim tag riveted to the brace beneath the glove box assembly, which contains information on body color, interior color, seat material, and body build date. This example is from a Tuxedo Black convertible with Bright Blue leather seats. The body number, S1820, indicates that this was the 1,820th convertible body made in St. Louis (some bodies were made under contract by A. O. Smith in Ionia, Michigan, and start with "A" instead of "S"). The body build date, just visible in the upper left, is "D09," which translates to November 9.

To authenticate, evaluate the engine stamping, which is located on the block's deck surface in a machined pad just forward of the passenger-side cylinder head. One section of the stamping, called the assembly sequence, indicates the engine size, application, and assembly date. Each engine stamping contains a second sequence that is the latter part of the serial number of the car the engine was originally installed into.

1
9
6
7

1967 Corvette
Replacement Costs for Common Parts

Convertible top	$175.00
Windshield	$450.00 (correct reproduction)
Seat upholstery (per pair)	$190.00 (correct vinyl reproductions), $400.00 (correct leather reproductions)
Carpet	$275.00
Door Panels (pair)	$350.00 (reproduction with upper metal supports and window felts installed)
	$630.00 (reproduction with upper metal supports, window felts, and all trim installed)
Headliner	$210.00 (correct reproduction)
Hood	$850.00 (correct press-molded reproduction)
Front fender	$195.00 (correct press-molded reproduction)
Wheel	$125.00
Wheel cover	$150.00 (good used)
Front grille	$375.00 (correct reproduction)
Headlamp assembly (including bucket, cup, ring, adjusters, bezel mount kit, and bulb)	$50.00
Tail-lamp assembly	$75.00
Exhaust system	$275.00
Shock absorbers	$75.00
Front wheel bearing	$15.00
Front springs (pair)	$150.00
Brake master cylinder	$100.00 (functional replacement)
Front brake cylinders (pair)	$40.00
Rear brake cylinders (pair)	$30.00
Radiator	$800.00 (correct dated reproduction for small block)
Radiator support	$350.00
Water pump	$75.00 (rebuilt original)
Ignition shielding	$360.00
Cylinder head (pair)	$300.00 (small block rebuildable originals)
Rear leaf spring	$110.00 (functional replacement)
Complete tune-up kit (ignition points, condenser, plugs, distributor cap, rotor, ignition wires)	$60.00
Fuel tank	$200.00

1967 Corvette Ratings Chart

Collectibility ★★★★★
Smoothness of Ride ★★★★
Reliability ★★★★
Comfort Cruising Speed: 80 miles per hour
Passenger Accommodations ★★★★
Part/Service Availability ★★★★★

The 1967 models are considered by many to be the most popular Corvettes ever made. Highly optioned and big-block-equipped cars are the most valuable. As with all Corvettes, excellent unrestored cars are worth more than comparable restored examples. If you are planning to purchase a rare car, do your homework or enlist the services of an expert, because deceitful practices like altering engine numbers, converting small blocks to big blocks, and adding rare options to cars that did not originally come with them are not uncommon.

As is always the case with Corvettes, originality and technical correctness of components is important to the value of any 1967. Familiarize yourself with the correct location, appearance, and significance of the casting numbers, casting dates, part numbers, and assembly codes that are found in most major components. Especially important areas to evaluate include the VIN tag, the chassis number, and the engine numbers.

1967 interiors were available in Black, Saddle, White, Bright Blue, Teal Blue, Green, and Red. Standard seat covers were vinyl, and leather was available as an option. In addition to leather, this unrestored interior has AM-FM radio, telescopic steering column, air conditioning, headrest, speed warning, and power windows.

Original paperwork such as a window sticker shown on the left or a build-sheet seen on the right add value and desirability to a vintage Corvette. 1967 marks the first year that build sheets were permanently attached to Corvettes as they progressed down the assembly line. The build sheet (also commonly called a "tank sticker" because they were supposed to be glued to the top of the gas tank) contains a wealth of information about the car it is attached to, including its body and interior color, selling dealer, and options.

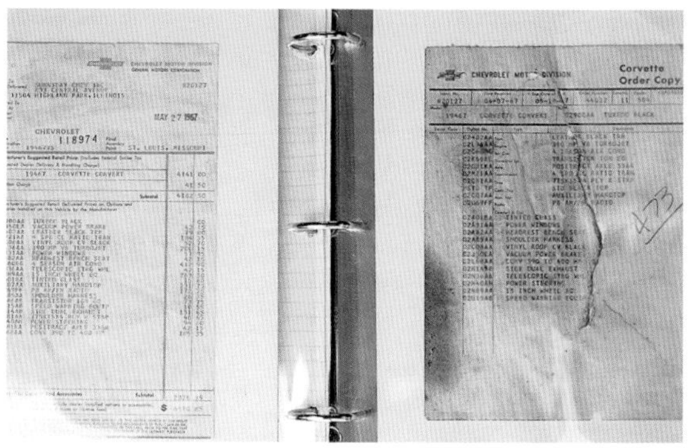

Only 815 cars were painted Tuxedo Black in 1967, making it the rarest color by far. This example has extremely low mileage, is documented by every item of paperwork imaginable, is equipped with the highly desirable combination of a 400-horsepower engine and air conditioning in addition to 17 other options, and is in beautiful unrestored condition. These are all of the characteristics serious collectors seek out, making this car extremely valuable and a once-in-a-lifetime find.

In the 747 1967 Corvettes built without an optional AM-FM radio, the dash was not cut out for it. The two plugs seen here beneath the clock fill the holes where the heater and defroster controls normally go. This original L88 is one of 35 cars that came with option C48, heater and defroster delete.

This 400-horsepower coupe has had the same owner for nearly 25 years and is exercised regularly. 1967s are wonderful drivers and excellent investments, but in spite of their popularity they do suffer from the same maladies as other Corvettes of the era. They are prone to chassis rust, particularly in the side rails beneath the rear areas of the doors. Also, they tend to run too hot, particularly air-conditioned cars and big blocks.

All 1967 L88 Corvettes were fitted with a larger-than-normal radiator. As with all Harrison aluminum radiators, including those found in all 1967 small-block cars, the part number and manufacturing date code are stamped into the top. The date in this example is 67E, which translates to May 1967, and the part number is 3007436. The date is actually stamped into a separate piece of aluminum that is welded to the radiator rather than directly into the radiator. All small blocks used radiator number 3155316 and all non-L88 big blocks used a large copper radiator that did not have anything stamped into the top.

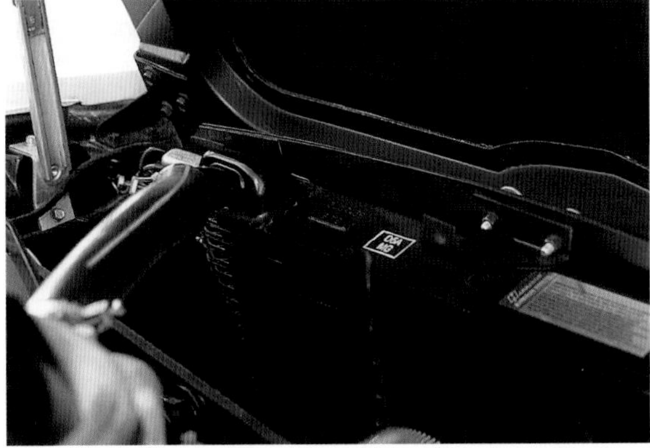

Factory-original big-block cars are especially valuable and therefore especially susceptible to counterfeiting. Familiarize yourself with the many components and features typical of big blocks, such as heavier axle retainers, a rear sway bar, a larger fuel line, special radiator and radiator support, and so on. Take the totality of circumstances, including your research into past owners and any authentic documentation that accompanies the car, into consideration when forming a conclusion. This gorgeous Silver Pearl convertible is one of only 16 L89s built in 1967 and has the kind of authentic documentation collectors love to see.

1967

What They Said in 1967

The Corvette's cockpit has the specific gravity of a P-51 Mustang, and that's the way it should be. No end of pleasure can be derived from watching all the gauges and needles doing their stuff every time you fire up.

The specs on our engine were straight out of racing-land: 11.0:1 compression; .5197-inch lift solid-lifter cam; 2.195- and 1.725-inch-diameter intake and exhaust valves; 3 Holley carbs.

When they dropped in the heavy 427 engine, one of the penalties imposed by the swap was higher spring rates. As such, the 427 model is strictly a smooth-road machine at the posted speed limits. Granted, once you get wailing, the suspension evens out and sticks to the ground doing it, but there are few places left to run 120 for sustained periods.

As you might expect, steering under all conditions was quick and light, and though power-assisted, provided an excellent feeling of changing road surfaces.

The Corvette, like many of the corporation's hot machines, will go on and on, shutting down would-be challengers with minimum maintenance. GM may not be in racing, but its divisions build the best darned line of production competition cars in the world. The 435 Sting Ray is kind of king of these kings. —*Hot Rod,* May 1967

The Sting Ray is in its fifth and probably last year with that name and body style, and it finally looks the way we thought it should have in the first place. All the funny business—the fake vents, extraneous emblems and simulated-something-or-other wheel covers—is gone, and though some consider the basic shape overstyled, it looks more like a finished product now.

For this test we selected an almost basic version of the Corvette: A convertible hardtop with the standard 300-bhp 327 engine, 4-speed gearbox and power assists. With the exception of the power assists, we concluded that this is the Corvette for the thinking driver.

It is a credit to the American way of doing things that the performance is achieved in a remarkably silent, smooth and economical manner. Our test car had the optional 4-speed gearbox, which is smooth, quiet and easy shifting. . . .

It's hard to find fault with the Corvette's handling; it's as near neutral as any car we know and of course there's always enough torque available to steer with the throttle. It is quite stable directionally in a cross wind and imparts an immense feeling of security out on the open road.

Over smooth roads the Corvette has a pleasing, almost big-car ride. Noise level is low from most sources, and thus this is a car for long-distance travel. Its effective heater, excellent AM/FM radio and good weather protection (regardless of top ordered) place it near the top of the list of sports/GT cars for pure comfort. On rough roads the ride deteriorates as the progressive-rate springs, limited wheel travel and willowy body structure combine to put up quite a fuss.

The Corvette's interior abounds with niceties. There are handy new center-mounted handbrake, seat-belt hooks that solve the problem of where to stow them, large, readable instruments and handy controls.

Disc brakes on all four wheels are powerful, smooth and consistent. . . . All things considered, the Sting Ray is a big value for the money.

The improvements we would most wish for in the next Corvette series would be lighter weight, improved body structure and quality control, and a better ride on poor surfaces. But in the meantime the Corvette ranks with the best sports/GT cars the world has to offer, regardless of price. —*Road & Track,* February 1967

I Bought a 1967 Corvette

I purchased my 1967 L88 Corvette, serial number 194377S120407, in 1979 after hearing about it from a friend who ran a Corvette shop in Perrine, Florida. I bought it from Corvette shop owner Paul Langbein, who had discovered the car at a repossession shop in Turtle Creek, a suburb of Pittsburgh. That was a time when L88s were not well recognized, and after I spent many hours under and all over the car, and carefully studied the original tank sticker, I was sure that it was one of the 20 factory-built 1967 L88s.

David Ziegler, the original owner, purchased the car in Washington, D.C., at Curtis Chevrolet. He drove it on weekends and drag raced it extensively both on the street and at the track. It was known as "The Flying Dutchman" and, according to David, "always won unless it broke." The L88 engine was too powerful for almost every part behind it, including the clutch, transmission, drive shaft, differential, axles, and chassis, all of which broke numerous times. When it didn't break, the car ran in the high tens at 130-plus mph.

The car was not drivable when I bought it in 1979. With help from many friends, including Gary Licko, Gerry Yursis, and Mike Schreiber, I finished restoring the chassis in 1988. It was displayed without a body at the Bloomington Gold show that year. The restoration was completed early in 1992. I chose to restore it to its period racing look, complete with American Racing mags, Blue Streak tires, Hurst shifter, and Stahl headers.

Everything you've ever read about how L88 Corvettes behave is essentially true. It's difficult to start in cold weather, doesn't like to idle below 1,200 rpm, has a voracious appetite for racing fuel, and will overheat if caught in traffic. You forget all of that, however, once you get behind the wheel and experience the most exciting and awe-inspiring drive you can imagine. *—Dave Walters*

I raced a new Corvette each year from 1958 to 1968 in regional SCCA races, Daytona, and Sebring. For 1967 our Sunray DX-sponsored car came to life while I watched our ordered white Corvette move down the production line at the old Corvette factory in St. Louis.

The 1967 failed the leak test miserably, because they left body putty off to save weight. I left the factory in a bright shiny Corvette late in the day with a light rain falling, slick streets and street tires. Any power applied in any gear would put the car sideways. Because of the tires, weather, and excessive power, you couldn't be in a hurry and go in a straight line or around a curve—particularly without a defroster to sort of see where you were going.

Don Yenko and I shared this L-88 at its first outing at Sebring in 1967. It was very fast and we had a very good run. In 1968 for Daytona the 1967 L-88 had its best showing. Jerry and I won Grand Touring and 10th overall. The car was fast going down the back stretch at Daytona, reaching speeds between 188 and 192 miles per hour.

It was thrilling seeing the same car perfectly restored 25 years later with the red, white, and blue American colors that I had insisted on.

The car is now valued at one million dollars! *—Dave Morgan*

Appendix 1

Engine Codes and Engine Block Casting Numbers

1953–1967 Corvette Engine Codes

1953

Code	Engine Size	Description
LAY	235	six-cylinder, 150 hp, three one-barrel carburetors, Powerglide

1954

Code	Engine Size	Description
YG	235	six-cylinder, 150 hp (155 hp beginning mid-production due to camshaft change), three one-barrel carburetors, Powerglide

1955

Code	Engine Size	Description
YG	235	six-cylinder, 155 hp, three 1-barrel carburetors, Powerglide
FG	265	V-8, 195 hp, four-barrel, Powerglide
GR	265	V-8, 195 hp, 4-barrel, 3-speed

1956

Code	Engine Size	Description
FK	265	210 hp, 4-barrel, Powerglide
GV	265	210 hp, 4-barrel, 3-speed
FG	265	225 hp, 2x4-barrel, Powerglide
GR	265	225 hp, 2x4-barrel, 3-speed
GU	265	240 hp, 2x4-barrel, high-lift cam, 3-speed

1957

Code	Engine Size	Description
EF	283	220 hp, 4-barrel, manual transmission
FH	283	220 hp, 4-barrel, Powerglide
EH	283	245 hp, 2x4-barrel, manual transmission
FG	283	245 hp, 2x4-barrel, Powerglide
EM	283	250 hp, FI, manual transmission
FK	283	250 hp, FI, Powerglide
EG	283	270 hp, 2x4-barrel, high-lift cam, manual transmission
EL	283	283 hp, FI, high-lift cam, manual transmission
EN	283	283 hp, FI w/air intake, high-lift cam, manual transmission

1958

Code	Engine Size	Description
CQ	283	230 hp, 4-barrel, manual transmission
DG	283	230 hp, 4-barrel, Powerglide
CT	283	245 hp, 2x4-barrel, manual transmission
DJ	283	245 hp, 2x4-barrel, Powerglide
CR	283	250 hp, FI, manual transmission
DH	283	250 hp, FI, Powerglide
CU	283	270 hp, 2x4-barrel, high-lift cam, manual transmission
CS	283	290 hp, FI, high-lift cam, manual transmission

1959

Code	Engine Size	Description
CQ	283	230 hp, 4-barrel, manual transmission
DG	283	230 hp, 4-barrel, Powerglide
CT	283	245 hp, 2x4-barrel, manual transmission
DJ	283	245 hp, 2x4-barrel, Powerglide
CR	283	250 hp, FI, manual transmission
DH	283	250 hp, FI, Powerglide
CU	283	270 hp, 2x4-barrel, high-lift cam, manual transmission
CS	283	290 hp, FI, high-lift cam, manual transmission

1960

Code	Engine Size	Description
CQ	283	230 hp, 4-barrel, manual transmission
DG	283	230 hp, 4-barrel, Powerglide
CT	283	245 hp, 2x4-barrel, manual transmission
DJ	283	245 hp, 2x4-barrel, Powerglide
CR	283	250 hp, FI, manual transmission
CU	283	270 hp, 2x4-barrel, high-lift cam, manual transmission
CS	283	290 hp, FI, high-lift cam, manual transmission

1961

Code	Engine Size	Description
CQ	283	230 hp, 4-barrel, manual transmission
DG	283	230 hp, 4-barrel, Powerglide
CT	283	245 hp, 2x4-barrel, manual transmission
DJ	283	245 hp, 2x4-barrel, Powerglide
CR	283	275 hp, FI, manual transmission
CU	283	270 hp, 2x4-barrel, high-lift cam, manual transmission
CS	283	315 hp, FI, high-lift cam, manual transmission

1962

Code	Engine Size	Description
RC	327	250 hp, 4-barrel, manual transmission
RD	327	300 hp, 4-barrel, manual transmission
RE	327	340 hp, 4-barrel, high-lift cam, manual transmission

RF	327	360 hp, FI, high-lift cam, manual transmission
SC	327	250 hp, 4-barrel, Powerglide
SD	327	300 hp, 4-barrel, Powerglide

1963

Code	Engine Size	Description
RC	327	250 hp, 4-barrel, manual transmission
RD	327	300 hp, 4-barrel, manual transmission
RE	327	340 hp, 4-barrel, high-lift cam, manual transmission
RF	327	360 hp, FI, high-lift cam, manual transmission
SC	327	250 hp, 4-barrel, Powerglide
SD	327	300 hp, 4-barrel, Powerglide

1964

Code	Engine Size	Description
RC	327	250 hp, 4-barrel, manual transmission
RD	327	300 hp, 4-barrel, manual transmission
RE	327	365 hp, 4-barrel, high-lift cam, manual transmission
RF	327	375 hp, FI, high-lift cam, manual transmission
RP	327	250 hp, 4-barrel, a/c, manual transmission
RQ	327	300 hp, 4-barrel, a/c, manual transmission
RR	327	365 hp, 4-barrel, a/c, manual transmission
RT	327	365 hp, 4-barrel, high-lift cam, TI, manual transmission
RU	327	365 hp, 4-barrel, high-lift cam, a/c, TI, manual transmission
RX	327	375 hp, FI, high-lift cam, TI, manual transmission
SC	327	250 hp, 4-barrel, Powerglide
SD	327	300 hp, 4-barrel, Powerglide
SK	327	250 hp, 4-barrel, a/c, Powerglide
SL	327	300 hp, 4-barrel, a/c, Powerglide

1965

Code	Engine Size	Description
HE	327	250 hp, 4-barrel, manual transmission
HF	327	300 hp, 4-barrel, manual transmission
HG	327	375 hp, FI, high-lift cam, 4-speed
HH	327	365 hp, 4-barrel, mechanical lifters, 4-speed
HI	327	250 hp, 4-barrel, a/c, manual transmission
HJ	327	300 hp, 4-barrel, a/c, manual transmission
HK	327	365 hp, 4-barrel, mechanical lifters, a/c, 4-speed
HL	327	365 hp, 4-barrel, mechanical lifters, TI, 4-speed
HM	327	365 hp, 4-barrel, mechanical lifters, a/c, TI, 4-speed
HN	327	375 hp, FI, high-lift cam, TI, 4-speed
HO	327	250 hp, 4-barrel, Powerglide
HP	327	300 hp, 4-barrel, Powerglide
HQ	327	250 hp, 4-barrel, a/c, Powerglide
HR	327	300 hp, 4-barrel, a/c, Powerglide
HT	327	350 hp, 4-barrel, hydraulic lifters, 4-speed
HU	327	350 hp, 4-barrel, hydraulic lifters, a/c, 4-speed
HV	327	350 hp, 4-barrel, hydraulic lifters, TI, 4-speed
HW	327	350 hp, 4-barrel, hydraulic lifters, a/c, TI, 4-speed
IF	396	425 hp, 4-barrel, TI, 4-speed

1966

Code	Engine Size	Description
HE	327	300 hp, manual transmission
HH	327	300 hp, K19, manual transmission
HO	327	300 hp, Powerglide
HR	327	300 hp, K19, Powerglide
HT	327	350 hp, high-lift cam, 4-speed
HD	327	350 hp, high-lift cam, K19, 4-speed
HP	327	350 hp, high-lift cam, a/c, p/s, 4-speed
KH	327	350 hp, high-lift cam, K19, a/c, p/s, 4-speed
IL	427	390 hp, special cam, hydraulic lifters, 4-speed
IM	427	390 hp, special cam, hydraulic lifters, K19, 4-speed
IQ	427	390 hp, special cam, hydraulic lifters, Powerglide
IR	427	390 hp, special cam, hydraulic lifters, K19, Powerglide
IP	427	425 hp, special cam, mechanical lifters, 4-speed
IK	427	425 hp, special cam, mechanical lifters, M-22 4-speed

1967

Code	Engine Size	Description
HE	327	300 hp, 4-barrel, manual transmission
HH	327	300 hp, 4-barrel, K19, manual transmission
HO	327	300 hp, 4-barrel, Powerglide
HR	327	300 hp, 4-barrel, K19, Powerglide
HT	327	350 hp, 4-barrel, high-lift cam, 4-speed
HD	327	350 hp, 4-barrel, high-lift cam, K19, 4-speed
HP	327	350 hp, 4-barrel, high-lift cam, a/c, p/s, 4-speed
KH	327	350 hp, 4-barrel, high-lift cam, K19, a/c, p/s, 4-speed
IL	427	390 hp, 4-barrel, special cam, hydraulic lifters, 4-speed
IM	427	390 hp, 4-barrel, special cam, hydraulic lifters, K19, 4-speed
IQ	427	390 hp, 4-barrel, special cam, hydraulic lifters, Powerglide
IR	427	390 hp, 4-barrel, special cam, hydraulic lifters, K19, Powerglide
JC	427	400 hp, 3x2-barrel, 4-speed
JF	427	400 hp, 3x2-barrel, K19, 4-speed
JD	427	400 hp, 3x2-barrel, Powerglide
JG	427	400 hp, 3x2-barrel, K19, Powerglide
JE	427	435 hp, 3x2-barrel, mechanical lifters, 4-speed
JA	427	435 hp, 3x2-barrel, mechanical lifters, K19, 4-speed
IU	427	435 hp, 3x2-barrel, aluminum heads, 4-speed
JH	427	435 hp, 3x2-barrel, aluminum heads, K19, 4-speed
IT	427	430 hp, 4-barrel, heavy-duty L88, M22 4-speed

1953–1967 Corvette Engine Block Casting Numbers

1953

Casting #	Description
3701481	235 cubic inch six-cylinder cast prior to mid-October 1953
3835911	235 cubic inch six-cylinder cast after mid-October 1953

1954

Casting #	Description
3835911	235 cubic inch six-cylinder

1955

Casting #	Description
3835911	235 cubic inch six-cylinder
3703524	265 cubic inch V-8

1956

Casting #	Description
3720991	265 cubic inch V-8

1957

Casting #	Description
3731548	283 cubic inch V-8

1958

Casting #	Description
3737739	283 cubic inch V-8
3756519	mid-to-late production 283 cubic inch V-8

1959

Casting #	Description
3737739	early production 283 cubic inch V-8
3756519	283 cubic inch V-8

1960

Casting #	Description
3756519	283 cubic inch V-8

1961

Casting #	Description
3756519	283 cubic inch V-8
3789935	very late production 283 cubic inch V-8

1962-64

Casting #	Description
3782870	327 cubic inch V-8

1965

Casting #	Description
3782870	327 cubic inch V-8
3858180	327 cubic inch V-8, very few of this casting number block was utilized. These came from the passenger car engine block foundry in Tonawanda, New York and it is believed that they were supplied to the Corvette plant while the foundry in Saginaw, Michigan that normally supplied Corvette engine blocks was shut down.
3855962	396 cubic inch V-8

1966

Casting #	Description
3858174	327 cubic inch V-8
3892657	very late production 327 cubic inch V-8
3855961	very early production 427 cubic inch V-8
3869942	427 cubic inch V-8

1967

Casting #	Description
3892657	327 cubic inch V-8
3869942	very early production 427 cubic inch V-8
3904351	427 cubic inch V-8
3916321	very late production 427 cubic inch V-8

Appendix 2

Corvette Glass Date Codes and Paint Codes

All factory installed 1953-67 Corvette glass, which was manufactured by a company called Libby-Owens-Ford, contains a two letter manufacturing date code. The first letter represents the month and the second letter represents the year.

Month Codes

January 1953-1956:	L
January 1957-1967:	N
February 1953-1957:	M
February 1958-1967:	X
March 1953-1956:	N
March 1957-1967:	L
April 1953-1957:	K
April 1958-1967:	G
May 1953-1967:	J
June 1953-1967:	I
July 1953-1957:	H
July 1958-1967:	U
August 1953-1967:	T
September 1953-1957:	E
September 1958-1967:	A
October 1953-1957:	F
October 1958-1967:	Y
November 1953-1967:	C
December 1953-1967:	V

Calendar Year Codes

1953, 1966:	A
1954, 1967:	Z
1955:	X
1956:	V
1957:	T
1958:	N
1959:	Y
1960:	U
1961:	L
1962:	L
1963:	C
1964:	G
1965:	J

1963-1967 Paint Codes

1963

Paint Code	Color
900	Tuxedo Black
912	Silver Blue
916	Daytona Blue
923	Riverside Red
932	Saddle Tan
936	Ermine White
941	Sebring Silver

1964

Paint Code	Color
900	Tuxedo Black
912	Silver Blue
916	Dark Blue
923	Riverside Red
932	Saddle Tan
936	Ermine White
940	Satin Silver

1965

Paint Code	Color
AA	Tuxedo Black
CC	Ermine White
FF	Nassau Blue
GG	Glen Green
MM	Milano Maroon
UU	Rally Red
XX	Goldwood Yellow
QQ	Silver Pearl

1966

Paint Code	Color
900	Tuxedo Black
972	Ermine White
974	Rally Red
976	Nassau Blue
978	Laguna Blue
980	Trophy Blue
982	Mosport Green
984	Sunfire Yellow
986	Silver Pearl
988	Milano Maroon

1967

Paint Code	Color
900	Tuxedo Black
972	Ermine White
974	Rally Red
976	Marina Blue
977	Lynndale Blue
980	Elkhart Blue
983	Goodwood Green
984	Sunfire Yellow
986	Silver Pearl
988	Marlboro Maroon
989	

Appendix 3

Final Monthly Serial Numbers

The exact assembly date for each 1953-1967 Corvette is not known with certainty. For most years, the serial number of the last car assembled in each month is known. From this information you can determine in most instances the approximate date your car was assembled. First, compare your car's serial number to the final monthly serial numbers for your year to determine which month your car was assembled. Then deduct the previous month's final serial number from the final serial number for the month your car was assembled to determine the total number of cars assembled the same month your car was assembled. Then divide that total number of cars by the total number of working days in the month to determine approximately how many cars were assembled each working day. Use this total to determine approximately which day of the month your car was assembled.

1953

June:	E53F001002
December:	E53F001300

1954

December, 1953:	E54F001014
May 18th:	E53F002628

1955

January:	VE55S001027
February:	VE55S001110
March:	VE55S001150
April:	VE55S001200
May:	VE55S001300
June:	VE55S001389
July:	VE55S001489
August:	VE55S001555
September:	VE55S001599
October:	VE55S001634
November:	VE55S001688
December:	VE55S001700

1956

August 8th:	E56S001003844

1957

October, 1956:	E57S100580
November:	E57S101070
December:	unknown
January, 1957:	unknown
February:	unknown
March 29th:	E57S103098
April 9th:	E57S103268
May:	E57S104331
June:	E57S104924
July:	E57S105584
August:	E57S106229
September:	E57S106339

1958

October, 1957:	J58S100486
November:	J58S101443
December:	J58S102511
January, 1958:	J58S103677
February:	J58S104789
March:	J58S105779
April:	J58S106544
May:	J58S107489
June:	J58S108192
July:	J58S108840
August:	J58S109168

1959

September, 1958:	J59S100409
October:	J59S100632
November:	J59S101587
December:	J59S102641
January, 1959:	J59S103962
February:	J59S104921
March:	J59S106033
April:	J59S107144
May:	J59S107934
June:	J59S108702
July:	J59S109437
August:	J59S109670

1960

October, 1959:	00867S101168
November:	00867S101454
December:	00867S102059
January, 1960:	00867S103158
February:	00867S104360
March:	00867S105711
April:	00867S107011
May:	00867S108167
June:	00867S109149
July:	00867S109846
August:	00867S110261

1961

September, 1960:	10867S101052
October:	10867S102301
November:	10867S103355
December:	10867S104306
January, 1961:	10867S105203
February:	10867S105966
March:	10867S106889
April:	10867S107804
May:	10867S108960
June:	10867S110160
July:	10867S110939

1962

August, 1961:	20867S100443
September:	20867S100827
October:	20867S102065
November:	20867S103465
December:	20867S104766
January, 1962:	20867S106234
February:	20867S107585
March:	20867S109116
April:	20867S110519
May:	20867S112035
June:	20867S113459
July:	20867S114520
August:	20867S114531

1963 (for the fourth digit, "3" indicates a coupe and "6" indicates a convertible)

September, 1962:	30867S100675
October:	30867S102756
November:	30867S104047
December:	30867S105972
January, 1963:	30867S107976
February:	30867S109814
March:	30867S111833
April:	30867S114128
May:	30867S116409
June:	30867S118524
July:	30867S120990
August:	30867S121513

1964 (for the fourth digit, "3" indicates a coupe and "6" indicates a convertible)

September, 1963:	40867S101741
October:	40867S104045
November:	40867S106063
December:	40867S108091
January, 1964:	40867S110297
February:	40867S112322
March:	40867S114570
April:	40867S116865
May:	40867S118805
June:	40867S120920
July:	40867S122229

1965 (for the fourth digit, "3" indicates a coupe and "6" indicates a convertible)

August, 1964:	194675S100227
September:	194675S101425
October:	(Labor strike)
November:	194675S103347
December:	194675S105754
January, 1965:	194675S108442
February:	194675S111059
March:	194675S113936
April:	194675S116516
May:	194675S118753
June:	194675S121216
July:	194675S123562
August:	194675S123564

1966 (for the fourth digit, "3" indicates a coupe and "6" indicates a convertible)

September, 1965:	194676S102031
October:	194676S104384
November:	194676S107186
December:	194676S109892
January, 1966:	194676S112587
February:	194676S115283
March:	194676S118091
April:	194676S120664
May:	194676S123016
June:	194676S125469
July:	194676S127720

1967 (for the fourth digit, "3" indicates a coupe and "6" indicates a convertible)

September, 1966:	194677S102110
October:	194677S102685
November:	194677S104981
December:	194677S107110
January, 1967:	194677S119465
February:	194677S112264
March:	194677S115316
April:	194677S117395
May:	194677S119747
June:	194677S122214
July:	194677S122940

Index

Other MBI Publishing Company titles of interest:

Porshe 911 Buyer's Guide
ISBN 0-7603-0947-7

Corvette 1968-1982
ISBN 0-7603-0418-1

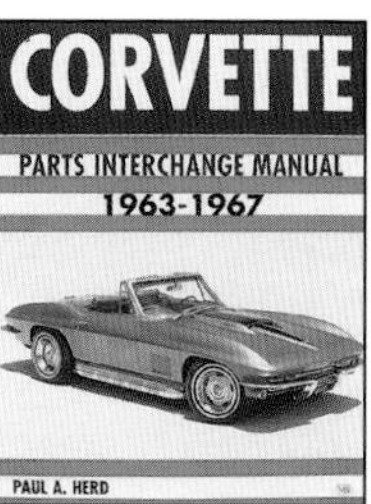

Corvette Parts Interchange Manual 1963-1967
ISBN 0-7603-0970-1

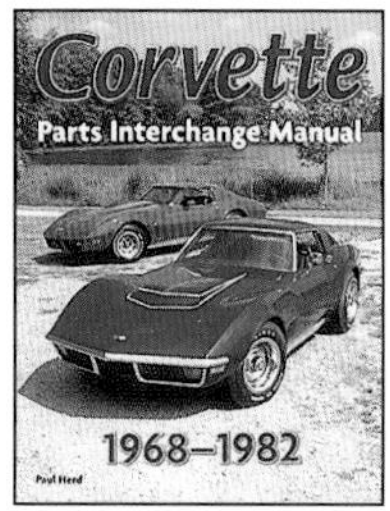

Corvette Parts Interchange Manual 1968-1982
ISBN 0-7603-0520-X

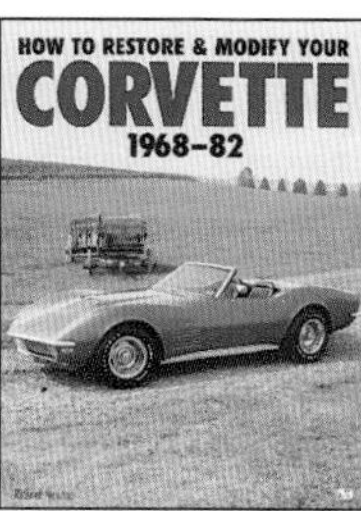

How to Restore and Modify Your 1968-1982 Corvette
ISBN 0-7603-0052-6

Corvette Restoration Guide 1963-1967
ISBN 0-7603-0179-4

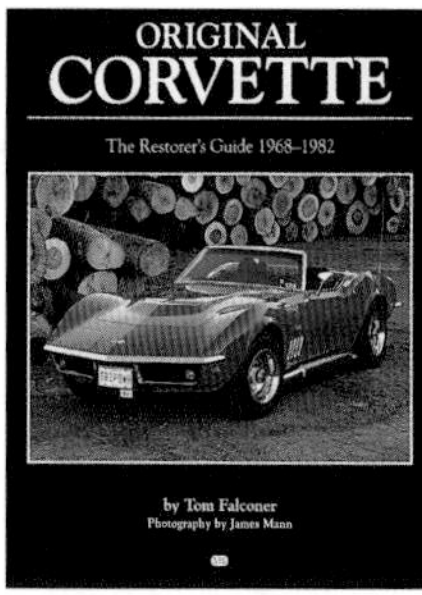

Original Corvette
ISBN 0-7603-0897-7

Corvette C5
ISBN 0-7603-0457-2

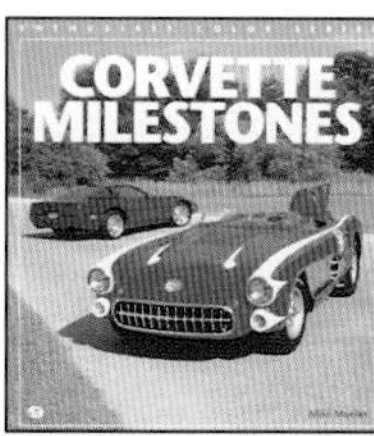

Corvette Milestones
ISBN 0-7603-0095-X